Diversity and Multiculturalism
in Libraries

**FOUNDATIONS IN LIBRARY AND
INFORMATION SCIENCE, Volume 32**

Editors: Thomas W. Leonhardt, *Dean, University Libraries, Wm. Knox Memorial Library, University of the Pacific*

Murray S. Martin, *University Librarian and Professor of Library Science Emeritus, Tufts University*

FOUNDATIONS IN LIBRARY AND INFORMATION SCIENCE

A Series of Monographs, Texts and Treatises

Edited by
Thomas W. Leonhardt
Holt Library, University of the Pacific
and
Murray S. Martin
University Librarian and Professor of Library Science Emeritus,
Tufts University

Diversity and Multiculturalism in Libraries

Edited by: KATHERINE HOOVER HILL
Dry Memorial Library
Erie Community College
Williamsville, New York

 JAI PRESS INC.

Greenwich, Connecticut   London, England

Z
711.7
D58
1994

Library of Congress Cataloging-in-Publications Data

Diversity and multiculturalism in libraries / edited by Katherine
Hoover Hill.
    p.   cm.—(Foundations in library and information science ;
v. 32)
    Includes bibliographical references and index.
    ISBN 1-55938-751-3
    1. Libraries and minorities—United States.   2. Multiculturalism—
United States.   3. Academic libraries—Services to minorities—
United States.   I. Hill, Katherine Hoover.   I. Series.
Z711.7.D58   1994   94-28566
                                                    CIP

CONTENTS

INTRODUCTION

At the end of the twentieth century, the United States is in a period of profound social change driven by the gradual changes in the constituent elements of its population. The increasing numbers of Americans who are not of white European descent are changing our perception of the way an "American" looks. Dramatic shifts in patterns of immigration, the passage of the Americans with Disabilities Act in 1990, and the election of Bill Clinton on a platform of change all contributed to increasing awareness of diversity issues in the 1990s. Corporations have established programs to address the complex issues this diversity brings to the workplace. Libraries, along with businesses and other social institutions, are considering these issues in terms of both their patrons and their own employees.

The emphasis on diversity and multiculturalism in library literature and in advertising for the library market has at times seemed to be a fad that would be overtaken by the next management crisis or buzzword before libraries could make any substantive changes. E. J. Josey described the persistence of the status quo in libraries as long ago as 1979 in Volume 13 of this series, *Library Management Without Bias*. Josey summed up the situation in two sentences. "Whatever the organizational structure, women and minorities are inadequately represented as administrators.... Native Americans, Chicanos, Puerto Ricans, Asian-Americans, and Afro-Americans are grossly underrepresented in all areas and at all levels in library and information science positions."[1] Fifteen years later, the American library establishment is still changing more slowly than the society it serves.

At the same time, library administrators may feel, each time they pick up the latest professional publication, that Thurber's Get-Ready Man is urging them to "prepare for the end of the world."[2] Clearly some response is in order, but it is less clear how to take these dire warnings of demographic change and apply them to a local situation, especially where, as in many cases, that change may not yet be apparent, and where many other pressing management issues clamor for attention.

The chapters of this volume show how library leaders have anticipated change and taken the initiative to make their institutions more useful and responsive to a multicultural society. Each chapter illuminates an aspect of diversity and service. Taken together, the theoretical and practical ideas presented not only give a portrait of library leadership in diversity and multiculturalism, but also are applicable in a wide range of libraries and local situations. These administrators and librarians, working "on the front lines" with diverse staff and patrons in diverse settings, have sought out ways to meet new kinds of information needs; and they offer examples of change that can serve as models for the rest of us.

I would like to thank Murray Martin, series editor for *Foundations in Library and Information Science;* Glendora Johnson-Cooper, Acting Director, Undergraduate Library, University at Buffalo; and Maryruth P. Glogowski, Acting Director, Butler Library, Buffalo State College, for their advice and encouragement during the preparation of this volume.

Katherine Hoover Hill
Volume Editor

NOTES

1.   Institute on Library Management without Bias, *Library Management without Bias,* ed. Ching-Chih Chen, in *Foundations in Library and Information Science,* Volume 13 (Greenwich, CT: JAI Press Inc., 1979), 63.

2.   James Thurber, "The Car We Had to Push," in *The Thurber Carnival* (New York: Harper, 1945), 182.

LEADING THE WAY TO DIVERSITY:

THE ACADEMIC LIBRARY'S ROLE IN PROMOTING MULTICULTURALISM

Rush G. Miller

Changing demographics in American society compels academic institutions toward less homogeneity within student bodies and faculties alike. Today one out of five Americans is a person of color, according to the latest Census.[1] Universities must cope with increasing numbers of minority students whose needs and concerns are not the same as the majority population. At the same time, the university's mission to prepare students for an economic, political and social environment that is increasingly global and diverse by nature creates pressure not only to provide educational experiences relevant to minority students but to enrich the educational experiences of majority students with an appreciation for and an understanding of other cultures. By the 1980s, merely acknowledging the importance of developing diverse campus communities evolved into a requirement of higher education's mission in society. Predominantly white institutions of higher education are recruiting minority students and faculty with a new fervor in order to make campuses more diverse and to provide to all students the benefits of the cross fertilization that derives from interactions within a multiracial and multicultural society.[2]

Academic libraries have also had to face challenges brought about by the changing demographics of society and the new emphasis on cultural diversity within universities generally. Despite the paucity of publications in the area of cultural diversity and the academic library, some notable work has been done in recent years. Successful efforts at Stanford University were reported by Roberto G. Trujillo and David C. Weber in 1991.[3] The Stanford program is similar to efforts in a number of academic libraries in that it focuses on increasing the numbers of minority staff in the libraries, mentoring and internship programs for minority librarians, staff development activities to increase awareness of diversity issues within the library staff, developing outreach services to minority students, and building library collections that address the needs of minority students and faculty.

C. Martin Rosen and other members of the Bowling Green State University library faculty and staff, in an article prepared for *The Reference Librarian,* place the academic library's role in a broader context.[4] They state,

[L]ibraries, as key centers of university culture with institutional links that cut across departmental and disciplinary boundaries, can play a key role in setting an inclusive tone—not only by building collections capable of meeting the scholarly and research needs of new constituencies, but also by offering an environment conducive to cross-cultural social and intellectual interaction.

An article in *Library Administration and Management* by Janet Welch and Errol Lam of Bowling Green State University provides an overview of the issues that have faced university administrators in recent years relating to minority and international student populations.[5] Welch and Lam call for academic libraries to take a leadership role at their campuses "to develop compatible environments for the students and faculty of diverse cultures who will be a large component of library patrons in the twenty-first century." In their view, the potential of minority and international students to enrich the lives of other Americans has been thwarted by racism and other barriers to full participation. It is important for majority individuals who have not been exposed previously to individuals of other cultures to become sensitized to them. This can be done, they maintain, by developing sensitivity programs that involve both majority and minority staff and students, with strong support from administrators.

This chapter focuses primarily on the efforts of Bowling Green State University's Libraries and Learning Resources to address the need not only to develop an atmosphere conducive to proactive services to minority students and faculty, to meet affirmative action goals and increase minority representation within its work force, and to sensitize staff to issues of cultural diversity; but also to play a major role in creating a more tolerant and inclusive environment for the campus as a whole. This program goes beyond most such programs at university libraries in that it had almost from the outset a broader perspective and participation than just the libraries on campus, and therefore, it is a prime example of how academic libraries can play a leadership role at a university that transcends their traditional mission within the institution.

THE NEED FOR CHANGE

Bowling Green State University is a residential university within the state university system of Ohio, located in a rural, conservative community of 35,000 in the northwestern section of the state. As of the fall of 1993, the student body included 17,502 students, of which 2,411 were graduate students. The university offers 170 undergraduate degree programs, 13 master's degrees in more than 60 fields and 14 doctoral programs in more than 60 areas of specialization.[6] The university has a limited, capped enrollment and practices selective admissions, resulting in a stable and level enrollment pattern. The number of minority undergraduate students has fluctuated somewhat over the past decade, but generally African American students make up about four percent of the student population. In addition, Asian/ Pacific Island and Hispanic students each account for about one percent of the total. At no time during the decade of the 1980s did the minority undergraduate student population exceed 900. Minority graduate students were represented in only slightly higher percentages during this period. By the end of the 1980s the number of minority faculty was also small, with only 19 African-American and 7 Hispanic faculty members.[7]

As at many predominantly white institutions, progress made in attracting minority students and faculty during the 1960s and 1970s in a national political climate conducive to providing educational opportunities for minorities was frustrated by reductions in the federal commitment during the 1980s. Bowling Green State had made progress in recruiting minority students, had created positions to assist minority students such as the Associate Vice President for

Minority Affairs and the Director of Affirmative Action, and had formed a Black Student Union and a Center for Ethnic Studies. The African American student population rose from 1.4 percent in 1970 to 4.7 percent in 1975. But from 1975 until 1983, minority student representation at the university dropped 22 percent to 843 from 1,085.[8]

In 1983, the newly appointed president, Paul J. Olscamp, prompted by concerns regarding the decline of minority students, formed a committee and charged its members with investigating means by which the university might increase the numbers of minority and nontraditional students on campus.[9] After a thorough investigation, the President's Committee on Recruitment and Retention of Minority and Nontraditional Students issued a sweeping report and set of recommendations. In particular, the Committee discovered "…a feeling among some minority students that they were being excluded from job opportunities in several areas" and that "…racist attitudes within the institution…make it less likely that minority students will receive equal access to work study jobs."[10] The Committee called for programmatic and curricular initiatives in addition to steps to change the image of the university in the media. They also recommended that financial aid and student employment practices be modified and that departments be given incentives to recruit minority students and faculty. Finally, they addressed changes needed to improve the quality of life on campus.

The campus committee's report to the president triggered a campus-wide initiative to address the issues of cultural diversity. In April 1983, then Dean of Libraries and Learning Resources, Dwight Burlingame, appointed an ad-hoc human relations committee representing the various departments within Libraries and Learning Resources to study the issue within LLR and to make recommendations for improving the multicultural environment. The committee's charge included investigation and recommendations dealing with the following categories: (1) staff and student assistant hiring practices, (2) employee and patron perceptions related to sexism, racism, or cultural differences, and (3) ways in which LLR might assist the campus community in creating a more positive multicultural environment for students and staff.[11]

Information gathered through surveys and interviews yielded data showing that LLR departments followed general university patterns noted earlier regarding the employment of minorities. Of 103 faculty and staff employed within LLR departments, only four individuals were members of minority groups. Of these four individuals, only one was a librarian who identified himself as an Asian Pacific Islander. Of 251 student assistants, only 36 were African American, and four were Hispanic. Roughly 4 percent of the staff and 14 percent of the student assistants were minorities. More disturbing to the committee than the overall statistics was the fact that fully half of the employing departments within LLR reported no minority student assistants.[12]

Attitudes expressed by staff members generally reflected a lack of appreciation for and understanding of university affirmative action and cultural diversity goals and objectives. Common perceptions included the idea that less qualified minority candidates were given preference over more qualified and capable white candidates. While a clear majority of staff and student assistants reported that no overt racism was evident on a day-to-day basis, others expressed the opposite view, reporting a prevalence of racist jokes by some employees and snide remarks about international students' accents.[13]

The committee concluded in its report that "...problems do exist in several areas of human relations in Learning Resources." To alleviate these problems, the committee recommended: (1) a staff member in the Dean's Office should be designated by the dean to receive and deal with confidential reports of racist and other inappropriate behavior by staff; (2) hiring patterns for student assistants and staff within each department should be monitored for two years to encourage greater multicultural representation in all employment areas; (3) a program of workshops should be developed for staff on topics concerning employee relationships, affirmative action policies, stereotypes, and the many facets of sexism and racism; (4) an investigation into charges of preferential treatment should be conducted; (5) a mechanism should be implemented to ensure that incidents of racism or discrimination or harassment can be reported without fear of intimidation or retaliation; (6) collections should be added to promote multiculturalism; and (7) an effort should be made to improve publicity for services, events, acquisitions, displays, and so forth, related to multicultural topics.[14]

FROM RECOMMENDATIONS TO ACTIONS

Despite the work of the report of the ad-hoc Human Relations Committee, no tangible change occurred until October, 1987, when Dean Rush G. Miller, who was appointed in June, 1986, appointed an ad-hoc Committee on Minority Affairs for LLR.[15] This new committee, with a much broader and larger representation, was given a charge similar to the first one to study indepth issues relating to the recruitment of minority faculty, staff, and student assistants within LLR; the working environment for minorities within LLR; services of LLR to minority students, including the sensitivity of staff and faculty and student assistants to minority concerns; and the special needs of minority students at the university relative to LLR services.

Like many institutions of higher education, Bowling Green was receiving negative publicity because of racial incidents occurring on campus. The university administration was concerned about these incidents and the underlying tensions between majority and minority students on campus. The President and Vice President for Academic Affairs asked each dean to establish collegiate committees to work toward the recruitment of minority faculty and to address issues of cultural diversity at the university through academic programs. The Libraries and Learning Resources ad-hoc committee had been formed prior to and independent of this initiative. From the beginning, the LLR effort had a broader and more inclusive focus than did most of the collegiate committees. Since LLR serves the entire university community, the mission of its program to address cultural diversity not only dealt with behaviors among the LLR staff and student assistants, but it also had to determine how minority students from all areas of the campus related to its services and programs.

A typical observer may have perceived LLR as an area of the university unlikely to become involved with issues such as cultural diversity. Except for the efforts of a few individual faculty or staff members, the libraries had remained "neutral" on campus. Overt racist statements, while not condoned by the administrators, were more or less tolerated or ignored. Efforts to recruit minority librarians and staff were passive and resulted in little progress. Lack of progress was blamed on the overall community environment or the lack of interest on the part of minorities when jobs were advertised. No staff development programs dealt with issues of ethnicity or diversity, and no services were enhanced to accommodate special needs of minority students at BGSU. It was this situation that the ad-hoc minority affairs committee was asked to study and address. Unlike the first committee in 1983, this one was given written assurance that their recommendations would be implemented fully or they would have a full and written explanation why not.[16]

One of the more enlightening activities this committee engaged in was to invite various university officials who dealt regularly with minority concerns to discuss them. The Assistant Vice President for Minority Affairs in Student Affairs, Dr. Jack Taylor, was particularly forthright in discussing the situation at the university. He stated bluntly that he had seen little improvement in racial attitudes in the past two decades and that campus racism was on the rise. Bigotry existed both in the residence halls and in the classrooms and all one had to do to discover it was to talk to a minority student. He further pointed out that the most important barriers against recruiting minority students to attend the university were: (1) a lack of minority role models among the faculty and administration; (2) an environment that is not supportive of non-white cultural values, one that does not affirm minority cultural dignity; and (3) an atmosphere which generates a feeling of isolation for minority students. The visit from Dr. Taylor, coupled with the viewing of Dr. Charles King's guest appearance on the Phil Donahue Show[17] and other sensitivity videotapes, gave members a renewed commitment to making a difference that has been the hallmark of the entire LLR effort to date.

In June of 1988, the committee submitted its report to the Dean. The report was thorough in its analysis and far-reaching in its recommendations. The introduction began with "...we recognize that racial prejudice does exist on campus and within Libraries and Learning Resources....[W]e are committed to making a positive contribution toward enhancing the multicultural atmosphere on campus." The first recommendation of the committee was to name a permanent representative standing committee on minority affairs to implement, oversee, and further develop the suggestions of the report and act as a resource on the subject. Other recommendations were divided into those dealing with the creation of an environment within LLR that enhances the atmosphere for a multicultural world and those dealing with the development of a proactive minority recruitment program at all levels of employment within LLR.[18]

To build a more tolerant and understanding environment within LLR, the committee concluded that one key was to develop sensitivity to cultural differences by various methods, both short range and long range. As a short-range strategy, the group recommended sensitivity training for staff members who are engaged in hiring student assistants. The viewing of Charles King's "racial sensitivity" tapes with the assistance of a facilitator and the videotape of a national teleconference entitled "Racism on Campus: Toward an Agenda for Action"[19] were specified as particularly helpful in this effort. Other short-range plans included placing minorities working in LLR in positions more visible to minority patrons; increasing the number of displays focused on events such as Black History Month, Hispanic Awareness Week, among others; and inviting minority groups to utilize library facilities for meetings. Long-range responsibilities to be assigned to a standing committee might include collection development efforts in the areas of minority cultures and literatures; an ongoing series of workshops for staff; increased use of LLR facilities to promote and publicize campus ethnic and cultural events; and social activities within LLR to promote an awareness of minorities such as potluck meals with an ethnic theme and brown bag luncheons with ethnic guest speakers.

The employment of minorities at all levels was a major focus of the committee's report. The committee recognized that demographics of the profession and, more especially, of the region of Northwest Ohio predicted that minority pools for positions within LLR would remain small. In an effort to overcome the dismal demographics, the committee established the ambitious goal of attaining an employment level of five percent minority librarians by 1993. That would mean employing an additional two persons within five years. Goals were also established for increasing the employment of minorities as support staff and student assistants.[20] Dean Miller endorsed most of the committee's recommendations.

A PERMANENT COMMITTEE

Serendipitously, LLR was beginning a serious effort to develop a strategic plan at the time the report was completed and accepted. Immediately the committee's report was forwarded to the Strategic Planning Committee so that the various recommendations and suggestions could be incorporated into the goals and objectives of the strategic plan.[21] Short-range recommendations were implemented more readily. A standing LLR Minority Affairs Committee (later renamed the Multicultural Affairs Committee) was formed. Employment goals were accepted and an aggressive and broad-based minority recruitment program was initiated, resulting in the attainment of the hiring goal for faculty librarians in only two years. Since 1988, the "MAC," as it has come to be known internally, has been a driving force behind both the LLR and the university-wide effort to promote awareness of cultural diversity issues.

The original role outlined for the Multicultural Affairs Committee (MAC), as defined by the dean and the ad-hoc committee, was to coordinate and promote cultural diversity within LLR, to improve the climate for minority employees, to reduce the potential for discriminatory behavior, and to improve services to minority and international students in the libraries. In an initial flurry of activity, the standing committee combined efforts with the dean's office to successfully launch a series of awareness sessions. In September, 1988, for example, a sensitivity session was held for all staff within LLR, but targeted at those who supervised minority student assistants. The two-part workshop included viewing the videotape of Dr. Charles King's appearance on the Phil Donahue Show followed by discussion facilitated by a staff member from the university's Multicultural Affairs Office. Dr. King, an educator and founder of Urban Crisis Inc., impressed viewers as a hard hitting, confrontational, and provocative speaker. He compelled the LLR audience to confront subtle racism and stereotyping indicative of any predominantly white group. A heightened sensitivity to cultural differences led to the development of a series of internally-focused workshops and guest speakers for the next two years, and a renewed emphasis upon cultural diversity issues in the LLR strategic plan and other planning activities. Staff who had not previously given these issues much thought suddenly became active in promoting programs and urging those who had not attended these sessions to do so. The dean and his administrative team endorsed these efforts, attended most of the sessions personally, and encouraged supervisors to allow release time for MAC activities for the staff who were willing to participate.

Programming

Between November 1988 and April 1991, MAC sponsored more than 20 different functions and activities that were attended by large numbers of LLR faculty and staff, and a growing number of university faculty and students. Following the King tape sessions, the committee sponsored a Multicultural Holiday Party in December of 1988. In January 1989 it sponsored a session for staff with the Associate Vice President for Multicultural Affairs to discuss racism on campus and what LLR areas could do to create a better climate for minority students. A major display entitled "Cultural Diversity at BGSU" was mounted in the large and centrally-located display cases of the main library. By September 1989 the committee sponsored the first of what has become an annual event, a Welcoming Reception for new multicultural students on campus to allow LLR staff and students an opportunity to meet each other. A handout was distributed to students who attended which listed LLR staff members serving as contact persons for minority students (approximately 20 staff had volunteered for this program).

By the fall of 1989, the committee was beginning to broaden its role to include programming that would have a campus-wide appeal. It presented a series of programs entitled "Valuing Diversity." These four programs gradually attracted audiences from ethnic studies faculty and classes, interested faculty and students, and other groups, including campus administrators. Topics in this first major series of programs based on videotapes included "Racism 101."[22] Also in the spring semester, 1990, the committee sponsored the first annual Undergraduate Essay Contest dealing with a multicultural topic. To attract a large number of interested applicants, the Undergraduate Essay Contest was listed in the University Scholarship Guide. Winning entries are awarded first, second, and third prizes, and the first-place contestant is invited to present his/her essay at a reception following the contest.

When this programming began, there were few such efforts in place at the university. An annual ethnic studies conference sponsored by the Ethnic Studies Department and a few forum-type programs sponsored by Women's Studies or the Office of Multicultural Affairs, which did not attract large audiences, were the primary activities directed at discussion of multicultural issues. The university had taken a bold step to require each student to take a course devoted to cultural diversity in the United States as part of the revised general education curriculum. Soon the LLR MAC programs became a major focus of the university's promotion of multiculturalism and one of the most influential aspects. The committee worked closely with other groups such as the Affirmative Action and Multicultural Affairs Offices, the multicultural affairs committees of other colleges, particularly Arts and Sciences, and the Ethnic and Women's Studies programs to coordinate programs and co-sponsor major events.

Diversity programming sponsored by the MAC gained recognition on campus for its quality and currency. Gradually initial audiences of 30 to 40 LLR staff swelled to 60 to 80, with more than half and often a higher percentage from outside LLR areas. During 1990-91 the committee built upon its earlier success with a series entitled "Dispelling the Myth" including programs that dealt with myths about affirmative action, the myth that uniformity is best (entitled "We Beg to Differ"), and myths about aging. "We Beg to Differ" brought together a panel of individuals representing various minority groups, including a homosexual student, a physically challenged student, an African American faculty member, a Hispanic faculty member, and others to talk about the university atmosphere from each perspective. Also during that year 22 of the staff underwent the BaFa BaFa simulation game.[23] Films were shown on racism and Chicanos, with facilitators for each. The second annual undergraduate essay contest was held, and the winners read their essays at a reception during National Library Week in the spring of 1991.

A survey mailed to the LLR staff in May 1991, to assess response to the Cultural Diversity/Dispelling the Myth series, revealed that one third of the LLR staff had attended four or more programs that year and 50 percent had attended at least half of them. It is clear from the survey comments that the committee's efforts were reaching staff and having a positive impact upon their views. Many expressed that they had developed a better understanding of other people and felt more empathy for them. Others pointed out the need to continue to promote not only the acceptance of cultural differences, but that they should be valued as well.

Collections and Personnel

Early in the implementation of the LLR strategic plan, funding was deemed essential to the plan. To attempt to make the strategic goals more effective in charting the direction of LLR, funds were routinely set aside from the operating budgets to fund special initiatives tied to strategic goals. Since multiculturalism was a strong component of the plan from the beginning, the Instructional Media Services department developed a proposal to establish a special video collection of titles dealing with multicultural topics. Funded at $5,000 per year beginning in 1989, this collection has become an important one to the entire university community. Titles were purchased for use in classrooms as well as in cultural diversity programming by various groups on campus.

Efforts to recruit minority librarians met with equal success between 1988 and 1991. Steps were taken to improve the hiring practices to enable LLR to meet its hiring goals for faculty (librarians). Vacancy announcements were revised to reflect the emphasis and commitment on the part of LLR to recruit and hire qualified minority candidates. These announcements after 1988 were sent to targeted minority audiences through publications such as *Black Issues in Higher Education and the Affirmative Action Register*. The University Personnel Services Office advertised job vacancies in two area publications targeted to minority populations (the *Toledo Journal,* an African American newspaper, and *La Prensa,* which is directed at the Hispanic population); additionally, job announcements are distributed to agencies such as the Ohio Commission on Spanish Speaking Affairs and the Veterans Affairs Office, which also have established links with minority populations.

The Library took a more aggressive and innovative approach to recruitment by attracting an intern from the Wayne State University library science program who was African American. The intern attended library science classes at WSU two days per week and worked at the BGSU Library 20 hours per week. In return, BGSU covered the cost of her tuition and fees as well as a stipend for her work at the BGSU Library for two years. Although no guarantees of employment were included in the agreement, when she graduated from WSU in 1990, the Library obtained funding from a special minority pool reserved by the Vice President for Academic Affairs to add a faculty position. Following a recommendation from the MAC, she was named Multicultural Services Librarian within Information Services in 1990. Her responsibilities after 1990 were to not only work as a member of the reference staff, but to assess services to minority students, to co-chair the MAC, and to design, establish

and promote library services to minority and international students.[24]
In addition to this position, the dean was able to identify a minority
candidate for the position of Director of Collection Management,
who was subsequently employed.

Other networking activities led to the recruitment of an African
American administrative staff member in the Instructional Media
Services division of LLR, an area that had had no recent minority
staff members. This individual had worked in the IMS as a graduate
student and had remained in touch with the director and staff after
graduating. Although he was employed with a major national
corporation, he was recruited successfully to fill an open position in
the IMS through personal contact. LLR began to participate in the
Pre-College Enrichment Program, placing two to three minority high
school students each summer in temporary student assistant
positions.

As a result of these activities, LLR had met its hiring goals for
faculty and administrative staff and exceeded them within three years.
Despite this success, MAC urged the LLR administration to continue
a vigorous effort to recruit and retain minority candidates for faculty
and administrative positions. Unfortunately, institutional constraints
on classified staff hiring practices, coupled with several years of stable
or shrinking employment, hindered LLR's ability to hire minority
individuals for classified staff positions to the degree desired by the
committee.

Improvements were noticeable in the employment of minority
student assistants as a result of the committee's report and the ensuing
emphasis on encouraging minority students to apply for LLR
positions. In 1988, minority students represented 8.3 percent of the
student work force in LLR. By 1991 that percentage had climbed
to 11.7 percent. It was clear from statistical and anecdotal evidence
that in 1988 that many departments discouraged or simply refused
to employ minority students. Many of the MAC's efforts at sensitivity
training were directed at supervisors of student assistants. Within a
few short years, that situation was relieved noticeably, and
complaints by student assistants of inappropriate or insensitive
behavior practically disappeared altogether.

By 1991, it was clear that the Multicultural Affairs Committee had
become less focused on internal staff programs and hiring practices
and more involved with campus-wide programs. The reasons for this
shift in emphasis were that (1) many of the initial recommendations

of the committee related to the LLR environment and employment practices had been implemented fully and had resulted in the achievement of the original goals; and (2) most of the issues the committee dealt with were university issues not unique to LLR and they had successfully provided programs that appealed to a wider audience.

Assessment and Future Direction

In April 1991, Dean Miller met with the committee and charged the members to conduct an assessment of the progress made toward implementing the 1988 report recommendations and to recommend future directions for the committee.[25] An assessment was conducted and a formal report presented to the dean in May 1992. As part of this process, the committee invited Dr. Mary Ellen Ashley, Vice Provost of the University of Cincinnati to lead a workshop for LLR staff entitled "Combating Racism on Campus." In one segment of the workshop Dr. Ashley led the staff in an assessment of the committee's programs in combating racism. This gave the committee additional insight into its activities and programs.

After evaluating progress made in critical areas over the preceding three years, the committee strongly urged the dean to continue the present strong support for MAC programming and activities in that their long range goals would require long range support to be achieved fully. The MAC assessment report concluded with a strong call for continued support:

> Since its inception in 1988, LLRMAC's activities have tangibly affected the working and living environment both in the library and across the Bowling Green State University campus. Measurable progress has been made toward achieving the goals enumerated in the 1983 report by the President's Committee on Recruitment and Retention of Minority and Nontraditional Students. In particular, LLRMAC's activities have fostered the process of "establishing a milieu for the intellectual, cultural, and social development of minorities." Nor are the benefits of LLRMAC's activities restricted only to the personal and professional development of minority members of the university community. Abundant evidence suggests the LLRMAC programming has enriched the environment for all members of the library staff. It is important to recognize that attitudinal changes occur incrementally over time; the gains made during the past four years could be lost in much less time in the absence of a continued effort. LLRMAC believes that its present structure is extremely effective and urges that this structure be

maintained and that the LLR administration continue to support LLRMAC activities as it has during the last four years.[26]

Despite the emphasis in 1991-92 on assessment, the MAC continued to sponsor outstanding programs for the campus. The Issues in Cultural Diversity series was continued with the theme of Articulating Identity. Programs centered on such topics as religious and gender themes from African history and culture, Asian Americans as the "model" minority, the Native American experience, and Mexican Americans. Each of these programs was led by one or more university faculty members with expertise in the field. Another program sponsored by the MAC was a panel discussion of the legacy of Martin Luther King, Jr. held in January 1992. The annual essay contest sponsored by the committee also carried the theme of articulating identity and requested papers on the topic of challenging labels in the 1990s. With support from the dean, the prizes for the essay contest were $100, $50 and $25. The committee also co-sponsored two teleconferences; one dealing with racism on campus and the other exploring the recruitment of minorities in the 1990s.

Beginning with the spring semester, 1993, self directed teams replaced the traditional committee structure in Libraries and Learning Resources. Although a Human Relations Team was established and given broad discretion to assess and develop services to minority and international students and to monitor the recruitment process to assure continued commitment to affirmative action, the Multicultural Affairs Committee continued to convene with a change in focus. Rather than dealing with all diversity issues, the Committee charge was modified to deal primarily with cultural diversity programming within LLR and the university as a whole. It would work closely with the Human Relations Team and some overlap in membership assured close communication between the two groups.

LLRMAC has continued to offer multicultural programming to the campus community. The programs are so relevant to discussions being held within courses offered through the general education program component on "cultural diversity in the United States" that professors often require their classes to attend them. The program thrives to the extent that it has become generally recognized as the best such effort on the entire campus, as evidenced by their receiving the 1993 BGSU Human Rights Commission's Award for Excellence in promoting multiculturalism. The MAC has a close working relationship with all other groups working at the university to enhance the atmosphere of inclusiveness and understanding.

The LLRMAC does not operate in a vacuum. Other noteworthy efforts at BGSU include giving every undergraduate student an opportunity to learn how the cultures of minority groups has enriched American history and life and implementing a general education component that addresses "Cultural Diversity in the United States" through a number of approved courses developed within traditional disciplines which focus on the impact of minority cultures. In addition, the university implemented a comprehensive development program for graduate assistants which includes sessions dealing with cultural diversity as well as more traditional subjects such as information technologies and effective teaching techniques.

The LLR effort, as part of a larger effort at Bowling Green State University, has been one of the most successful such efforts in the history of the university. Why? Perhaps students may view the library as a safe place where they feel less threatened, and they may be more willing to express themselves concerning sensitive topics at a library program than in the classroom where they are afraid to disagree with their instructor. Perhaps through Herculean efforts of highly motivated and hard working staff members wanting to make a difference at the university and in the LLR environment, the resistance gradually wore down. Whatever the reasons, one thing is clear above all else: no one at the university would have ever asked LLR to undertake such a mission on behalf of the entire university. No library will ever be assigned this task. The administrators and staff of a library must want to play a broader role for it to happen. But in the final analysis, a library system can be the "heart of the university" in more than one sense. It can be the center not only of the intellectual life of the university but the center of its efforts to reflect society by bringing together a community of diverse peoples and cultures.

ACKNOWLEDGMENTS

The author would like to acknowledge the assistance of Mary Wrighten, Multicultural Services Librarian, and Beverly Stearns, Assistant to the Dean at BGSU Libraries and Learning Resources, in preparing this chapter.

NOTES

1. Bureau of the Census, *Statistical Abstracts of the United States, 1990* (Washington, 1990), 14-15.

2. Otis A. Chadley, "Addressing Cultural Diversity in Academic and Research Libraries," *College and Research Libraries* 53 (May 1992): 206-208.

3. Roberto G. Trujillo and David C. Weber, "Academic Library Responses to Cultural Diversity: A Position Paper for the 1990s," *Journal of Academic Librarianship* 17 (July 1991): 157-161.

4. C. Martin Rosen, Mary Wrighten, Beverly Stearns, and Susan Goldstein, "Student Employees and the Academic Library's Multicultural Mission," *Reference Librarian,* in press.

5. Janey E. Welch and R. Errol Lam, "The Library and the Pluralistic Campus in the Year 2000: Implications for Administrators," *Library Administration and Management* 5 (Fall 1991): 215.

6. "Annual Report of the President, 1991-92." (Bowling Green, OH: Bowling Green State University, 1992), 69-71.

7. "Resource Planning Handbook, 1990-91." (Bowling Green, OH: Bowling Green State University, 1991).

8. Ibid.

9. "President's Committee on Recruitment and Retention of Minority and Nontraditional Students [Report]." (Bowling Green, OH: Bowling Green State University, 1983).

10. Ibid., 7-8.

11. "Ad-Hoc Learning Resources Human Relations Committee" [Report]. (Bowling Green, OH: Bowling Green State University Libraries and Learning Resources. February 14, 1984), 3.

12. Ibid., 5.

13. Ibid., 6-10.

14. Ibid., 19-22.

15. "Ad-Hoc Minority Affairs Committee [Report]," (Bowling Green, OH: Bowling Green State University Libraries and Learning Resources, 1988), 1. Hereafter cited as 1988 Report.

16. Rush G. Miller, "Memorandum to Ad-Hoc Committee on Minority Affairs." (Bowling Green State University Libraries and Learning Resources, 26 October 1987).

17. "Racial Sensitivity: Interview with Charles King," (The Phil Donahue Show, Dick Mincer, producer, WGN Continental Broadcasting Company, 1981, Videotape).

18. 1988 Report, 1-5.

19. "Racism on Campus: Part 2." Teleconference sponsored by Governor's State University and the Johnson Foundation, 1988.

20. 1988 Report, 6-8.

21. "Libraries and Learning Resources Strategic Plan 1988-93." (Bowling Green, OH: Bowling Green State University Libraries and Learning Resources, 1989).

22.   Thomas Lenon and Orlando Bagwell (producers), "Racism 101," Frontline. Public Broadcasting System, 1988.

23.   R. Garry Shirts, *BaFa BaFa: A Cross Culture Simulation* (Del Mar, CA: Simile II, 1977).

24.   Mary G. Wrighten. "The Significance of a Minority Reference Internship Program," (Bowling Green, OH: Bowling Green State University Libraries and Learning Resources, Typescript).

25.   "Libraries and Learning Resources Multicultural Affairs Committee [Report]," (Bowling Green, OH: Bowling Green State University Libraries and Learning Resources, May 1992), 2.

26.   Ibid., 7.

VOICES OF DIVERSITY IN UNIVERSITY OF CALIFORNIA LIBRARIES: IMPACT, INITIATIVES AND IMPEDIMENTS FOR CULTURAL AND RACIAL EQUITY

Carol J. Yates, Rafaela Castro and Lillian Castillo-Speed

VOICES OF COMMITTEE MEMBERS: VOICES OF DIVERSITY

Racism is an ever-evolving force in this country. At times it is overt, at times it is covert.

...the constant problem of being the warrior scholar: the constant emotional oppression; the daily fight for legitimacy; the daily struggle for visibility.

...the need for strategies for survival; strategies of resistance.

...never being heard; [my] comments only heard, accepted and made legitimate when repeated or restated by a white person.

The dynamics of the committee have been a problem because it has been a struggle to be heard. At times I have felt like an outsider.[1]

These are the voices of diversity, the voices of members of the Ad Hoc Committee on Librarians' Association of the University of California (LAUC) Workshops on Cultural Diversity in Libraries. Voices of members struggling with issues of race, class, gender and internalized oppression. Voices eventually coming together as one in the report, with more clarity about what cultural diversity is and is not. Committee members were able to assess what cultural diversity meant not only for the report, but also for themselves in relation to the library network of the University of California.

THE UNIVERSITY OF CALIFORNIA AS A MICROCOSM OF CULTURAL DIVERSITY

The nine campuses of the University of California (UC) comprise an academic arena within which approximately 166,000 students, 7,700 faculty and 560 librarians make use of resources in over 90 main and special libraries. Among the special libraries and collections, four are East Asian/Chinese; two are Black/African American; three are Native American/American Indian; five are Chicano/Hispanic; and one is a multicultural archival collection. It is estimated that all 15 of these special collections house less than five percent of the total library resources in all special libraries and collections for the university. By contrast, the Office of the President of the University has reported that for 1992, over 30 percent of the student population, 14 percent of the faculty and 17 percent of librarians are from one of the four underrepresented ethnic groups in the state of California. (These figures are based on self-reported ethnic identity.)[2] As of 1993 no comprehensive analysis had yet been completed to determine the actual percentage or extent of ethnic resources in all of the University's libraries.

Infrastructural impediments to cultural diversity and equity are apparent from the Office of the President of the University of California, all the way to the campus level. At the time of the committee's deliberations there was very little ethnic or racial permeation in the Office of the President, or in the top-level administration of the nine campuses. Sytemwide library committees, such as the policy-making University Librarians' Library Council and Heads of Public Services and Collection Development Council, lacked ethnic and racial integration. The absence of cultural diversity experience in these policy-making bodies has set the pattern for policy decisions throughout the libraries. For these reasons, the ad hoc committee began its deliberations on cultural diversity with a heavy burden on its shoulders—an absence of policies and university tradition, as well as a history of deficiency in areas dealing with ethnic and cultural diversity.

In order to maintain its eminent position as a global research institution in the twenty-first century, the University of California will need to make immediate adjustments in resources, staffing and services to reflect the increasing proportion of the underrepresented ethnic groups among the state's student and general population. Since the late 1980s, the University has made some renewed efforts toward cultural diversity. Library-related initiatives have included: a systemwide conference on cultural diversity in undergraduate education, where faculty and librarians explored ways to integrate multicultural issues into the curriculum; the establishment of cultural diversity advisory committees and programs at various libraries; and the procurement of funding via the systemwide librarians' association for a systemwide workshop on cultural diversity and the meetings required to organize it.

Within the past 10 years, several UC campus libraries have initiated programs to recruit and hire librarians whose professional responsibility would be specifically in the area of cultural diversity. The Los Angeles and San Diego campus main libraries had designated Ethnic Studies Librarian positions since the early 1970s, however, these positions primarily entailed collection development responsibilities rather than an extension of library services to a culturally diverse faculty and student body. In 1985 the Santa Barbara campus library established an internship program for ethnic minority library school graduates. Among the goals of the program was the employment of ethnic minority librarians in an academic library; the provision of role models for undergraduate students; and the creation of a more heterogeneous professional staff.[3] At least two of the interns have been hired in career positions by a University of California library. The Santa Cruz campus library created a Multicultural Services Librarian position with the primary responsibilities of providing outreach and leadership in library services for the campus multicultural community.[4] Following these successes, the Davis campus library recruited an Ethnic Studies Librarian in 1989, and the Irvine campus library created a Multicultural Outreach Librarian position based on the Santa Cruz model. Additionally, UC libraries jointly established a two-year residency program to recruit two librarians of color each year.

Prior to the Librarians' Association of the University of California's sponsorship of the workshop, a study was conducted to determine which issues librarians considered most urgent and important within the University's libraries. Unfortunately, cultural diversity was among the lowest priorities. The president of LAUC at that time reprioritized the items in order to place cultural diversity at the top of the priority list, and recommended that workshops be held statewide for all librarians. Thus cultural diversity was moved from margin to center as a concern for the University's libraries and forced to become a real and unavoidable issue.

These endeavors initiated among the campus libraries culminated in the conception of a statewide committee of librarians charged with organizing a workshop on cultural diversity for all librarians. The workshop was designed not only to raise the level of awareness about library cultural diversity issues, but also to allow an open dialogue in an environment where Latinos, Asian Americans, American Indians and African Americans could be represented and contribute in their own voices.

BIRTH OF THE COMMITTEE

In 1989 the President of the Librarians' Association of the University of California (LAUC) established the Ad Hoc Committee on LAUC Regional Workshops on Cultural Diversity in Libraries. In the charge issued to the committee, the President requested that the nine librarians and two faculty members on the committee plan two regional workshops on cultural diversity issues in UC libraries. Recommendations from these workshops would be used as a springboard for new or modified programs and services in the key areas of bibliographic access, collection development, reference services and bibliographic instruction. The committee later added recruitment/retention/promotion of librarians from the four underrepresented ethnic groups as a fifth area of concern, because they felt these personnel issues were a vital component of the other key areas and of the concept of cultural diversity. These recommendations would also provide a framework upon which positive changes in library services and resources related to the undergraduate curriculum, new ethnic studies requirements, and new faculty research interests could be built. Members of the committee were independently selected by the LAUC chairs of their respective campuses, and the resulting ethnic composition was three African

Americans, five Chicanos/Hispanics and one person of eastern European ancestry. The two faculty appointees were Chicano and African American. It was quickly noted that no Asian American or Native American librarians were selected for the committee.

THE COMMITTEE'S "REAL TASKS"

Members soon realized that this committee was unlike others they had served on. The conventional work of planning a workshop was secondary to two other important tasks before them: learning to work on ethnic issues as a multiethnic group; and creating a definition for cultural diversity. The real work of the group involved not only the analysis of professional library issues, but also the examination of personal ethnic identities; identities reflected in the work of each committee member. While committee members shared common concerns, it was soon apparent that each member had unique cultural formations, cultural differences and culture-based interpretations of reality. Since committee members were appointed on the basis of race or ethnicity, efforts were made to make members more sensitive to and understanding of each other's cultural issues. Committee members had to talk through personal issues in order to write about professional library issues. Eventually, in order to address the real issues of cultural diversity and follow through on the committee's responsibilities, members decided to participate in a special workshop to facilitate intragroup dialogue, trust and respect. It became clear through the workshop processes that cross-cultural and intra-cultural issues were as important to consider as multi-cultural issues. The members valued this process and felt it was essential to completion of the committee's responsibilities.

One of the most time-consuming tasks for the committee, however, was defining cultural diversity. Not until the preparation of the final draft of the report was the committee able to establish a common vocabulary and language which could be used as a base and parameter for the report. To facilitate understanding of the final report, the preface included the following definition: "...cultural diversity...pertains to the conditions, expressions and experiences of four historically under-represented groups. Under federal regulations these are Asian Americans/Pacific Islanders, Latinos, African Americans, and Native Americans/American Indians."[5]

Several initial responses to the report were critical of this working definition. It was considered too narrow, since it did not include gender, disability or sexual preference as components. The term "diversity," which the committee felt was much broader in scope but often used to mean "cultural diversity," continues to be debated within the University. To date, there seems to be no generally accepted definition, and no consistent conceptualization of cultural diversity. Many campus and systemwide reports about "cultural diversity" not only focus on the four traditionally underrepresented groups but other minority constituencies as well. Beyond the boundaries of the University of California, definitions of cultural diversity seem even more elusive, with many sociopolitical overtones and innuendos. Members of the committee, while in agreement about the definition derived for the report, were uncertain about whether the adopted definition was an oppressive or liberating one; one that could be used to hinder or support the committee's mission.

From its inception, the committee felt it was thrust into a vacuum to complete its work. Standing library committees already existed to examine prevailing issues in areas such as collection development, resource sharing, and professional development. The Ad Hoc Committee was established to examine new, more sensitive issues which had never before been the focus of a LAUC committee. Given that the work of the committee was totally non-traditional, committee members felt more respect and support could have been directed toward its mission. Instead, the committee often felt that barriers seemed to be continually cast in the pathway of its progress.

An example of an obstacle which the committee felt was constructed to delay its progress was the issue regarding the chair of the committee. The initial chair, appointed by the LAUC President and Executive Committee, was a very proficient librarian, and highly respected by committee members. This librarian was removed from the position as chair by the LAUC Executive Board, without consultation with the committee members. This occurred at the very beginning of the committee's deliberations. While committee members were attempting to reinstate the chair, the Vice-President of LAUC was appointed as a replacement LAUC by the Executive Board, again without notification to committee members. The committee felt that these actions not only demonstrated an unnecessary level of control, but prevented the committee from effectively commencing with its charge.

The committee also had no authority to obtain funding or to establish its own process. After 18 months of meetings and workshops, an extensive amount of data was collected, analyzed and summarized by the committee. A request for funds to hire an editor for the final drafting of the report was denied. Consequently, the rewriting and editing of the report had to be done by committee members and was a tedious, laborious and drawn-out process. To the committee these actions highlighted the fact that the higher goals of cultural diversity were not as significant in reality as originally stated by the University administration and by LAUC.

THE COMMITTEE REPORT: THE MANY VOICES OF DIVERSITY

In May, 1992, more than two years after its first meeting, the committee submitted its final report and recommendations to the systemwide LAUC. After many questions, negotiations and revisions, LAUC accepted the report and its consequences, thereby converting it from a committee report to a LAUC document. It was at this point, that committee members realized an important shift of responsibility had finally taken place. Of the 27 recommendations the first six considered most important by the committee were to:

1. Establish a permanent system-wide committee to deal with issues of cultural diversity in the University's libraries as well as implement the recommendations of this report
2. Provide training in multicultural communication and sensitivity for all library employees, including training for all librarians in understanding and valuing cultural differences and incorporating these differences into professional duties and initiatives.
3. Proactively recruit, hire and encourage the advancement of librarians from the underrepresented groups.
4. Prepare as part of the Committee's annual report, analyses of reports and initiatives on cultural diversity generated by LAUC, the LAUC divisions, the Office of the President, and/ or other academic institutions as appropriate.
5. Encourage California library schools to continue to recruit and matriculate culturally diverse students, employ faculty, and develop and diversify courses in ethnic studies bibliography

and services to diverse cultural groups.
6. Establish funding from the Office of the President to initiate, develop, and implement cultural diversity recommendations.[6]

By September 1992, the first recommendation, to establish a standing Committee on Cultural Diversity, had been approved by the 500 members of LAUC. The sixth recommendation regarding funding was partially implemented in December 1992, when the first Chair of the standing Committee on Cultural Diversity prompted the LAUC Executive Board to pass a resolution supporting efforts to secure university and external funding for restrospective electronic conversion of collections in five of the ethnic studies libraries. The other 26 recommendations, also planned for implementation, involve the access to as well as the evaluation and enhancement of culturally diverse resources; the increased valuation of and sensitivity to cultural differences in reference and bibliographic instruction; and most important, the recruitment, retention and advancement of librarians from the four underrepresented ethnic groups.

IMPACT AND FOLLOWUP OF THE REPORT

After its acceptance by LAUC in May 1992, the report was distributed by the LAUC President to other LAUC standing committees, the systemwide Vice President for Academic Affairs, the Chair of Library Council (organization of library directors), and the deans of all three library schools in California. In the cover letter that accompanied the report, the LAUC President stated the hope that "these recommendations will be acted upon and that the results will reverberate through all levels of UC libraries, and will also have a more general influence on the library profession and scholarly community both in California and in the larger academic world."[7]

The larger library world received a review of the report during the 1992 annual conference of the American Library Association in San Francisco, where several copies of the report were circulated. Some committee members also discussed the report in their presentations at the conference. Committee members realized a growing awareness of the report among California librarians when they were asked at meetings for copies of the report. To ensure easy future access to the report, plans are being made to make the document available through the ERIC Clearinghouse.

Although it is too soon to assess definitively the impact of the report within UC libraries, it should be noted that the Berkeley campus has established a LAUC-Berkeley task force to consider recommending the first formal committee on library cultural diversity for that campus.

The first meeting of the new standing committee on cultural diversity was held in the fall of 1992. At this meeting the following four subcommittees were formed to tackle the 26 remaining recommendations: Collections and Access; Workshop on Cultural Diversity in Bibliographic Instruction; Recruitment, Retention and Promotion; and Diversity Initiatives. Tasks and goals outlined for these subcommittees will undoubtedly occupy its members throughout the remainder of this decade. The fall 1993 workshops on bibliographic instruction are to focus on cultural sensitivity and communications. By Fall 1994, a process should be established for describing and assessing ethnic collections in the UC system as a means of preparing funding proposals for retrospective conversion. Preliminary information was being compiled by another subcommittee for analysis of the recruitment, retention and advancement of ethnic librarians in the University. As a result of the letters sent by the 1991/92 LAUC President, bridges to important systemwide library committees are forming; particularly the collection development and public services committees of Library Council.

Committee members old and new are hopeful that these energies and activities will assist in the further, more significant development of a more equitable multicultural university.

AN AFTERWORD: VOICES OF THE AUTHORS

It is amazing to think about how different the report would have been if we had approached it at the same level as we approach other committee work. It would have been just another superficial and forgettable document. Because of the sensitive nature of racism and the discovery that, in our own particular ways, we were all profoundly affected by it, we were forced to take our deliberations to a deeper level. We took the risk that we might touch raw nerves–and this did happen. But at some point we reached a level of trust that encouraged us to keep going until the job was done.

–Lillian Castillo-Speed

If a value judgement is overly apparent in this document, it is because our private selves were so intimately involved in the work of the committee and the writing of the report. As ethnic librarians performing professional ethnic library services, it is difficult to distinguish between our ethnic identities and our ethnic labors.

—Rafaela Castro

Cultural diversity seems like a new toy, to be used for playing the same old political games. Even though terminology to describe certain ethnic groups has evolved from 'culturally deprived' to 'cultural diversity', there is still a long way to go before the inevitable term of 'cultural equity' is understood and accepted.

—Carol Yates

NOTES

1.   Librarians Association of the University of California, "The Many Voices of Diversity; Report of the Ad Hoc Committee on LAUC Regional Workshops on Cultural Diversity in Libraries," (Los Angeles: University of California, 1992), Photocopy, 9-10.

2.   Percentages are based on 1992 figures for self-reported ethnicity for students, faculty and librarians. (Office of the President, University of California, Oakland, March 1993).

3.   Joseph A. Boisse and Connie V. Dowell, "Increasing Minority Librarians in Academic Research Libraries", *Library Journal* 112 (April 15, 1987): 53.

4.   Allan J. Dyson, "Reaching Out for Outreach," *American Libraries* 20 (November 1989): 952.

5.   Judy Horn [LAUC President 1989/90], Charge to the Ad Hoc Committee on LAUC Regional Workshops on Cultural Diversity in Libraries, 8 December 1989 [appended to "The Many Voices of Diversity"].

6.   "The Many Voices of Diversity," 1.

7.   Ellen Meltzer [LAUC President 1991/92], cover letter sent with copies of "The Many Voices of Diversity" to systemwide library committees and to library schools of the University of California, 13 August 1992.

CULTURAL DIVERSITY STAFF TRAINING:

THE CHALLENGE

Cheryl Gomez

DESIGNING A TRAINING PROGRAM: IS IT WORTH IT?

In 1991, the University of California, Santa Cruz Libraries were faced with the reality that the year 2000 had arrived nearly a decade early. The Hudson Institute's *Workforce 2000,* published in 1987, had alerted us all, management, librarians and staff alike that radical shifts in our demographic reality at the local, state and national levels would impact our workplace practices in ways we could only imagine.[1] We learned that we would need to accommodate an "increasing number of women, minorities, and immigrants" into our work force; that the historical focus on affirmative action hiring would not do justice to the complexity of issues raised under the heading of multiculturalism;[2] that we would need to seek new and creative ways to successfully ride the "second wave of affirmative action" beyond access for minorities and towards full participation and collaboration of all our colleagues.[3]

Historical, Social and Economic Context

Our project needed to be seen in the context of both a national and local agenda that ranked cultural diversity as a priority for our future

Looking to our own community, we needed to understand the local context in which we would be approaching such an undertaking. We live in a seaside resort town, recovering from a major earthquake, beset by issues of growth and environmental protection. Santa Cruz is a community with a rich tradition of eccentricity and social responsiveness in which local residents are increasingly faced with issues that besiege larger cities: dwindling municipal and county resources, decline in social services, underemployment, hate crimes, Immigration and Naturalization Service raids, gang activity, and so forth. If we were to address issues of cultural sensitivity we needed to take into account the reality of the communities in which our colleagues lived.

Creating a Committee

In May 1991, the Cultural Diversity Task Force was created to recommend to the University Librarian a cultural diversity staff training program and to oversee the implementation of that program. (I use "staff" throughout this chapter to include all career staff, librarians, supervisors and managers, unless otherwise stated.) The organizing principles of the project were (a) to offer a variety of activities and events with broad appeal that would serve as an introduction to diversity awareness (these events led to a series of formal workshops facilitated by an outside consultant on skill-building in the workplace); and (b) to seek input, feedback and evaluation of programs and events from library employees.

The mission of the Task Force was to foster cultural diversity competency through a combination of knowledge, awareness and skill-building. The overall goal was to develop and maintain a positive working environment in which all persons would be able to achieve their full potential through acceptance and mutual respect.

Describing Organizational Culture

When we began to look around at our co-workers and to actually open a dialogue on "differences" with them, we discovered that "diversity" came in guises that went beyond the categories we were reading about in the projections for the year 2000.[4] We were looking at designing a training program that could take into account the cultural intersections between ethnicity, race, class, gender and sexuality; but we were also uncovering a remarkable universe of diversity that included religion and spiritual values, urban and rural upbringings, age, physical abilities, political philosophies and much more.[5]

Our library was culturally diverse and we certainly met the required affirmative action standards; it was not, however, an integrated workplace. Out of 132 employees, 13 of us were people of color. At the time the Cultural Diversity Task Force was charged, we had 17 supervising librarians, 6 white men, 1 Latino, and 10 white women; 17 non-supervising librarians, 7 white men, 7 white women, one African American woman, 1 Asian woman, and 1 Latina; out of 20 supervising staff members we had 5 white men, 1 Latino and 14 white women; all other staff numbered 78 and included 22 white men, 2 African American men, 1 Asian American man, 48 white women, 1 African American woman, 3 Asian American women, and 1 Latina. Clearly, we would need to aggressively pursue an organizational shift from monoculturalism to multiculturalism in our library, if we were to keep pace with history in our state and the social reality of our own organizational culture.

Influenced largely by UC Berkeley's Project DARE, we recognized the need to focus on skill building as well as awareness of cultural differences in the work place.[6] I do not think we understood at the outset how very challenging this task would be. Many of us assumed that some cataclysmic event, similar to the Loma Prieta earthquake of 1989 that measured 7.1 on the Richter scale, would jolt us into awareness and activity. What actually happened over the course of the next two years was quite different, but equally transforming. It was a very exciting and enlightening time.

While other committees in the library were grappling with such issues as a wiring project that would link us to a campus network and the world; an automation plan that could see us into the twenty first century; a budgetary crisis resulting in serials cancellations, hiring freezes, equipment and supplies reductions, and early retirements, we, the Cultural Diversity Task Force, were discussing issues of trust and communication in the library. We were examining issues of cultural, ethnic and racial identity, respect, difference, the cultural significance of our own names, heritage, lineage, our prejudices and our preconceptions about one another.

Long-term Planning

Our first and most important bit of advice to libraries embarking on staff training is to be patient and plan for the long term. Systematic oppressions have been constructed historically in this country; they target groups of people as "less than" in our culture in ways that are ever-present in our workplace.[7] Vesting a multicultural philosophy that promotes the acknowledgment, appreciation and use of cultural differences in the life of an organization takes time, a lot of time, and hard work.

This chapter describes our experience at UCSC with designing a two-year staff training program on diversity and offers guidelines for how to accomplish a program in your own library. To answer the question, "Is the process of designing a program worth the time and effort?"—the answer is an unqualified yes.

Guidelines

1. Analyze the historical, social and economic context in which you will be designing your program. Social reality at the national and local levels seriously influences the lives and attitudes of your co-workers.
2. Be patient. Keep an open mind. Plan for the long term.

DIVERSITY AND LIBRARY ADMINISTRATION

The Role of Management

The single most important element in designing a staff training program is commitment from the top.[8] Training will undoubtedly involve all levels within your library; but without enthusiastic support from the director, or in our case the University Librarian, expectations of success will be less than effective. Your staff will want to know specifically how much time and money and how many people the head of your library is willing to invest in diversity training. At UC Santa Cruz, we were fortunate to have a University Librarian who validated the process through funding, release time for staff to attend our programs and the freedom for the Task Force to explore the dimensions of diversity and difference in our library. If a criticism could be made on the role of top management in the design of the program, it was that the Task Force failed at some critical moments in the process to communicate to staff the support lent by management; the effect of this was sometimes to isolate management from line librarians and staff.

Composition of the Cultural Diversity Task Force

In December, 1992, on the recommendation of the Task Force, the University Librarian established a permanent Library Committee on Cultural Diversity. The Committee consists of one ex-officio member of top management (i.e., the Assistant University Librarian for Human Resources) and 12 appointed members selected from various classification levels of librarians and career staff, with librarians constituting not more than half of the total membership. The Committee includes one member from each of the eight library departments; a representative each from middle management (the Library Management Group); the Librarians Association of the University of California, Santa Cruz; the Library Affirmative Action Committee; and one member-at-large who is selected on the basis of interest, experience and/or training. Appointed members serve staggered two-year terms and, to the extent possible, represent the full spectrum of diversity within the library. The University Librarian appoints a Chair and Vice-Chair as coordinators; however, all committee members share equal status and all are responsible for maintaining the committee's environment of mutual trust, openness and respect for one another's opinions.

A critical quality of the Cultural Diversity Committee is the ability to problem solve in an environment of trust and creativity. When the Committee is reconstituted annually, the group schedules a retreat moderated by a trained facilitator to enhance collaboration skills. The significance of commitment and cooperation amongst members becomes clear under the pressure of the work the committee undertakes. I will describe below the specific activities we organized at Santa Cruz. The point, here, is that everyone on the committee must participate actively in the work of subcommittees, for example, if the work is to go forward. Accountability is key. In our library, we had several subcommittees coping with programs, exhibits, the hiring of a workshop facilitator, coordinating a new employee sponsorship program, and so forth. Everyone was required to perform.

Guidelines

1. Enlist the commitment of the chief administrator of your library. Commitment must be specified in terms of money, people and time as well as visible moral support.
2. The selection and charge of a diversity committee must be integrated into the administrative structure of the library; otherwise it appears peripheral to the stated mission of the library.
3. Committee members should represent the full range of diversity among library employees.
4. Each newly constituted diversity committee should undergo a facilitated skill-building workshop as preparation for planning a program for all library staff.
5. The diversity committee must be based on trust and accountability; the sensitivity issues involved in designing an awareness training program and the work involved demand this.

DEFINING DIVERSITY IN YOUR LIBRARY

Research and Dialogue

After securing the support of management, the most important task a cultural diversity committee undertakes is creating a clear and honest definition of diversity as it applies to the organizational culture of your library. R. Roosevelt Thomas Jr. speaks to the inherent tension between coping with "racism" in the workplace on one hand and on the other promoting an active appreciation of cultures other than our own. "The wrong question: 'How are we doing on race relations?' The right question: 'Is this a workplace where "we" is everyone?'"[9]

Defining the "we," in all its dimensions of "difference," is critical to the success of any training program. Your committee should make an honest evaluation of the intersecting variables of race, ethnicity, gender, sexuality, economic status, abilities etc. in your library's particular environment. This information should inform all activities around staff training. The idea is to make your environment multicultural, not to accede to an ideal standard of "correctness" that is unrelated to your specific organizational culture.

How do you achieve this? You achieve this through research and dialogue. I cannot overstress the importance of discussion.

Discussion is time-consuming and, for co-workers whose workdays are inevitably overburdened, can seem unproductive. Ultimately, however, the time that colleagues spend talking with each other and above all listening to one another provides the most important empirical data you will collect.

Reading and discussing what you read is also very important. Racism, sexism, ageism, classism are learned systematic oppressions. At the personal level, target and non-target groups consciously or unconsciously learn to be either perpetuators of oppression or perpetuators of the victim position.[10] No one is born with oppressive attitudes and beliefs.

Modern "isms" can be expressed at the personal, interpersonal, institutional, or cultural levels.[11] Organize a subcommittee to prepare a bibliography of readings that apply to the particular diversity needs of your library; update the bibliography; hold informal discussion groups on these readings. It is sometimes easier to acknowledge negative attitudes if we approach them with some intellectual distance and then attempt to integrate what we have learned into our daily behavior.

The Process of Change

Personal and interpersonal change involves acknowledging and valuing one's own cultural background and recognizing the particular dynamics found within different cultural groups.[12]

> Changing institutional and cultural racism involves a commitment by all members of an organization to examine norms, values, and policies. Overt power discrepancies must be changed. More subtle reward systems that reinforce, differentially, status quo behaviors must give way to systems that include diversity at every point....[13]

Assuming that our Task Force represented the diversity of our libraries at UC Santa Cruz, "we" were defined initially as a circulation supervisor, a media specialist, a bibliographer, two department heads, the head of personnel, two reference librarians, a conservation specialist, two library assistants from serials, a science librarian and the library accountant.

We asked everyone we could think of on campus and in the community to give us advice on how to do a training program. In the process of this activity and in attempting to define diversity in our library, we became much more to each other than a job description.

We became Asian American, African American, bicultural-cultural, white American, Jewish, immigrants from Asia, Scandinavia, Eastern and Western Europe and the Caribbean, with rich cultural traditions and assumptions. We also became for each other women, men, mothers, fathers, gay, lesbian, working-class, middle-class, young, old, blondes, brunettes, redheads, white-haired, artists, designers, musicians, collectors, poets, explorers, dancers, crafts people, surfers and computer buffs.

We learned that we had all at one time or another been part of both a target and non-target group on the basis of our diversity and that the experience could open our hearts and minds to acknowledge and appreciate our "differences" and to understand that while all forms of oppression are not equal in our culture, no one form should be impugned.

This process was not easy. We unlocked doors that had been safely locked against interaction with co-workers. We steadfastly maintained an atmosphere of inquiry, not blame, which was essential, and everyone was committed to the task. If you think, however, that you know the people you work with, let a facilitator organize a few "identity" exercises for you and find out how very little you actually do know. It is fascinating.

Guidelines

1. Analyze the organizational culture of your library. What brings people together; what keeps them apart? "Multicultural" includes a wide variety of variables which constitute "diversity." Find out who your people are; do this through research and group discussion at the committee level and with the staff at large. Trust your conclusions.
2. Record what you learn.

THE PROGRAM

Design: A Mixed Strategy Approach

You probably will not feel as if you have begun the process of diversity training until you hold your first event and follow-up with staff evaluation. As outlined above, a lot of time and effort is expended in getting to this point. It is tempting to think that an on-going program should have a linear design, a beginning, middle, and an end. A straight line is not, however, the most direct route to awareness and in this section, I will advocate a mixed strategy for organizing events and workshops. Remember, there is no ideal model for multicultural awareness training; there is only the informed intent to plan events that will stress the inclusiveness of a wide variety of variables that constitute diversity in your library.[14]

There are risks as well as advantages to a pluralist approach. It is a challenging and sometimes frightening prospect to try and select the best vehicle for raising awareness on an issue that is as sensitive as intercultural communication. Sometimes you will get it wrong; but when it is working it is well worth it.

A mixed strategy approach to diversity training attempts to draw on as many different resources as possible. Experts in the field of diversity awareness can come from every walk of life and each has his/her contribution to make; the skills and talents of outside consultants, local scholars, community activists, and co-workers should be explored. Find out what people know and are willing to share, for example, personal narratives, dance, song, story-telling, individual research, workshop facilitation, and so forth. Use surveys/questionnaires, informal discussions with staff, and visits to departments in the library to solicit ideas for programs. Take advantage of the multidimensional lives of your co-workers; they represent an untapped well of creativity that will enhance any training program. The idea is to encourage an inclusive organizational culture that consists of commonalities; who better to create this than the members of that culture?

Implementation

Local Resources

At Santa Cruz, we spent a full year researching consulting firms who offered diversity awareness training. We knew that we wanted a comprehensive training for all employees that would take into account the cultural climate of our library and provide follow-up to a program which we assumed would raise a number of sensitive issues. I will evaluate the advantages and disadvantages of such a program after a quick look at the manner in which we utilized local resources. During the year leading up to the workshops, we offered a variety of events and activities for staff that functioned as preparation for the formal facilitator-led sessions:

1.   We started by organizing an employee sponsorship program. Each new employee was assigned to both a librarian and a member of staff who introduced the new person to the library and campus community. The sponsor was available to answer questions of an informal nature that were not covered by the relationship with a supervisor. The intention was to make new members of the staff feel welcome, by providing them with contacts outside their immediate department.

2.   At the same time, we organized a series of panel discussions on the general topic, "Working in a Multicultural Environment." For these events we recruited faculty and staff members from other departments on campus to share their experiences. We videotaped these sessions, which included a panel presentation of three people and a substantial period of open discussion with library staff. Over a period of several months, we were able to participate in a dialogue with colleagues from the Asian American, Chicano/Latino, African American and Native American communities on campus. Obviously, there is opportunity for organizing future programs that focus on many more variables of diversity.

3.   We sponsored lunch-time video showings of popular feature films with multicultural themes from the library's collection, followed by staff-led discussions.

4.   A book group meets regularly to discuss books and films on multicultural themes.

5.   Library exhibits regularly feature multicultural themes, such as Dia de los Muertos (Day of the Dead); The Twenty-fifth anniversary of the Watts Riots; Visioning the Next 500 Years; History and Culture of California Indigenous Women.

6.   A Cultural Diversity Staff Bulletin Board announces local cultural events, speakers, poetry readings, films, dance, theater, and so forth.

These kinds of activities serve two functions. Not only are employees brought together across rank and department in thought-provoking discussion, the library's collection is also challenged to support a multicultural program.

Outside Consulting Firms

We hired an outside facilitator to offer three all-day workshops on diversity awareness. Initially we wanted the consultant to conduct a "climate survey" in the library and ensure follow-up to the workshops, including a written report with recommendations for future programs. Staff and librarians were free to sign up for any one of the three workshops. We had decided not to divide the sessions by rank or department, but to seek a genuine cross-section of diversity variables in each session. Prior to the first visit by the facilitator, Task Force members, acting in teams, visited every department of the library to answer questions and address concerns regarding the workshops. Each session was addressed by a senior university administrator which affirmed the importance of the work to the mission of the university.

Outside consultants can be very expensive. Our research revealed that service averaged between $800-$1200 per day. We were very careful, therefore, to solicit recommendations for firms from reliable sources on campus and in the community. We also prepared a detailed list of questions relevant to our organizational climate for the two facilitators we eventually interviewed.

The workshops accomplished our primary objective, to provide career staff and librarians with a shared learning experience that could serve as both a foundation and a catalyst for continued examination and discussion of broadly defined diversity issues across hierarchical structures.

An invaluable contribution by the facilitator was the outsider's unbiased evaluation of an organizational environment. This was not always easy for people to hear; management in particular was challenged by an evaluation that stressed improved communication across ranks as a condition for a healthy work environment.

The responses to the workshops, both before and after, were as varied as the people with whom we work. The spectrum of opinion on the effectiveness of the workshops ranged from "a complete waste of time" to "one of the most enlightening workplace events ever experienced." We met a substantial degree of resistance to the workshops from some employees, while others were eager to evaluate and change an environment of low morale. The Cultural Diversity Task Force welcomed all of these responses, as every opinion indicated involvement. We had created an open forum for opinion on multiculturalism in our library and needed to consider every contribution.

In times of fiscal crisis, libraries will not always be in a position to hire expensive outside consulting firms. It is important to stress again that other local, less expensive resources, can be utilized effectively. It is often the case that members of your community have been trained in workshop facilitation and are willing to offer their services at a more modest rate.

Guidelines

1. Learn by doing. Vary your programs.
2. Call on local talent and expertise from your library, community, college and university when planning events. Seek input from staff and librarians.
3. Investigate carefully before hiring an outside consulting firm. Questions regarding specific costs, methodology, program materials, and quality of follow-up should be determined before hiring a facilitator.
4. Listen to and evaluate the feedback of your co-workers.

EVALUATION OF THE PROCESS

It is important to remember that diversity training is not an end in itself; change is the goal, change in behavior and change in attitude.[15] The definition of change is the act or process of transformation. I would like to close this chapter, in that spirit, with an evaluation of the process rather than with a formal conclusion.

At the end of the first phase of awareness training in our library at Santa Cruz, we submitted a report to the University Librarian, evaluating two years of planning and activity and making recommendations for the future. The most significant was the recommendation to establish a standing library committee on cultural diversity with membership rotating throughout the staff, affirming the necessity for on-going programs on the "isms" of our organizational culture. In addition, we encouraged management to hold regular library-wide, open discussions on diversity issues and concerns; we recommended that supervisors be offered training to help in developing specific policies related to cultural sensitivity in the workplace; we encouraged all library departments to evaluate and improve communication structures and encouraged managers to communicate with staff in general and express appreciation for a job well done. We stressed the need for staff to take responsibility for addressing communication issues with supervisors and managers; supervisors and managers were encouraged to listen and respect the ideas of staff. We recommended the continuing use of campus and community resources to present workshops, programs, and cultural events that would promote multiculturalism in the library. These may seem very common-sense principles of interaction between co-workers in the workplace. It is fascinating, however, how unconscious and historical neglect can easily lead to misunderstanding and frustration across ranks in an organizational culture.

A quote from the Task Force report summarizes, I think, our collective state of mind at the time of its presentation:

> The charge undertaken by the Cultural Diversity Task Force has been in large part an experimental process that led us into the uncharted territory of trust and communication amongst managers, supervisors and staff in a complex organization.... The road to diversity awareness has not been a smooth one and the horizon still lies before us.... [16]

The year 2000 is getting closer and has taken on a metaphoric significance for many of us that should neither intimidate nor paralyze our efforts to create change. Multiculturalism is not achieved by the accumulation of knowledge or "putting in" your hours in a skill-building workshop. If this were true it would be a lot easier to accomplish than it is. "Biases, prejudices and stereotypes run deep and die hard" in our society;[17] but struggle is the birthplace of change. An on-going program of awareness training does create a climate in which change can take place and for this reason it is certainly worth pursuing.

What we have learned at Santa Cruz is that some days you get it right and some days you do not, and that the increasing number of days in which you sense behavior in your colleagues that is genuine and enlightened and not compelled by the fear of "correctness" indicates that you are moving forward. We understand the mission of our project, to contribute to a more positive, supportive work environment through increased understanding, acceptance and mutual respect as well as the visible, externalized expression of appreciation for cultures other than our own. If we work hard, we might be half-way there by the year 2000; I think we would be pleased if we were.

NOTES

1. W. B. Johnston and A.H. Packer, *Workforce 2000: Work and Workers for the Twenty-first Century* (Indianapolis: Hudson Institute, 1987.)

2. University of California, Berkeley, Project DARE: Program Synopsis (December 1991), 1. Project DARE began at Berkeley as a pilot program for new

students in the residence halls during the 1988-1989 academic year. It was designed to orient new students to a complex, multicultural university environment. The program's focus has been on basic awareness about culture, stereotypes, and assumptions. As of Fall 1991, approximately 4000 students have participated in the program. Planning for a staff program began in 1991. Recognizing that approaches to staff and students may differ, focus was placed on awareness skill-building and an action plan for implementing new skills in the workplace.

3.   Robert G. Trujillo and David C. Weber, "Academic Library Responses to Cultural Diversity: A Position Paper for the 1990's. *Journal of Academic Librarianship* 17, no. 3(1991): 157.

4.   For definitions of "organizational culture," see Mary A. Fukuyama, "Taking a Universal Approach to Multicultural Counseling," *Counselor Education and Supervision* 30 (September 1990): 7; and E. H. Schein, "Organizational Culture," American Psychologist 45 (1990): 111.

5.   Derald Wing Sue, "A Model for Cultural Diversity Training," *Journal of Counseling and Development* 70 (September/October, 1991): 100.

6.   U. C. Berkeley, *Project DARE,* 1.

7.   Valerie Batts and Joyce Landrum Brown, *Assumptions and Definitions,* (Cambridge, MA: VISIONS, Inc. 1990), 2. VISIONS is a consulting firm offering diversity training to organizations. UC Santa Cruz hired a VISIONS facilitator for its diversity workshops. The above is one of many documents prepared and distributed at the workshops by consultants from VISIONS.

8.   "What to Do, What to Avoid and How to Begin," *Bulletin of the American Society of Newspaper Editors* 739 (March 1992): 3.

9.   R. Thomas Roosevelt Jr., "From Affirmative Action to Affirming Diversity," *Harvard Business Review* 90 (2) (March-April 1990): 109.

10.   Valerie Batts, *Modern Racism: New Melody for the Same Old Tunes* (Cambridge, MA: VISIONS Inc., 1989), 3.

11.   Batts and Brown, *Assumptions, 4.*

12.   Batts, *Modern Racism, 3.*

13.   Ibid., 3.

14.   Fukuyama, "Taking a Universal Approach," 7.

15.   "What to Do," 5.

16.   Cultural Diversity Taskforce, *Report to the University Librarian* (Santa Cruz, CA: University of California, Santa Cruz Libraries, 1992), 8.

17.   Sue, "Cultural Diversity Training," 105.

CULTIVATING WORKPLACE DIVERSITY AND EMPOWERING MINORITIES BY FOSTERING MENTOR-PROTEGE RELATIONSHIPS

Edward D. Garten

Cultural diversity has always been a fact of American society. However, today, that same diversity is growing more important to our collective future and is posing more challenges for the workplace. Our places of work are changing rapidly in gender, color, nationality, and cultural point of view. It has been noted that by the year 2000 women will make up about 47 percent of workers, with minorities and new immigrants by that time holding 26 percent of all jobs; up from 22 percent in 1990.[1]

On the day that I initiated the preparation for this chapter, my local metropolitan newspaper's lead editorial proclaimed that the character of the new President-elect was being revealed through his pick of appointees.[2] The editorial suggested that the soon-to-be new administration would be shaped, in part, by its inclusion of more women and minorities at many levels of government and through its active cultivation of workplace diversity. The editorial went on to suggest that what was becoming clear about the new President-elect was his emphasis on balance: male-female; white and people-of-color;

insider-outsider; and moderate-liberal. Indeed the editorial suggested that this diversity was being achieved with consummate skill, avoiding charges of "quotas" or "reverse discrimination." That same editorial ended by noting, quite forthrightly, that this commitment to balance and diversity may have a "down side." Diversity, itself, so suggested the editorial writer, may complicate the decision-making process and, perhaps, make it slightly messier. Conversely, the point was made that excluding diversity, whether it be racial, gender, or the diversity of thought, would be a pretty cowardly way to make future governance easier.

Any discussion which includes in its title the phrases "empowering minorities" and "cultivating diversity" is by its very nature a "messy" discussion and one laced with politics. Since the 1970s there has occurred a heightened sensitivity to race, gender, and multicultural issues as those played themselves out within the workplace. Libraries did not escape the multiple and animated debates surrounding these issues. Debates on affirmative action, quotas, hiring goals, and the value of diversity long have been debated within the popular as well as the academic press. Notwithstanding where individual librarians stood on these issues, the facts remained that we were increasingly becoming a nation of multiple cultures; a nation where the movement of history was toward a more radical equality between men and women in the workplace; and a society which would continue to assimilate the culturally diverse within itself. The very texture of our social system will continue to be altered and enriched by these trends. While there will continue to be individuals and groups within society who will resist these trends, the press of contemporary American society will be toward more diversity and a greater acceptance, not simply tolerance, of that diversity.

PRESUPPOSITIONS AND A DEFINITION

At the outset, one might posit the question of "why" cultivate a mentoring environment in libraries which will have, among its desired ends, the empowerment of minorities and women and the creation of more diversity in the workplace? Clearly, I believe that libraries certainly should not discourage diversity in any form. One of our important roles, at least since the 1960s, has been the provision of materials and services which incorporate cultural, ethnic, and gender-specific elements which will help achieve the objectives of the library and serve its diverse clientele.

Perhaps an answer to the "why" with respect to the fostering of leadership and the establishment of mentoring relationships within libraries which will encourage diversity is the simple suggestion that we must go beyond the provision of diverse materials reflective of our clientele. We must start to believe that diversity is also a personnel and staffing issue. Staffing in our libraries needs to be a reflection of the communities we serve. Indeed, within academic libraries at least, the role of equity and diversity is becoming more critical within both the university hiring process and the regional accreditation process.

Fundamentally, I believe that the nurturing of diversity and gender equity within libraries is more than the establishment of diverse collections reflective of the diversity of opinion which is America. It is also a learning attitude on the part of the library. We must move increasingly toward a posture predicated on the belief that a richness of learning—indeed a richness of personal growth—comes about through a recognition of the talents held by women and minorities. Operational processes, and the reflective processes within those processes, increasingly must be conditioned by a stronger acceptance and appreciation of workplace diversity.

A Guiding Definition for Mentoring

My assumption is that mentoring relationships within libraries simply don't develop through some magic. Rather, they are facilitated, guided, nurtured, and sustained over time. Perhaps one of the better definitions of facilitated mentoring is the one expressed by Morrison in her book *The New Leaders: Guidelines on Leadership Diversity in America* (1992). In her definition, "facilitated mentoring is a structure and series of processes designed to create effective mentoring relationships, guide the desired behavior change of those involved, and evaluate the results for the proteges, the mentors, and the organization."[3]

READYING THE ORGANIZATION FOR CHANGE

Diversity is an extremely sensitive topic. Quite often a broad range of emotion-packed reactions reflect strong and often disparate views on this workplace issue. Indeed, the very term diversity has been in use only within the last several years among human resource professionals. Phrases such as "valuing diversity" and "managing diversity" are now increasingly common within the literature of human resource management.[4] The now archaic-sounding word, "integration," is not much used these days; however, any grappling with what diversity means must take into account racial and ethic integration and, as Morrison notes, not simply an awareness of integration's value.[5] Most importantly, individuals with diverse backgrounds "must be integrated into the teams that plan and carry-out" our organizations' activities so that their ideas and skills are used and not merely acknowledged.[6] Diversity is more than a matter of numbers; it is more than accepting differences and variety within the workplace. Rather, it is a prevailing attitude centered on the overall belief that the richness of organizational learning (which we are also about) comes not so much from a focus on selected parts of the workplace, but instead, from the whole.

Planning for Diversity

Morrison has been among those who have advocated a number of simple, yet straightforward approaches to the planning for diversity. She notes that first one has to discover (and perhaps rediscover) the diversity problems which exist within one's organization. Senior administrators are urged to strengthen their commitment to diversity. In addition, Morrison suggests that all organization managers should be prompted to choose solutions to the creation of diversity which will fit a balanced strategy. In this regard she suggests that top administrators must select solutions to diversity which address challenge, recognition, and support, and which agree on at least a modest start. Morrison argues that organizations must continually demand results and then "revisit the goals." Finally she notes that organizations must use building blocks which will sustain momentum. Organizations must plan well beyond the short-term impact of any selected diversity practices. They must leverage successes and progress and they must "add diversity to diversity."[7]

Paradigms for Diversity

Kim has been most helpful in providing us with some specific paradigms for the discussion of diversity within workplaces.[8] Kim has suggested the "golden rule" approach to diversity; the assimilation approach to diversity; the "righting the wrongs" approach to diversity; the culture-specific approach to diversity; and the multicultural approach. Understanding and appreciating each of these possible approaches is important in preparing staff to grapple with the realities and implications of workplace diversification.

In the "golden rule" approach to diversity, the goal is simply to treat each individual within the organization with respect and civility. Following this paradigm, prejudice and oppression are not recognized; rather individual responsibility and a common moral system make diversity work. Unfortunately, as we know, this paradigm has its limits. We know only too well that the Golden Rule often is applied from one's own point of reference and the pretension of color-blindness has the tendency to weaken the traditions and preferences of those who are not in the majority.

The second paradigm suggested by Kim is described as the assimilation paradigm. This model calls for shaping individuals to the dominant work and cultural style already present within the workplace. Assimilation, generally, according to Morrison is now regarded as a dysfunctional workplace strategy simply because the drive toward homogeneity may stifle creativity.[9]

A third paradigm which Kim called "righting the wrongs" is simply an attempt to address historical shortcomings as they have worked themselves out (or not worked themselves out, as the case may be) in the workplace. We know this approach as being closer to prevailing definitions of affirmative action. And we know that under this paradigm, because group histories are accentuated, a "we-versus-them" tension may arise within organizations.

The fourth model for moving toward diversity which Kim offers can be called the culture-specific approach. In this model employees within the organization are taught the norms, practices, and values of other cultures and minority groups in order that they might begin to work more effectively within the organization. Sometimes, however, trainers and personnel officers report that only a shallow appreciation for the values of other cultures results from the training that may accompany this model. As Morrison has suggested, employees may only learn to fit in and relate to other cultures on a superficial level. Little substantive change may result.[10]

Finally, the multicultural approach to diversity, as suggested by Kim, involves raising the consciousness level for a deeper appreciation of individual and cultural differences and creating a higher level of respect for the individual. This approach assumes the need for a broader understanding of diversity as well as the need for a deepened appreciation for the many gifts which a rich cultural mix of people brings to the workplace. The workplace, according to this model, is strengthened by raising up and celebrating a host of differences. The emphasis on employee and interpersonal skill development, in theory, has the tendency, over the long run, to negate any polarization within the workplace.

Neurotic Tendencies Which Resist Diversity

Individuals within organizations, indeed entire organizations, may exhibit hostile attitudes toward minorities and the desire on the part of senior leadership to foster broader diversity within the workplace. Kets de Vries has described the type of organization that exhibits this persecutory preoccupation. He notes that the predominant concern associated with this suspicious style is the fantasy that no one within the organization can be trusted. Guardedness and secretiveness are pervasive within such organizations.[11]

Suspicious senior managers may help perpetuate this type of organizational culture where a constant fear of attack exists and where energy is expended on identifying the enemy and finding someone or some group on which to fix blame.[12] Individuals within such organizations are often highly suspicious, and even hostile, toward any attempts at racial, cultural, or gender diversification. It is rather easy to see, as well, where diversity programs which are imposed upon such persecutory cultures may become targets of blame on the part of paranoid, suspicious individuals who fear a new organizational model. Kets de Vries is among a group of organizational behavior specialists who have used the insights of psychoanalysis through which to understand organizations. Abraham Zeleznik suggests that "you should realize that thinking with psychoanalysis as a frame of reference puts you in a position of despising pretense." Zeleznik suggests that we really need to understand what happens within organizations and zeros in on the "infinite variety of ways people have of obscuring what is real" within organizations.[13] This obscuring of what is real, this illusion of false claims which can somehow come to guide an organization is a very real phenomenon. Ann Morrison points out that the roadblocks to diversity are substantial. As she notes, no one knows the definitive cure for prejudice or for the other barriers that prevent individuals from advancing within organizations, but strong managers have made substantial headway on diversity issues "by using information and their own judgment to create solutions that fit their situations."[14] Indeed the commonly accepted characteristics of good leaders—insight, courage, skill in building organizational consensus, and energy—may be what is required, plus the intangible elements of good timing and luck!

Controlling Assumptions Which Resist Diversity

Morrison has noted that one serious mistake that many managers make is to assume that "no news is good news when it comes to hearing about advancement barriers" for minorities which might be perceived to exist within the organization.[15] She notes that many women and people of color do not feel free to comment on workplace barriers which they encounter simply because doing so separates them even more so from traditional managers. They feel like (and are often perceived like) complainers.[16] Library managers need to get at the root of such perceptions and feelings, allowing those feelings to surface in order that they might be examined and resolved, posing, ultimately, less harm to the organization.

One of the other assumptions which offer resistance to furthering diversity, and indeed, in measuring diversity, comes in part, according to Morrison, from many managers' negative reactions to government regulation of equal employment opportunity. We know that during the 1980s, in particular, some managers resented the goals and timetables which the federal government often mandated. Morrison, among others, has noted that these timetables and quotas have often come as "measures to be avoided at all costs."[17] Other managers insist, however, that quotas "are the backbone of any diversity effort because the numbers have to change if progress is to occur.[18] Clearly, we need a better understanding of how deeply held beliefs about— and prejudices toward—quotas and timetables control our attitudes toward workplace diversification.

Valuing Diversity in Libraries

Valuing diversity and establishing opportunities and programs for the enablement of mentoring relationships—which, in turn, will foster and nurture individuals who will add to organizational diversity—will accrue other short- and long-term benefits for any information service organization. These benefits include:

- Helping the minority protege generally to feel more closely connected to the cultural fabric of both the library and the library's parent institution. This integration makes it less likely that the protege will leave the library and take his or her acquired skills along.
- Helping the minority staff member survive the adjustment period. Becoming part of and feeling comfortable with a new organization is difficult for most people, but perhaps especially so for minorities who must contend with a host of other workplace barriers.
- Having a mentor "friend" or "guide" within the library can help dispel the sense of uncertainty which the minority person may be prone to feel about the new organization. The organization is viewed as a positive, goal-oriented place in which to work.
- Giving the new minority employee a "safe" environment in which to explore new ideas or to offer suggestions for library improvement. All new employees—minority and non-minority alike—are sometimes fearful of offering suggestions early in their tenure. This may be especially true for many minorities who are at the same time dealing with the internal feelings of "does this organization really want me?" and "does this organization really accept me?" A mentor can create an environment in which new ideas or untested ideas can find a safe haven.
- Evidence suggests that performance and productivity ratings are higher for proteges than for nonproteges.[19] Certainly we want evidence that those we mentor are performing at a higher level and are being viewed by others as models for productivity.

ENLISTING THE SUPPORT OF
DEPARTMENTAL ADMINISTRATORS

A library leader working to create a minority mentoring program should seek ways of suggesting to first and second tier supervisors that the effort, if successful, will have both short and long term benefits to the library. It will have benefits in terms of recruitment. Successful minority proteges most likely will speak highly of the library outside of the library. And the library, subsequently, will develop a reputation for providing a welcoming and supportive working environment for minorities. The library will, if the program is successful, experience less minority attrition. Fewer minorities will leave the library and take their newly acquired skills with them if they are exposed to a supportive, developmental mentoring environment. Additionally, a successful program will allow many minorities who may, at present, lack certain desirable skills to achieve a readiness for higher level responsibilities with the library.

First and second line managers and supervisors need to be shown by example, and through rewards for success, that they can aspire to flexibility in their communications with individuals of varying backgrounds. I would suggest a four-step approach whereby supervisors can improve their relations among people of differing backgrounds. There exists the need for planning and programming which will allow supervisors to (1) understand at a deeper level that cultural differences do exist; (2) develop self-acceptance of one's own cultural background and style; (3) learn about other cultures; and (4) aspire to a higher degree of flexibility as one interrelates with minorities in the workplace.

Additionally, library administrators need to gain a deeper appreciation for the rather simple—yet easily overlooked—notion that women, men, and minorities often do not share a common culture within organizations. Each group often identifies, defines, and organizes its workplace experience in unique ways. Because of these deeply rooted differences in understanding the workplace, each person often may be unable to see or understand the experiences of others. Several factors may account for these differing experiences. First the context of organizational life is often different for each group. Second, each group appears most comfortable communicating within its own group. And third, the cultures of race and gender often offer unique perspectives on organizational or workplace experience. That is, they often have remarkably different "histories" of workplace relationships. It is little wonder that many library managers feel themselves ill equipped to handle cultural differences in the workplace, since they often have such limited contact with other races or cultures. In moving to create mentoring environments which will engender a rich staff diversity which, in turn, will persist over time, one may still encounter, unhappily, a few managers who may exhibit tendencies toward wanting to "protect" minorities or who continue to rely on stereotypes or untested assumptions in dealing with minorities and women. Clearly there is a need for a better understanding of the differences among the foreign born and among women as groups; a need for a better appreciation of the sources of misperception and misunderstanding of cultural contributions; a need for a stronger understanding of the work dynamics that make some within the workplace feel part of the larger organization and others feel excluded; and a need to understand and act upon the specific areas in which managers can make a difference in fostering a more humane and diversified workplace.

My experience in engendering mentoring relationships among those who have had little experience in mentoring is that people often harbor a number of unspoken relationship, gender, and culture concerns. My experience suggests to me that mentoring relationships which will promote diversity within libraries never really get off the ground until these unspoken concerns are raised for conscious inspection and addressed in candid, honest fashion. For example, we need to acknowledge that there will be people on our library staffs who view any diversification as "social engineering." The truth remains that forms of subtle racism and sexism exist within all organizations and workplaces. Library administrators who believe in staff diversity and who believe that such diversity can be fostered, and then given impetus, through structured and facilitated mentoring programs, must be honest and candid in the face of covert or overt opposition or resistance. Most staff members, of course, are not racist, nor are they resistant to change. It's often a matter of not sharing a common experience. A white male is more likely to relate to a white male than he is to a Hispanic male. With someone of my own background I don't have to explain where I am coming from.

Staff members who are under consideration as possible mentors for a minority person may express considerable concern about "racial-type" issues emerging at some point in the mentoring relationship. For this reason they may be somewhat reluctant to take on a mentoring responsibility where such a personally daunting area of discomfort lurks just below the surface. Overcoming this often subliminal uncomfortableness may take much patience and extensive discussion with a potential mentor. The mere acknowledgment that some level of uncomfortableness exists will certainly be a start toward securing ways and means through which to address racial issues were they to arise within the mentoring context.

Women and Mentoring Relationships

With respect to women, there still exist a number of barriers to the mentoring relationship. Ragins notes that mentors not only have the opportunity to train women in organizational politics, they can also serve as buffers against discrimination. Unfortunately, she notes major barriers such as women not actively seeking mentors and male mentors not selecting female proteges.[20] Libraries wishing to overcome these apparent barriers should provide more opportunities for female supervisors to interact with potential mentors and should cultivate more female mentors at lower organizational levels where a less prominent mentor-protege relationship might be developed. Obviously, there will be those who will be overly concerned about sexual issues which may arise in pairing a male mentor with a female protege. As Morrison has pointed out, the "spontaneous attraction between two people can stimulate positive energy for both and result in increased productivity for the organization. An arranged match may miss that spontaneous surge of excitement yet still be productive by all measures.[21] For arranged matches to be successful, according to Morrison, it may be wise to identify multiple candidates for the mentor role and then allow the proposed protege to spend a brief amount of time with each and see how the personal chemistry develops.[22] To be fair, however, it should be noted that much of the literature in this area has dealt with the other extreme, that of completely avoiding the relationship that tends toward the very personal. There is really little more advice which can be offered here. The mentor creation leader will need to assess the compatibility of male-female mentor-protege relationships with great care, and only after substantial discussion with those under consideration.

Characteristics of Effective Mentors

When looking for possible mentors among your departmental heads, always look for individuals who can both listen and talk. Many minority mentoring relationships have soured early due to a mentor who talked more than he or she listened. Obviously when looking for an initial group of mentors one needs to look for people who have successfully managed people within their own departments. These people should also be individuals who have been successful at chairing library taskforces or committees. As one identifies promising minority proteges one will, naturally, be cataloging skills for which these individuals need development or reinforcement. Subsequently, one will be identifying departmental managers who have many of the skills which are needed in the protege. Often skills will include both technical and professional/organizational ones. Finally, as one identifies potential mentors among present supervisors, at all levels of the library's organization, one needs to look for individuals who are well respected by other staff and whose opinion is readily sought after on a range of work-related problems. When those who consciously, or unconsciously, resist the creation of a minority mentor-protege program actually see those whom they respect highly succeeding in mentoring efforts, many earlier resistances may fall.

In addition to the observations above, I would suggest a range of other characteristics which will be found in strong mentors. These include: strong interpersonal skills; organizational knowledge; technical competence; personal power and charisma; willingness to be responsible for someone else's growth; ability to share credit; and a high degree of patience and willingness to take risks.

Above all, the first mentors chosen for an initial effort at what I call "mentoring diversity" must be enthusiastic about doing so. And they must be actively involved in the tasks of mentoring. My own definition of mentoring in the context emphasizes the astute pairing of a more skilled staff member with a less experienced (and less, we assume, organizationally attuned) minority person.

Potentially successful minority mentoring programs fail when mentors lack the time to work with their proteges or when they delude themselves into believing that mentoring need only take a few minutes for coaching and feedback in a given week of work and activity. Mentors must recognize that mentoring is hard and time-consuming work. It is both quantity of time and quality of time.

CREATING PRACTICAL AND EFFECTIVE MENTORING ENVIRONMENTS

The most important aspect of any mentoring program undergirding a diversity thrust is the clarification of goals for the program. My experience is that these goals must be straightforward, practical, and amenable to formal and informal evaluation. In a very practical sense a library administrator should expect his or her first and second line managers to be role models for minorities and women who may be in the mentoring relationships. Role models must be people who can model success, who exhibit the ability to get things done in a timely fashion, who are knowledgeable of the library's history, goals, and strategies for moving into the future, and who enjoy the work they do and exhibit explicit satisfaction in that work. First and foremost, a minority person who is involved in a mentoring relationship needs to be in a relationship that models the very best behaviors and ideas of the workplace.

Managers chosen as mentors have a role to play in helping minority proteges make effective working connections within the library. Effective manager mentors will help minority proteges make connections to state and national professional organizations, will offer guidance with respect to the most effective way of getting things done within the larger organization of which the library is part (i.e., city government, the corporation, or the university), and will facilitate the protege's entry into library meetings or committee structures.

In a practical fashion, mentors may also choose to offer minority proteges some of the following guidance as suggested by Morrison:[23]

- Act as a source of information on the mission and goals of the larger organization.
- Provide insight into the organization's philosophy of human-resource development.
- Tutor specific skills, effective behaviors, and how to function within the organization.
- Give feedback on particular, work-related observed performances.
- Serve as a confidant in times of personal crises and problems.
- Assist in plotting an appropriate career path.
- Agree to a "no fault" conclusion in the mentoring relationship in the event that the relationship does not sustain growth.

My own experience would suggest that many minority proteges desire a mentor who can exhibit a number of organizational skills for which, unfortunately, secondary schools and colleges rarely model. These attributes include modeling of on-the-job decisiveness, the effective and creative use of personal authority and power, the ability to deal effectively with workplace stress, and the ability to tolerate uncertainty and ambiguity. In selecting potential mentors within the library environment, one is well advised to consider individuals who model these behaviors and characteristics at a high level.

Obviously not all of the burden-of-proof should be placed on the mentor with respect to desirable characteristics. Minority proteges who are either library-identified or self-identified should, themselves, possess personality and attitudinal characteristics which suggest their receptivity to feedback and coaching and their willingness to assume responsibility for their own growth and development. In addition, it is desirable that minority proteges will have assessed their potential and will have some reasonable sense that they will be able to succeed at one or more levels above their present position.[24]

Mentoring Effective Written Communication

Morrison's list, noted above, includes the possibility of tutoring specific skills and effective behaviors. My own experience suggests that one of the most critical tasks in this category is the mentoring of effective communication. Arguably, most organizations employ more than a few individuals, minority and non-minority alike, who exhibit less-than-desirable writing skills. Either through inadequate attention to writing skill development in earlier education or jobs, or through lack of opportunity to practice good written communication on the job, many employees lose out in their quest for advancement and ultimately, job satisfaction, because of these inadequate skills. Regrettably, one must be honest in noting that there are those few staff members who are predisposed to believe that many minority individuals do not communicate well in writing. When they see less-than-desirable or less-than-effective examples of written communication from these individuals—which may be overlooked by supervisors or even mentors—their prejudices and preconceptions are reinforced. Given the growing importance of excellent writing in the library management environment, it is not unrealistic, nor is it patronizing, to suggest that some mentors for minority proteges may wish to explore the explicit strengthening of written communication, if needed, as one of the departmental objectives in the mentor-protege relationship. Assuming mentors who are, themselves, effective communicators through written reports, letters, and memoranda, the most important and valuable objective that can be gained here is that of modeling effective writing. We know that the most important elements that managers look for in the written work of their subordinates are organization, clarity, conciseness, spelling, and grammar. Moreover, because so many taskforce reports and other library planning documents are now developed by teams or taskforces, it is important that library mentors consider involving the minority protege in team or collaborative writing efforts where some level of both development and success can be attained. While seemingly a self-evident area for goal attainment in the mentor-protege relationship, one would be surprised to learn how often this area of skill development is ignored or overlooked.

Rotational Job Assignments

Within an effective minority mentoring program which is intended to enhance diversity, rotation of job assignments may have considerable value in exposing the protege to a broader array of organizational tasks, thus helping assure that the protege will become more flexible on the job. Job rotation allows participants to experience a wider variety of challenges within the library workplace. These challenges can stretch their skills, challenge some of their assumptions, and help them identify interests early. In planning rotational job assignments, one caution applies: Keep the mentor with one protege until experience and competence on that particular job emerge.

Sponsorship for Professional Development

All library managers who serve as mentors have an important and very practical role to play in helping sponsor minority proteges' attendance at state and national meetings of the American Library Association, the American Society for Information Science, or other related professional groups. While I assume that all library leaders will encourage their minority librarians and female librarians who are seeking broader staff roles to attend state and national association meetings on a regular basis, I am often surprised to learn how few libraries support even the occasional staff person's attendance at state and national meetings. Many of those whom we should be mentoring are now in junior or senior clerical or administrative support roles. My own experience would suggest that one of the most fruitful elements of sponsorship, especially for the paraprofessional protege, is the moral and financial support for that person's attendance at state, regional, and national association meetings. Having an experienced library leader "walk" a minority protege through an annual meeting of the American Library Association can be an eye-opening experience for that protege. Opportunities for networking are extended and the protege's horizons are opened to a more promising and professionally rewarding future.

Attributes of Successful Programs

What are the traits associated with successful programs? I would suggest that the administrator wishing to nurture mentoring relationships which will undergird and foster a more extensive staff diversification effort must be able to explicitly tie expectations of the protege, and goals set forth for the protege, to specific skills and activities within the workplace. Thus the "agreement" which the mentor and minority protege strike must be focused and straightforward. Steer away from elusive and hazy goals which resist evaluation. If, as an administrator, you are establishing mentor-protege relationships make certain that the proteges' immediate superiors (assuming these persons are not the mentors) are involved in the development of the written agreement. The protege's immediate supervisor may have suggestions for the protege's development which could be incorporated into the agreement. Indeed, it is important that the immediate supervisor be involved, periodically, in any formative evaluation of the mentor-protege relationship.

ARL Spec Kits

In 1992 the Association of Research Libraries (ARL), Office of Management Services offered a range of services which would assist librarians in establishing organizational and programmatic responses to diversity issues. As prelude to the development of the various services which ARL offers in this area, the project examined a range of issues including the impact of diversity on library services, interactions with library users, and the development of collections which would support the growing emphasis on diversity. Systems and

Procedures Exchange Center (SPEC) kits in this area include *Affirmative Action Policies and Practices in ARL Libraries, Cultural Diversity Programming, and Minority Recruitment and Retention in ARL Libraries.* The reader is urged to consult these resources for other programmatic options in structuring a mentoring and development program which will undergird planned staff diversity.[25]

EVALUATING MENTOR-PROTEGE RELATIONSHIPS

Clearly the effectiveness of any minority mentoring program which is designed to enhance and strengthen staff diversity will be premised on whether (1) that program provides the support for the developing minority person so that he or she is able to do what they were trained to do and (2) there is evidence over the long term that minority persons and women persist within the library, take on new and broader responsibilities, and therefore help create a climate in which the library is viewed by other minorities as a favorable climate in which to work. Conversely, however, the library leadership may have determined and agreed among itself that an indicator of success may well result in minority or women interns moving on to other library or information environments in more advanced positions. Practically, one may see a combination of the two as an indicator of success: some minority and women proteges persisting and advancing within the organization and others moving on to other workplaces in higher level roles.

As part of the summative evaluation of the relationship, the individuals who have been part of that relationship need to be able to consciously articulate the life cycle of that relationship. How did the relationship begin? Where did "sticking points" occur? How were these barriers or roadblocks to the relationship remedied? How did the relationship (if so) move on to a higher stage of shared and mutual learning? When did the relationship "jell" in the minds of both the mentor and the protege?

Fundamentally, the real test of a mentoring program which is intended to foster further organizational diversity is the level of long-term commitment to the program on the part of the senior library department managers. Do we have a fundamental commitment to helping minorities and women grow and respond to change within our organizations or would we rather believe a brief show of action is all that is required?

In evaluating a diversity program one should also, at some point, make a determination as to whether the organization has furthered the development of structures and policies which recognize and affirm gender differences. Are more women who were formerly not generally viewed as "leaders" now included in library leadership teams and taskforces? Is the exchange of ideas between the genders and the perception of both women and men a more vital part of the decision-making processes engaged in by the library's leadership? Are the support structures in the larger organization, that is, university, corporation, city government, perceived to be more sensitive to women as a result of the educational efforts attendant to the diversity program?

PREPARING FOR THE FUTURE: CONCLUDING THOUGHTS

Perhaps Ann Morrison has expressed it best and in simplest fashion when she said that "developing diversity is a struggle." Elaborating, she notes:

> The time and other resources required to make diversity come to life in an organization are truly staggering. What's more, there are no guarantees that certain practices will indeed foster meaningful diversity, and there is no proof that diversity will pay off for an organization. Yet some of the largest, most profitable, and most admired organizations in the United State have made diversity a priority. Their leaders are convinced that the struggle is worthwhile.[26]

Nearly all leaders, from whatever life or cultural experience they may come, are highly proficient in learning from experience. As Bennis and Nanus have suggested, most leaders have been able to identify a small number of mentors and key experiences that have powerfully shaped their philosophies, personalities, aspirations, and operating styles within the workplace.[27] Establishing the administrative goal of cultivating leadership which will derive the most value from the increasingly more diverse talents of our present and future workforce is only the smart thing to do. The reward is found in having had a hand in unlocking the voices and talents which will move our libraries and information agencies forward in progressive and successful ways.

As I conclude the writing of this chapter, the soon-to-be-new President is talking about making his administration a "reflection of America." This reflection is intended to say "yes" to the diversity which characterizes the America of the very late twentieth century. During the presidential campaign of 1992, Bill Clinton, during a televised speech at Notre Dame, observed: "To the terrible question of Cain—am I my brother's (and sister's) keeper?—the only possible answer for us is a thunderous yes." As this century nears its end, the fundamental struggle within the workplace will continue to be the struggle to achieve a broader recognition that people of worth do not need to be identical. We know that today's minorities are rapidly becoming tomorrow's new majorities. To create a vibrant workforce within the workplaces we know as libraries will mean, in the future, that we will be required to explicitly recognize that we are our brothers' and sisters' keepers and that those of us in leadership positions within libraries are called upon to foster explicit mentoring and enabling environments which will allow the richness of talent available to us to take root and grow.

NOTES

1. Audrey Edwards, "Cultural Diversity: The Enlightened Manager—How to Treat All Your Employees Fairly," *Working Woman* 16 (1) (1991): 45-51.

2. Editorial, Dayton Daily News, 10 January 1993.

3. Ann M. Morrison, *The New Leaders: Guideline on Leadership Diversity in America* (San Francisco: Jossey-Bass, 1992), 5.

4. Ibid., 4.

5. Ibid.

6. Ibid.

7. Ibid., 263, 264.

8. J. Kim, "Issues in Work Force Diversity" (Panel discussion at First Annual National Diversity Conference, San Francisco, CA, May 1991).

9. Morrison, *The New Leaders,* 6.

10. Ibid., 7.

11. Manfred F. R. Kets de Vries, *Organizations on the Couch: Clinical Perspectives on Organizational Behavior and Change* (San Francisco: Jossey-Bass,1991), 247.

12. Ibid., 249.

13. Zeleznik, Abraham."The Leadership Gap," *The Academy of Management Executive,* 4(1) (1990): 7-22.

14. Morrison, *The New Leaders,* 267.

15. Ibid.,165.

16. Ibid.

17. Ibid.,227.

18. Ibid.

19. American Society for Training and Development, "Benefits of Mentoring," *ASTD Info-Line Series,* September 1986, 2-4.

20. Belle Rose Ragins, "Gender and Power in Organizations: A Longitudinal Perspective," *Psychological Bulletin* 105(1) (1989): 51-88.

21. Morrison, *The New Leaders,* 173.

22. Ibid.

23. Ibid., 13.

24. Ibid., 13-14.

25. Association of Research Libraries, Spec Kit *v*163, *Affirmative Action Policies and Practices in ARL Libraries;* Spec. Kit *v*167, *Minority Recruitment and Retention in ARL Libraries;* and Spec Kit *v*165, *Cultural Diversity Programming.* Washington, D.C.: Association of Research Libraries, Office of Management Services, 1992. These publications are available from ARL for $33.00 ($22.00 for ARL members). For information call the Office of Management Services Publications Department, (202)232-8656, or order from ARL at 1527 New Hampshire Avenue, N.W., Washington, D.C. 20036.

26. Morrison, *The New Leaders,* 266.

27. Warren Bennis and Burt Nanus, *Leaders* (New York: Harper & Row, 1985), 188.

THE MANY WE ARE:

GUIDELINES FOR MULTICULTURAL COLLECTIONS
BASED ON THE BLOOMFIELD COLLEGE PROJECT

Danilo H. Figueredo

It might not be problematic for research-driven think tanks like the Library of Congress, the Research Libraries of New York Public, and Harvard University to develop a multicultural collection. As these institutions attempt to document the human experience at a given moment in history, they acquire, with book budgets in the millions and generous endowments, a diversity of materials that is—be it by accident, coincidence, or intentionally—truly multicultural. But this is not so with smaller academic libraries where the creation of a collection on diversity might lead to territorial conflicts, especially if the curriculum does not include multiculturalism.

It is not uncommon for a faculty member to question the selection of a title on multicultural education over a required text on science. The instructor might protest, "Specific gravity is what we need. My students don't need to know about a multicultural society. Specific gravity is the thing." Persuading this faculty member could be onerous, and asserting academic and intellectual freedom in the selection process, while certainly an academic librarian's right, might not resolve the dispute. To minimize the conflict, the library intent on building a multicultural collection must have a written policy statement supportive of diversity, and a library committee supportive of the policy.

The collection development policy is the product of hours of work. It is the written expression, edited and refined, of the dialogue amongst committee members. It "is a crystallization of each library's understanding of how its collection can serve its mission...an assertion of the library's place in its institution...."[1] The policy is the document that states explicitly the beliefs of the committee. For a policy to support multiculturalism, the committee must want it to do so. It is therefore crucial, and obvious, to recruit committee members who perceive diversity as a genuine academic agenda.

This might not be easy. There are two camps on the issue and the division is almost biblical, for few are neutral. Scholars like Arthur Schlesinger and the late Allen Bloom champion the cause against diversity. Schlesinger warns, "What happens when people of different ethnic origins, speaking different languages and professing different religions, settle in the same geographic locality and live under the same political sovereignty? Unless a common purpose binds them together, tribal hostilities will drive them apart."[2] Allen Bloom dismisses the notion that "all knowledge claims are self-contained within a particular culture"[3] and maintained that at a particular instance in history one civilization might be more advanced than another. Other scholars affirm that diversity "bashes" Western European civilization. Writes Schlesinger, "'Multiculturalism' arises as a reaction against Anglo- or Eurocentrism...."[4] The underlying concern is the abandonment of Western culture. "Can any education be serious that does not focus centrally on Western civilization?" asks an educator.[5]

These writers believe that multicultural education and scholarship war on Eurocentrism and that multiculturalism is, in fact, turning away from plurality to particularism. Explains Diane Ravitch, "pluralistic multiculturalism must contend with a new, particularistic multiculturalism....Advocates of particularism propose an ethnocentric curriculum to raise the self-esteem and academic achievement of children from racial and ethnic minority backgrounds."[6]

The educators in the multicultural camp respond that there is no aggression toward Western European traditions. Affirms scholar Molefi Kete Asante, "There is space for Eurocentrism in a multicultural enterprise so long as it does not parade as universal. No one wants to banish the Eurocentric view. It is a valid view of reality where it does not force its way...."[7] What is being proposed is the study of Western culture in relation to the "interaction with other cultures and with its own subcultures."[8] Mexican poet and Nobel Prize winner Octavio Paz expresses it best: "The ideal of a single civilization for everyone, implicit in the cult of progress and technique, impoverishes and mutilates us. Every view of the world that becomes extinct, every culture that disappears, diminishes a possibility of life."[9]

Ultimately, what multicultural diversity does is to rearrange cultural priorities to invite a world view, to "allow us to hear all the voices that are used by the human race,"[10] explains educator John F. Noonan.

THE BLOOMFIELD COLLEGE PROJECT

Dr. Noonan is the President of Bloomfield College, an institution whose mission is to "prepare students to function at the peak of their potential in a multiracial, multicultural society."[11] Affiliated with the Synod of the Northeast Presbyterian Church (U.S.A.), the college has traditionally served diverse ethnic groups from northern New Jersey. It was founded in 1868 as a seminary that served the educational needs of newly arrived German immigrants and where courses were taught in German. By 1913, the curriculum was primarily in English and its students represented diverse nationalities. In 1987 Dr. Noonan, then a newly appointed president, "saw the college's multicultural identity as a unique resource and gave crucial support and leadership from the top."[12]

From 1989 to 1991, a grant from the New Jersey Department of Higher Education helped the college implement its mission through a unified project, "Toward A Multiracial, Multicultural Society." The project "supported programs that reached every sector of the campus."[13] A major activity was the revision of the curriculum.

The college "approached multicultural curriculum development through ...faculty development. Starting with the concrete goal to revise or develop one course, faculty restudied their disciplines for the content of perspectives of race, gender, ethnicity, and class." Diverse faculty members, including librarians, participated in five semester-long seminars conducted by preceptors-in-residence who were experts in diversity.[14] The readings included works of fiction, research papers, treatises, all emphasizing a world view. Participants also worked for a year with outside consultants from their own disciplines.

The project was successful because "faculty shaped and owned the program."[15] Likewise, the faculty responded favorably to the library's plan to develop a multicultural collection, a goal that emerged out of the librarians' participation in the seminar and for which funds were initially allocated from the grant. Obviously, finding support from such a predisposed faculty was not an issue. But the Bloomfield College experience is not universal.

LIBRARIANS AS ADVOCATES

When a college-wide initiative is not present, the administrator responsible for Bloomfield College's success recommends a departmental approach.[16] This is an appropriate strategy for the library: "academic libraries are in a key position to play a significant role in the infusion of ethnic studies into the core curriculum. Given the mission of the library...[it is] in an ideal position to help the teaching faculty add cultural diversity issues to their courses...."[17]

Academic freedom is in the province of the library. A library has as much liberty as faculty members to forge new intellectual directions. With the mandate to serve its community, the library's direction is evident. Even if the curriculum does not include multiculturalism, the diversity found within the college community yields a genuine need:

> [T]he composition of college and university student bodies has altered radically in the recent past. Two decades ago...it was a great deal easier to characterize 'average' college freshmen—how they looked, sounded, and how prepared they might be to use the library. Today, any past assumptions about patrons can hinder rather than expand public service. The patrons college and university libraries now serve represent a diverse mix of cultures, ethnic origins, gender groups, ages, socioeconomic classes, and physical abilities.[18]

Even opponents of diversity acknowledge this change. "[C]ultural pluralism is now generally recognized as an organizing principle of this society,"[19] writes Ravitch. Government sources, academic publications, and the popular press are replete with articles highlighting estimates that in the year 2050, Asians, Latinos, African Americans, and other nonwhite groups will make up nearly 47 percent of the population.[20] These are ethnic groups and minorities that to varying degrees are represented on campuses today and have demonstrated interest in their ethnicity.[21] Given the opportunity, these students inject into their assignments an international perspective. It is the role of the library to meet the needs of these students and to provide the required materials.

FORMING THE MULTICULTURAL LIBRARY COMMITTEE

The library director needs to share this vision since he or she is ultimately responsible for the collection. If there is lack of support at this administrative level, the librarians serving under the director must advocate the need for a multicultural collection. They may initiate change department by department. Multicultural reference sources, for example, may be added to the reference collection. Where the director does not sit on the library committee, the librarians might use the committee as an advocate. Where the director is part of the committee, the librarians must lobby members and seek succor from sympathetic colleagues. The intent is advocacy. The objective is the collection. The desire is support from the committee.

Forming a supportive committee demands shaping and activism on the part of the librarians. Rather than await appointments made by the faculty's ruling body or the department chairs, the librarians should identify supporters and urge them to volunteer, a welcomed action on many campuses where the library committee is not popular and in want of members.

Beyond the traditional membership of faculty and students, the committee should be opened up to the non-teaching community: administrators, representatives from student services, and even staff. This is not only philosophical, for multiculturalism is the participation of many, but also practical. The more who partake of the process, the more who take it to heart. The success at Bloomfield College is credited to a campus that took ownership of the project.[22]

The diversity of opinion of the diverse interests represented on the committee results in an inquisitive process that is similar to a self-study. Traditional approaches will be questioned. Standard responses will be dismissed. The library will be viewed from inside as well as from the outside. Emerging questions will flesh out the agenda: Who are we? where are we going? what do we want our collection to look like? The driving force will be the process to define multiculturalism.

ATTEMPTS AT DEFINITIONS

There is no consensus on a definition. There are writers who maintain that this is precisely how it should be, that multiculturalism is not static, definable; that it is an on-going activity.[23] Each institution, then, must arrive at its own definition.

The diversity within the library committee allows for a definition that is valid for the particular campus. The committee, however, should invite a wide array of views. Focus groups might be held. Faculty and librarians might interview students. The interviews and discussions could have a scientific, analytical base, but it might be just as effective to keep the conversations informal. The primary question is: What is your definition of multicultural diversity? The secondary question is: What types of books and what subjects would you like the library to purchase?

The emerging definition and inventory of interests and needs will draw a profile of the collection. However, the focus should not be limited to the particular ethnic groups on a campus. It is just as important, for example, to own a collection on African Americans and Latinos as materials on Italian Americans and Jews. As a guideline, the library should acquire materials on the experience of the groups that the American Library Association has identified as deserving attention: African Americans, Latinos, Native Americans, and Asian Americans.[24]

Beyond books on race and ethnicity, the collection should include works on gender, feminist literature, gay studies, aging and the physically challenged. The committee must also determine whether or not the library should purchase works written in languages other than English.

FOREIGN LANGUAGES

For many advocates of multicultural education, foreign languages are an intrinsic element of diversity. Others suggest that foreign languages should be included in the collection only if it supports the curriculum. The response varies from campus to campus. However, should the committee decide to obtain foreign language materials, it must define the scope and extent of the collection.

Foreign language acquisitions might be placed on opposing poles which are, in fact, a continuum. At one end is the research collection, at the other, a "drug store" collection. The research collection allows an independent researcher or doctoral candidate to complete a good portion of this work in one location. The research collection brings together as many documents as possible on a particular topic. The intent is to document humanity during a historical period. A foreign language collection of this type includes mainstream publications, vanity press, government documents, flyers, chapbooks, and so forth. The materials are obtained directly from the country of origin through a librarian's shopping tour of the region, exchange programs, and, most commonly, through foreign nationals contracted by the institution and working out of a home base in their country. Clearly, this is a collection that needs to be well funded. In most small colleges, the collection does not assist Ph.D. candidates.

The "drug-store" collection is funded on a much smaller scale. It is not meant to support and foster research but to meet the needs of the curriculum, the students, and the faculty. This is a collection that consists mainly of books published by major houses and of well-known periodicals. Acquisition is done through book vendors in the United States. It is possible that the books on the shelves at the college library could be found in a bookstore. For example, a reader wanting a recent novel from Latin America could find it at the library, but also purchase it at a Spanish bookstore in Manhattan or Miami. Thus the designation "drug store," suggesting titles readily available at foreign language bookshops based in this country.

POLICY STATEMENT

The commitment to foreign languages and to building a multicultural collection must be converted into practice by the production of a written policy statement. It is the statement that demonstrates support, that presents guidelines for a systematic approach to collection development.

Much has been written on the subject, and the American Library Association and the Association of College and Research Libraries continue to publish guidelines and manuals on collection development and policy statements. Of particular help are the monographs *Collection Management: Background and Principles* by William A. Wortman and *Guidelines for Collection Development,* edited by David L. Perkins.[25] The following is a summary of the basic elements found in policy statements:

- *Introductory Statements:* Mission and role of the library; community analysis; statement on intellectual freedom; rules under which libraries operate; purpose of policy; responsibility for development; timetable for review.
- *Body of Policy:* scope and limits of collection; subjects covered; number of copies to be purchased; selection criteria; formats; languages; weeding and retention; preservation; special materials; gifts policy; procedures for selection and weeding.[26]

In developing a multicultural collection, the policy statement must contain language that unequivocally supports diversity. It might be argued that the statement does not need to spell out multiculturalism, but the absence of specific language could relegate the multicultural collection to an outreach service, with a potential for neglect. On this terrain, the committee must be aggressive in assuring the written inclusion of multicultural diversity.

BLOOMFIELD COLLEGE'S COLLECTION DEVELOPMENT POLICY

Bloomfield College is revising its policy statement as this chapter is being written. As part of participation in the faculty development seminar, a librarian worked closely with a faculty member from Rutgers University Graduate School of Communication and Information Studies to write a document that reflected the multicultural mission of the college. A draft was prepared in the summer of 1991. A second statement was written during the fall semester of the same year. This document was revised in the winter of 1993 and the library committee planned to study it during the fall of 1993.

Adhering to the principle that commitment to multicultural diversity must be expressed from the outset, the introduction to the statement was rewritten. The original version expressed that the library would "meet the instructional needs of Bloomfield students."[27] The revision adds, "to support the mission of the college which is to prepare students to function at the peak of their potential in a multiracial, multicultural society."[28]

The statement referring to the library's general collection was changed from "The library maintains a general core collection and a course specific collection"[29] to "The library maintains a collection on multicultural diversity, a general core collection, and a course specific collection."[30]

In the area of faculty's responsibilities, language was introduced to reaffirm multiculturalism: "Faculty members should consider not only the specialized needs of their courses [when ordering materials], but also multicultural perspectives in their disciplines as well as general needs."[31]

Periodicals And Videotapes

The policy statement addresses the needs for multicultural periodicals. This decision was based on the concept that numerous publications reflect the historical circumstances of a particular ethnic group and document the existence of such a group. "The ultimate purpose of ethnic minority media is the peaceful preservation of the linguistic and cultural identity of a population that political and economic factors have put in a threatened position."[32] The policy statement's language indicates support of acquisition of these materials:

> [P]eriodicals are selected to supplement the book collection with current material. New periodicals will be added following these guidelines: Is it needed to support the curriculum? Does it fill a gap in the general collection? Is it indexed in the printed and online indexes available in the library? Does it document diversity?[33]

Videotapes were also added to the list of types of materials, a novelty in the policy statement. In the past, the acquisition of videos was regarded as a secondary activity of lesser importance than book materials. The popularity of videos within the student body and increased use of the medium by faculty, specifically in the teaching of multiculturalism, brought about a commitment to this non-print

type. Videos are regarded as equal in value to books, and the selection
of a video is not made on price but on the merit of the information
provided. The policy statement now reads: "Videos that support
curriculum and document multicultural diversity will be purchased
to complement information found on print."[34]

Allocation

The policy statement clarified allocation of funds for the support
of multiculturalism. The literature suggests diverse methods to
develop allocation guidelines. These include allocation by subjects,
by departments, by areas of subject strength, by priorities identified
by the institution, by unique collections. At Bloomfield College, the
staff opted to use at least 10 percent of the book budget to acquire
multicultural materials: "The library will acquire 10 percent of the
materials on multicultural diversity beyond the titles requested by the
faculty."[35]

BEYOND THE MULTICULTURAL COLLECTION

The Bloomfield College policy statement is not ambivalent in its
support of multiculturalism. The policy indicates that librarians are
responsible for acquisition and final selection. The document clarifies
that commitment to multiculturalism must appear from the outset
in the policy statement, that the collection must be described as a
multicultural collection, and that the faculty plays a role in the
development of a collection on diversity.

But beyond the supportive policy statement and the multicultural
collection, the library must adopt a service approach similar to public
libraries' service orientation. The collection will not be used if the
library does not promote it. Many of the students that emerge from
a multicultural background have been underserved educationally and
originate from American cities and foreign countries where library
service may be non-existent. The librarian cannot wait for these
students to walk into the library. The library must go to these
students.

It all comes down to a transformation of the role of the academic
librarian and the creation of paths that lead to growth for both the
librarians and the students. Writes a multicultural librarian,

[A]s libraries expand and adjust their roles to support the university's mission to create an open environment for culturally diverse populations, libraries can take advantage of the fertile ground offered by ethnic studies courses.... Librarians can... learn about student expectations of librarians. In like manner, librarians can express to the students of color... what expectations librarians may have of them. These open and honest exchanges of expectations and objectives should result in a rich and rewarding experience for all.[36]

NOTES

1. William A. Wortman, *Collection Management: Background and Principles* (Chicago: American Library Association, 1989), 124.

2. Arthur M. Schlesinger, Jr., *The Disuniting of America* (New York: Norton, 1992), 10.

3. Patrick J. Hill. "Multiculturalism: The Crucial Philosophical and Organizational Issues," *Change* 23, no. 4 (July/August 1991): 40.

4. Schlesinger, *Disuniting of America,* 74.

5. Hill, "Multiculturalism," 43.

6. Diane Ravitch, "Multiculturalism: E Pluribus Plures," in *Debating P.C.,* ed. Paul Berman (New York: Laurel, 1992), 276.

7. Molefi Kete Asante, "Multiculturalism: An Exchange," in *Debating P.C.,* Berman, ed., 303.

8. Hill, "Multiculturalism," 43.

9. Quoted in Hill, "Multiculturalism," 40.

10. Danilo H. Figueredo, "Developing a Multicultural Collection," *New Jersey Libraries* (Winter 1992), 13.

11. *Catalog, 1991-1992* (Bloomfield, NJ: Bloomfield College), 1.

12. Martha J. LaBare and Stuart G. Lang, "Institutional Transformation for Multicultural Education: Bloomfield College and St. Norbert College," in *Promoting Diversity in College Classrooms: Innovative Faculty and Institutions,* ed. Maurianne Adams (San Francisco: Jossey-Bass, 1992), 128.

13. Ibid.

14. Ibid.

15. Ibid., 132.

16. Martha J. LaBare, "The Inclusive Curriculum" (Paper presented at conference, "The Inclusive Curriculum: Setting Our Own Agenda," sponsored by The New Jersey Project, Parsippany, New Jersey, 17 April 1993, Photocopy).

17. Arglenda J. Friday-Dorsey. "Role of Libraries in Ethnic Studies and the Core Curriculum in Higher Education" (San Jose, CA: San Jose State University, Photocopy).

18. Phoebe Janes and Ellen Meltzer, "Origins and Attitudes: Training Reference Librarians for a Pluralistic World," in *Continuing Education of Reference Librarians,* ed. Bill Katz. New York: Haworth Press, 1990, 146.

19. Ravitch, "Multiculturalism: E Pluribus Plures," 274.

20. *Business Week.* 21 December 1992, 29.

21.   "Information Literacy: Developing Students as Independent Learners," American Association of Higher Education, National Conference on Higher Education (Valencia, CA: Mobil Tape Co, 1993).

22.   La Bare and Lang, "Institutional Transformation," 132.

23.   Ladson-Billings, G. "The Multicultural Mission: Unity and Diversity." *Social Education* 56, 308-322.

24.   Roberto J. Trujillo and Yolanda C. Cuesta, "Service to Diverse Populations," *ALA Yearbook 1989,* 7-11.

25.   William A. Wortman, *Collection Management: Background and Principles* (American Library Association, 1989) and David L. Perkins, ed. *Guidelines for Collection Development* (American Library Association, 1979).

26.   Betty Steckman, "The Collections Policy and How to Write It: A Brief Outline," (Paper presented at EMAnj/New Jersey Library Association Conference, New Brunswick, New Jersey, 28 October 1990).

27.   "Collection Development Policy," (Bloomfield, NJ: Talbott Library, Bloomfield College), Fall 1991, 1. Hereafter cited as 1991 Policy.

28.   "Collection Development Policy," (Bloomfield, NJ: Talbott Library, Bloomfield College), Winter 1993, 1. Hereafter cited as 1993 Policy.

29.   1991 Policy, 1.

30.   1993 Policy, 1.

31.   Ibid., 2.

32.   Stephen Harold Riggins, *Ethnic Minority Media.* (London: Sage Publications, 1992), 287.

33.   1993 Policy, 1.

34.   Ibid.

35.   Ibid., 4.

36.   Friday-Doresey, 10.

RETHINKING THEORETICAL ASSUMPTIONS ABOUT DIVERSITY:

CHALLENGES FOR COLLEGE AND UNIVERSITY LIBRARY PLANNING

William C. Welburn

INTRODUCTION

Ralph Ellison once said that "American diversity is not simply a matter of race, region, or religion. It is a product of the complex intermixing of all these categories."[1] What Ellison stated more than 20 years ago is still pertinent to the present discourse on diversity in colleges and universities throughout the United States. Diversity is indeed a complex issue for the higher education community, primarily because of the way in which people interact with one another on campus to determine the fate of the common square.

Crucial to the academic library's planning agenda is an advocacy within the library organization that is actively engaged in campus dialogue. Internal leadership can maintain an ongoing feel for change within the environs of the university resulting from the interactions of librarians, faculty, administrators and other staff, and most importantly the students. Leadership can also be the locus of the strategic considerations of the library in relation to the structure of the institution and the process through which new ideas travel. In developing this thesis, relevant ideas from organization theorists who write about diversity have been explored to see how strategies on diversity might evolve.

THE MILIEU OF HIGHER EDUCATION

Campus discourse, whether at Stanford University or Olivet College, the University of Wisconsin or George Mason University, illustrates how volatile diversity has been as an issue in higher education. Conversation also tells us that there is an important question for college and university planners: what kind of future is there for diversity in an organization that is *loosely coupled?* There are two features of the college as an institution that are crucial to our understanding of organizational change in the context of the present discussion: the *structure* of institutions of higher education and the *conceptualization* of diversity.

The Organizational Context

The accidental death of a building is always due to the failure of its skeleton, the structure.[2]

Many organization theorists have used colorful metaphors to describe the structure of colleges and universities, including the college as an organized anarchy, a web of subcultures, or a loosely coupled system. Kuh and Whitt observed that "few colleges are monolithic entities; dominant subcultures and subgroupings within them shape institutional change."[3] Clark, Astuto, and Kuh used Karl Weick's idea of a *loosely coupled system* to suggest that decisions and the organization of work in higher educational institutions can be better understood by examining the *strength* of coupling among subunits, between planning and decision making, or among other organizational elements.[4]

Loose coupling has been conjured up as a metaphor of organizational structure because it gives the observer of an organization a view of its activities that differs from those found in traditional theories of bureaucracy. In their recent reconceptualization of the idea of organizational coupling, Orton and Weick wrote:

> Loose coupling suggests that any location in an organization (top, middle, or bottom) contains interdependent elements that vary in the number and strength of their interdependencies. The fact that these elements are linked and preserve some degree of determinacy is captured by the word coupled in the phrase loosely coupled. The fact that these elements are also subject to spontaneous changes and preserve some degree of independence and indeterminacy is captured by modifying the word loosely. The resulting image is a system that is simultaneously open and closed, indeterminate and rational, spontaneous and deliberate.[5]

In other words, loose coupling represents an unpredictable relationship among units, decisions, and actions within a single organization. College campuses are connected by networks of activities that support the academic and nonacademic socialization or *cultural learning* of students, faculty, administrators, staff, and visitors.[6] Academic programs are far-reaching and often fragmented. They are sustained by a web of academic support programs, such as libraries, computing centers, advising and related student services, and counseling centers, many of which have emerged in their present form in recent decades. Despite overarching institutional responses, diversity is still defined and interpreted variously throughout the loose structure of the college.

Orton and Weick continued their description of loose coupling in organizations:

> If there is neither responsiveness nor distinctiveness, the system is not really a system, and it can be defined as a noncoupled system. If there is responsiveness without distinctiveness, the system is tightly coupled. If there is distinctiveness without responsiveness, the system is decoupled. *If there is both distinctiveness and responsiveness, the system is loosely coupled.* (emphasis added) This general image is described here as the dialectical interpretation of loose coupling.[7]

Dialectical indeed! Libraries seeking a clear definition of institutional purpose on diversity can be left dumbfounded by the fluidity of communication among agencies on a single campus. It is not uncommon that when planning for specific diversity initiatives, libraries may find two separate offices with similar programs and different interpretations of diversity, yet each knowing that the other exists. For example, on one large university campus a single office administers two different summer programs for pre-first year students. They are very aware of one another—-one was an outgrowth of the other—-yet they remain apart, assuming very separate identities and different budgetary allocations. An observer can distinguish one from the other only through careful analysis of the populations each serves: one contributes to the *cultural* diversity of the campus while the other contributes to the university's commitment to *socioeconomic* diversity.

ACADEMIC LIBRARY STRATEGY ON DIVERSITY

The two-pronged strategy chosen by a single office to address social and cultural diversities in the aforementioned example is particularly important for a library's own planning toward support for each program with, for instance, an instructional program. If we define diversity as the interactions of a mixture of people within a shared space, and our programmatic approaches are characteristic of loosely coupled organization, then libraries are faced with the task of creating strategies in which we interpret the meaning behind the public discourse of diversity on campus. One approach is to treat diversity as a dynamic construct, one that considers both the historical context and the institution's distinctive culture. The other approach is to agree on the very nature of the concept of diversity and its elements.

The Distinctive Culture

Despite the loose structure of colleges and universities that can lead to various interpretations of diversity, each institution shares a distinct culture and *saga*. Diversity on any campus has been defined not through proclamation but through the exchanges between people, ideas, knowledge, positions, and the use of power and authority over time. Thomas Sowell has argued that the failure of today's cultural diversity movement is due to its inability to see diversity as dynamic rather than static, to observe the temporal patterns in relationships between different cultures and subcultures over time, and to identify the contributions one group might make to create changes in another.[8]

Every college or university has its historical legacy in intercultural relations. The arrival of the first Native American students, quotas imposed on Jewish students, segregation and desegregation of African American students, the development of academic programs on culture, race, and gender, and the introduction of supportive services specifically for international students are just a few examples of the adjustments of higher education that are lodged in the memories of individual colleges and universities.

The development of the organizational saga can have a profound effect on where library planners choose to concentrate their efforts in diversity. For instance, if the creation of an African American or Women's Studies Program was initiated by student protest decades ago, it would be advantageous to understand the nature of the protest, the institutional response and long term commitment, and the changes that have occurred over time to shape the present condition of the program. The admission dates of the earliest students of color, where they lived (on or off campus in segregated housing), and how they succeeded, combined with subsequent fluctuations in the number of admissions can establish a historical context for today's rhetoric in institutional strategic plans.[9]

Elements of Diversity

Three dimensions of diversity can be illustrated by the conceptual framework used to formulate strategy on diversity at the University of Iowa Libraries (see Figure 1).

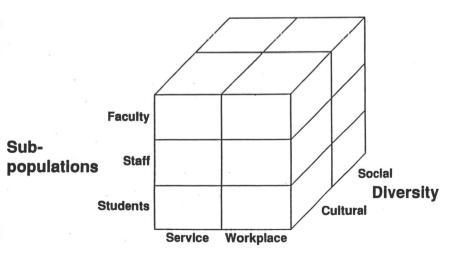

Figure 1.   3-Dimensional Matrix on Diversity

Distinctions are made among strategies on the introduction and management of diversity in the contexts of client-centered services and workplace or personnel-related activities. The matrix also distinguishes among the populations in and around the library: its staff, faculty, and other university employees, and students.

There are also important distinctions to be made among the dimensions of diversity itself, as illustrated in the earlier example of the campus office with concurrent summer programs. In the matrix, a distinction is made between social and cultural diversity because different strategies are employed to reach common goals. Unfortunately, there are too many instances where such distinctions are not considered, thereby creating situations where ideas for sound programs are misapplied. Reginald Wilson argued that academic achievement and culture must be differentiated from one another and proposed a "tripartite model based on the relationship between the valuation of oneself by others and the valuation of self by oneself."[10] While the model's most effective explanatory power lies in the clarity it brings to exploring differences in academic achievement and the reception of cultural groups in higher education, it is the distinction drawn between cultural identity and academic performance that is relevant to the present discussion of the library's strategic planning initiatives on diversity.

The manner in which *minority* and *at-risk* are used interchangeably in academic library outreach programming for students is an example of our failure to recognize the varieties of diversity and the importance of Wilson's argument. At times there can be an overlap between minority and at-risk student populations. Both Wilson and Claude Steele have noted that there is a correlation between "negated culture" and achievement.[11] Yet, strategies that work require library outreach program planners to delineate between the concepts of at-risk as a social situation and minority as a cultural signifier. A library's outreach program for a community of students with a higher than average chance of leaving college for academic reasons is likely to focus on a rigorous introduction to the college-level use of information sources and services, while programming geared toward students of color ought to be grounded in the institutions' valuation of culture. On the one hand, teaching strategies that are used for at-risk students might focus on skill-building experiences. On the other hand, programming geared toward students of color might take advantage of cultural frameworks that introduce students to collections, information resources and services that affirm the importance of multicultural contributions to the human record.

In essence, there are at least three aspects of diversity that should be considered in strategic planning: distinctions between client service and workplace issues, populations in and around the library, and the social/cultural dimensions of diversity. It is necessary to keep in mind that they will be interpreted in various ways, given the loosely coupled nature of higher educational institutions. However, when they are organized in a matrix, the matrix can provide a much clearer picture of how to frame questions and begin projects. When combined with an assessment of the evolution of diversity within the institution, the matrix places librarians in a better position to engage in strategic planning on diversity.

DIVERSITY STRATEGIES-IN-ACTION

If academic libraries are to formulate strategies for managing diversity in such a complex, loosely structured environment, then it is essential to encourage leadership from within their staffs. It cannot be expected that an entire staff will maintain a high level of interest in diversity initiatives over time. Besides, it is unlikely that they will agree upon a single definition and have time to assess or monitor changes in institution-level priorities. An approach emerging in recent years among academic libraries is to create the position of, or assign responsibilities as, a diversity officer to assume such a leadership role.

Whether an official position created by library administration or a more informal commitment taken on by staff, the diversity librarian has the potential to move the organization, if the librarian is handed both authority and accountability. In corporations, diversity officers are sometimes given vice presidential status within the organization.[12] Diversity librarians, however, are usually fairly low in the bureaucratic order. As a result, their ideas often are unheard by the larger organization at best, and at worst can be greeted with contempt, especially during times of fiscal retrenchment. Accordingly their planning becomes self-contained and there is, ultimately, a ghettoization of diversity rather than its extension throughout the organization.

Additionally, as with any other position, administrators also ought to set standards of accountability for diversity librarians. Crafting strategy on diversity can be subverted when expectations are not clearly mapped out and goals are neither set nor evaluated. And given the controversy surrounding diversity as an institutional initiative, it is essential to establish credibility for any aspect of library diversity planning.

The diversity librarian who is vested with both authority and accountability can function as a leader within the organization in identifying the elements of diversity on campus and in defining the distinctive character of the institution manifested in its history. What is also critical is that the diversity librarian has the opportunity to converse with other campus officials and engage the library in the informal networks established throughout the institution to support diversity as a planning initiative. This can be done through scanning the external environment and by conducting a cultural audit with the library to figure out the underlying cultural assumptions of library staff as a basis for creating strategies.[13]

Examples of Strategies in Action

By using the above considerations in formulating strategy on diversity and in allocating personnel to execute strategy, academic libraries that are seriously considering diversity as a key component of strategic planning will have a full range of options on programming to pursue. Two examples are given below.

First, many institutions are refocusing their attention on problems faced by new and untenured faculty, particularly those from underrepresented groups within their academic departments. Few libraries have staff time to allocate to conduct inquiries throughout their campuses to establish linkages with academic programs which are concerned about the fate of their untenured faculty. With the luxury of time, a diversity librarian can pursue leads throughout the campus to identify departments that provide support for untenured faculty and explore opportunities for library programming. The intent here is to seize any occasion for human contact.

Second, cultural diversity can be a workplace initiative concerning training student assistants. One approach is for the diversity librarian to develop strategies to recruit students of color into positions where mentoring relationships can be established by library staff. The underlying intent is to retain students through the duration of their college careers. Mentoring relationships can also lead some students to consider the library and information professions among their career options. Another approach is for the diversity librarian to develop mechanisms for training students from majority populations to understand the nature of multicultural societies. Strategies can be employed to promote ethics and responsibility in the workplace and in workplace behavior and to develop skills in intercultural communication.[14] In this instance, an assessment of the cultural assumptions of the organization—particularly of those who supervise students—may prove to be important to determine how to initiate diversity training for student assistants.

Both examples fit within the three-dimensional matrix discussed earlier. Neither example can be effective without some prior knowledge of institutional history. Most importantly, while both can be done within traditional staffing patterns, their chances for success, and for success in managing diversity in general, are greatly enhanced through the efforts of a diversity librarian.

CONCLUSION: THE INTEGRATION OF CULTURES

The future of diversity as an organizational strategy for academic libraries lies in our ability to turn Ralph Ellison's concern for the integration of race, region, religion, or other cultural categories into practice in the provision of library and information needs on campus. Assessments of the institution's many subcultures, combined with an internal audit of the cultural assumptions of the library itself, can provide an initial framework for managing diversity. Yet it is crucial that library managers foster support for individual staff who are ready and willing to carry out a sustained, long-term program.

The underlying assumption of this essay is that diversity cannot have a future if it continues to exist as a celebration of differences in an organization or community. Rather, diversity can be viewed in all of its complexities as the integration of cultures within a shared space. The challenge for the academic library community is not to buy into diversity. Instead, it must press forward on meeting the challenge of managing diversity.

NOTES

1. Ralph Ellison, *Going to the Territory* (New York: Random House, 1986), 37.

2.   Matthys Levy and Mario Salvadori. *Why Buildings Fall Down* (New York: W.W. Norton,1992), 2.

3.   George Kuh and Elizabeth Whitt, *The Invisible Tapestry: Culture in American Colleges and Universities* (College Station, TX: Association for the Study of Higher Education, 1988), 52.

4.   David L. Clark, Terry A. Astuto, and George Kuh, "Strength of Coupling in the Organization and Operation of Colleges and Universities" (Paper presented at the Conference on Research and Thought in Education Administration, New Brunswick, New Jersey, April 7-8, 1983).

5.   J. Douglas Orton and Karl E. Weick, "Loosely Coupled Systems: A Reconceptualization," *Academy of Management Review* 15 (1990): 204-5.

6.   Kuh and Whitt, *The Invisible Tapestry,* 37.

7.   Orton and Weick, "Loosely Coupled Systems," 205.

8.   Thomas Sowell, "A World View of Cultural Diversity," *Society* 29 (November 1991): 37-44.

9.   Roger Wilkins, "A Modern Story," *Mother Jones* 16 (September 1991): 12-13.

10.   Reginald Wilson, "Curricular Diversity and Academic Achievement," *Liberal Education* 77 (January/February 1991): 12-15.

11.   Claude Steele, "Race and the Schooling of Black Americans," *Atlantic* 269 (April 1992): 68-78.

12.   Julie Amparano Lopez, "Managing: Firms Elevate Heads of Diversity Programs," *Wall Street Journal,* 5 August 1992. It is also worth noting that in a survey of more than 1400 companies, 64 percent of those surveyed did not see diversity as a priority over the next two years. See Joan E. Rigdon, "Managing: Work Force Diversity Stirs Little Concern," *Wall Street Journal,* 22 May 1992.

13.   R. Roosevelt Thomas, *Beyond Race and Gender: Unleashing the Power of Your Total Work Force* (New York: AMACOM,1991), 34.

14.   William Welburn, "Diversity." Paper delivered at Conference, *The Role of the Student Assistant in the Academic Library,* of the Iowa Library Association/ Iowa Chapter of the Association of College and Research Libraries Staff Development Committee, 3 February 1993.

CULTURAL AWARENESS AND BIBLIOGRAPHIC INSTRUCTION IN ACADEMIC LIBRARIES

Scott B. Mandernack, Poping Lin and David M. Hovde

For the past several decades, educators and public service librarians in American academic institutions have become increasingly aware of the emerging nature of our multicultural society and the specialized needs of diverse user groups within our campus communities. Whether based on racial or ethnic background, country of origin, age, gender or other characteristics, all have become recognized in some fashion as distinct population groups with particular needs. These changing demographics are evidenced by both the ever-increasing numbers within each of these groups, and the increasing percentage of the total student population that these groups represent. While specific responses to these changes vary across the spectrum and from one institution to another, the common thread that pervades is the recognition that the individuals within these populations require special attention to instill confidence in their use of library facilities and to further their development of library research skills.[1]

From the earliest research it has been noted that the attainment of library skills is an important factor in the "non-traditional" student's overall development within American academic culture.[2] However, the unique cognitive styles of these diverse groups, drawn from a variety of cultural and environmental stimuli, may present barriers to achieving successful library research skills. These barriers, which may be numerous, and vary with the group in question, include: deference to authority figures; cultural perceptions of gender; learning styles and rates; differences in the role of libraries in the education process; cultural concepts of research and independent thinking; language proficiencies; educational disadvantages; and physical barriers and lack of appropriate equipment.[3]

Instructional design librarians must be cognizant of these special needs and be open to implementing appropriate and relevant programs. However, before one can begin to plan and design library services to address these particular needs, a basic, very fundamental premise must first be developed: an acute sense of cultural awareness. Throughout all aspects of program design and development, consideration must be given to the recognition of and sensitivity to the needs of individuals from a wide variety of backgrounds and experiences.

Culture is a notoriously ambiguous concept, the definition of which has baffled the minds and imaginations of many anthropologists and other scholars. Nevertheless, the fact that culture is all-pervasive and penetrates into every nook and cranny of human life is almost universally acknowledged. Culture is indeed commensurate with human life itself. Formulations of the concept of culture by some of the most prominent anthropologists may well illustrate this point. A. L. Kroeber and C. Kluckhohn, after reviewing 164 formulations of the concept of culture, presented their own:

> Culture consists of patterns, explicit and implicit, of and for behavior acquired and transmitted by symbols, constituting the distinctive achievement of human groups, including their embodiments in artifacts; the essential core of culture consists of traditional (i.e., historically derived and selected) ideas and especially their attached values; cultural systems may, on the one hand, be considered as products of action, on the other as conditioning elements of further action.[4]

Clifford Geertz, perhaps the most influential anthropologist in this country in recent decades, offers a much simpler but no less comprehensive definition:

> The concept of culture I suppose...is essentially a semiotic one. Believing, with Max Weber, that man is an animal suspended in webs of significance

he himself has spun, I take culture to be those webs, and the analysis of it to be therefore not an experimental science in search of law but an interpretive one in search of meaning.[5]

The definition offered by Kroeber and Kluckhohn sees culture as patterns of behavior with traditional ideas and values as its core. The second definition views culture as systems of meaning. Their approaches are different, but both stress two seemingly paradoxical points: first, culture is all-inclusive, in the sense that it permeates one's ideas, values and patterns of behavior; second, culture is specific, in the sense that different peoples have different cultures with different ideas, values, and patterns of behavior.

Just like the air we breathe, in every place and every moment, the all-inclusive nature of culture tends to dull our sense of its existence, especially the cultures of others. Cultural awareness, however, keeps alive that sense of the existence and presence of other cultures. The plural form "cultures" is used deliberately, because there is no "general culture" in the sense that culture is universal. All cultures are concrete, particular and specific to certain groups of people. Cultural awareness, therefore, by definition, embraces a multicultural approach and automatically rejects ethnocentrism or any other forms of cultural chauvinism.

Emphasizing the importance of cultural awareness is extremely relevant to the planning and development of library services in today's society. The first step in developing a cultural awareness is to identify the diversity of the population being served. There are different emphases in the interpretation of the meaning of "diversity." Some for instance, emphasize ethnic diversity, making ethnic or racial factors their major concern. To them, African Americans, Asians, Hispanics, and so forth, constitute diverse populations, in spite of the fact that some of these people actually embrace many of the same cultural constructs as the cultural mainstream of American society. Others emphasize gender (male vs. female), sexual orientation, age (adult vs. nontraditional students), or profession (majors in sciences vs. humanities). In addition to different *groups* of people, different *aspects* of people may also be considered in defining "diversity." Some emphasize the psychological aspects (such as aggressiveness vs. timidity in asking questions, or self-confidence vs. diffidence), while others concentrate on the communication aspects (such as the difference between verbal and non-verbal skills). Still others may emphasize physical aspects (those with physical disabilities), educational level, or socioeconomic status.[6] Different emphases bring to light different dimensions of the issue of population diversity.

In regard to library instruction, the authors believe, cultural awareness should be of utmost concern and given top priority. Some may argue that since learning is a cognitive process that can be scientifically described, and since science is universally applicable and not culture-specific, it follows that consideration to cultural diversity in instructional design is unnecessary. However, culture is the most pervasive and fundamental source of the formation of the self, including one's character and way of thinking. The authors believe, therefore, that although the *content* of library instruction—the knowledge to be transmitted and acquired—may be universally valid, both the transmitter and the learner of that knowledge are human beings and are, therefore, culture-specific. Both have certain culturally defined characteristics or "pre-structures" in their minds. These "pre-structures" influence not only the learning patterns of the audience but also the teaching style of the instructor. Library instructors should not only be aware of cultural diversity among the audience they are addressing, but must also consider the cultural assumptions they carry within themselves.

At Purdue University, enrollment over the past decade has experienced an overall growth rate of 12.5 percent. Distributions and growth rates among specific population groups have generally reflected the national trends, with the numbers of "ethnic Americans"—African Americans, American Indians, Asian Americans, or Hispanic Americans—international students, nontraditional students (undergraduates over the age of 25), and physically challenged students, all increasing at a faster pace than the general enrollment. The relative percentages of these diverse student groups have indeed changed the character of the campus population. In 1986/87, students identified with these groups constituted just over 27 percent of the general campus enrollment: 6.7 percent ethnic Americans, 5.5 percent international students, 14.8 percent nontraditional students, and 0.5 percent physically challenged or learning disabled students. By contrast, in 1993, over nine percent of the students identify themselves as ethnic Americans and nearly seven percent are international students from over 100 countries. Add to this the 19 percent of returning adult students and those with physical challenges or learning disabilities, and the figure of "non-mainstream" college students rises to over 35 percent, more than one of every three students on our campus.

Agreeing with Stoffle in her assertion that "the needs of students from cultures other than the dominant one...is the single greatest area of concern confronting undergraduate education in the next several decades,"[7] the Libraries seek to manifest cultural awareness through numerous efforts to implement services that better serve the wide range of learning styles and information needs represented on the campus. Library instruction in the Purdue University Libraries has evolved into a multi-faceted program of offerings reaching students with different interests, learning styles, backgrounds, and experiences. Many of the services have been designed not so much to target a particular audience within the campus community, but rather with a sensitivity to the variety of cultural and educational needs. Hence, the mix of services provided—perhaps not unique unto themselves, but the composite picture, as it were—conveys a general theme of inclusiveness, enabling us to accommodate the demands of many different users with differing viewpoints.

LAYING THE FOUNDATION

Adequate facilities and equipment, knowledgeable and well-trained staff, and well-developed collections are important prerequisites in providing effective instructional services. The building design and how it is equipped determine the accessibility to resources and, to some extent, influence the modes of instruction used. The composition of the staff, their service priorities, and their ability to communicate well shape the image and perception of the library, as well as the ability to effectively teach library concepts and resources. The scope and relevancy of the collections are important indicators of the library's ability to adapt to the needs of the users, and they provide the key resource for developing critical evaluation skills as an important part of the research process.

When considering the needs of a diverse clientele, each of these elements takes on added dimensions. The traditional thinking about each of them may no longer be valid or relevant for today's users. The changing campus populations require that we carefully reconsider each of these components to ensure that we maximize the potential for effective learning of library research skills and strategies.

Facilities

The Undergraduate Library at Purdue views itself, in some respects, as a cultural center. The building was designed with the undergraduate student in mind, and as such, includes a large number of study spaces. The Library regularly attracts large numbers of students, and has become a gathering place for groups from all walks of life. It is generally regarded as "the place to meet people," particularly for freshmen new to the campus and the community. The "study hall" concept is further supported through the provision of "incidentals," from printed guides and bibliographies to staples, paper clips, correction fluid and other supplies. While of little real significance in fulfilling the educational objectives of the Undergraduate Library, providing such token incidentals sets a tone and engages the students into the mindset that the library is available for their needs and that it supports their basic, immediate objectives— that of getting their papers or other research projects completed— as well as contributing to the long term goal of teaching them to become information literate. Encouraging an atmosphere of casual comfort and diversity, the library is promoted as a meeting place and thus serves as a foundation to a general climate of awareness and openness to a pluralistic society.

Further, recognizing that learning disabled, physically challenged, visually impaired, and hearing impaired students often require special assistance in meeting their educational goals, the Libraries received funding to develop a facility specifically designed to provide equipment and support to such students. The Adaptive Learning Programs (ALPS) center was established to offer four principal services: text services, allowing students to have their textbooks recorded on tape; adaptive equipment loan service, providing equipment for use in class or at home; ALPS center, providing access to a variety of assistive technologies for information access and other computing needs; and instructional services, offering training on the use of equipment and computer software. Use of the facility and services is restricted to students who have registered with the Office of the Dean of Students, who recommends appropriate services campus-wide to meet the needs of each individual.

Closely allied with ALPS, the Undergraduate Library also includes an Instructional Media Center, which supports a collection of audiovisual media and equipment for listening and viewing. In addition to providing information in formats other than print, it enables the Library to take advantage of computer technology for instructional purposes. A local area network was installed, including both Macintosh and IBM-compatible computers, which allows for group instruction sessions on using the online information system and also for the use of locally-developed computer tutorials on an individual basis. An outgrowth of this has been the addition of a large print software program to one of the CD-ROM workstations in the Reference unit, allowing visually impaired users to use resources that may otherwise be unavailable to them. Nonprint and computer options have proven very beneficial in expanding the availability of resources, and in providing access, both physically and bibliographically, through a variety of means, thereby addressing the needs of our diverse user groups.

Staffing

That the staff is a key resource in the provision of effective library service goes without saying. Whether at the Reference Desk or in a classroom setting, the interaction and communication between the staff and the patron often determines the success of that individual's comprehension and understanding of the information and concepts being presented. Effectively addressing the needs of a diverse user population introduces additional concerns, both in the hiring process and in training. The staff, in addition to being well trained in their jobs and able to communicate well, must also be able to understand the varying needs of a diverse user population, which includes awareness of and sensitivity to the differing experiences, perspectives, and values that individuals bring into the library. Staff members who have been sensitized to the issues of cultural differences will be more likely to serve each individual more effectively by making a better-informed assessment of the patron's actual needs, taking into account expectations, fears, attitudes, and so forth. A diverse staff, by its very nature, is much more likely to recognize differences in sensitivities, thus providing a "teaching laboratory" in the everyday work of the unit. Moreover, it also conveys to the users a greater invitation to utilize the resources of the library. By breaking down some of the initial barriers of approaching a staff member who may or may not understand—let alone appreciate—cultural differences, the library is much more approachable and presents itself in a more positive light.

Cultural awareness, then, is critical to a successful encounter with the patrons.

Approachability is one aspect of public services that includes a great many issues, from a simple smile, to how one dresses or wears their hair, as well as how he or she communicates with the patron. In many cases approachability issues are beyond the control of training or supervising. Racial and ethnic representation, young and old, male and female all contribute to the image of the service component of a library, so the hiring process is of utmost importance. While the primary concern is to recruit people with appropriate skills, representatives from the various population groups can provide the added dimension of improving this aspect of public services.[8]

The staff in the Purdue Libraries, while not absolutely representative of the general university population, has nevertheless succeeded in recruiting a truly diverse staff. For example, the Libraries administration, in recognizing the importance of a diverse staff and the development of the cultural dimension in library services, actively sought to fill a faculty position with a librarian who would bring a new perspective to strengthening library services to diverse populations. Clerical staff, graduate assistants and student assistants also reflect the diversity of the campus population, including nontraditional students, international students, ethnic Americans, physically challenged individuals, and some who are fluent in other languages, including sign language.

Training and staff development seminars or workshops have been utilized successfully in many institutions as a method to dispel stereotypes, examine cultural differences, and promote multicultural awareness among library staff.[9] Purdue University Libraries have held seminars on this and related topics. One seminar included a panel discussion entitled "International Students in the Libraries," composed of one of the authors, who is from China, and three graduate students from Kenya, India, and Costa Rica. The panelists reflected on their experiences in academic libraries both in their respective countries and in the United States. Five programs were presented in another large scale, system-wide seminar entitled "Survival At The Front." The topics encompassed a wide range of issues in dealing with the varied student populations. One session dealt with communication skills and cultural attitudes as they relate to the reference interview. Another was concerned with adult student learning styles and expectations of library service. A wide-ranging discussion was also held on perceptions that various international students have toward libraries and librarians, and vice versa. Examples of conflicting expectations based on custom were examined in relation to their effects on library service.

Collections

Collections serve as a powerful teaching tool in fulfilling the instructional objectives of the library and reflect strongly on the library's commitment to its mission. In expressing a commitment to promoting tolerance and sensitivity to cultural diversity, the library's collection should also represent these values. Materials that support research and teaching from a pluralistic perspective should be actively sought and acquired, and statements in support of this must be incorporated into collection development policies and practices. In some cases, appropriate materials may not be as readily available as are the mainstream publications, yet they are vitally important to the development of independent thinking among library patrons. This includes publications from minority and alternate presses, as well as from the literatures of other countries. It has been argued by some that, in the case of international students enrolled in American institutions, they should be expected to improve and expand their knowledge of English, and libraries need not be concerned with providing materials in their native languages. Such a view, however, may well undermine efforts to instill in patrons the sense of lifelong learning and independent curiosity. Indeed, cultural mores and attitudes are invariably reflected in language. The study of language, therefore, as a reflection of cultural values and beliefs, becomes a vital component of the educated person. Whether directed towards the international student or the American student studying a foreign language, materials in other languages can provide unique opportunities to a more thorough understanding of the world. Caution should be taken, especially in times of budgetary constraints, not to view such acquisitions as "supplemental" to the curricular needs of the university, but rather as enhancements to them.

Measures to ensure a broader scope for the collections of the Purdue Libraries have been incorporated into several collection development policies. One such policy which was rewritten was that of the recreational reading collection. For years, this collection of current materials had consisted largely of American bestsellers and popular fiction, with a small selection of English titles. However, because of an increased awareness and attention to cultural pluralism, it was decided that this collection could be expanded to provide more opportunities for "chance encounters" with literature from other countries or that expressing "alternate" viewpoints. As such, the collection development policy for this collection was enhanced to include contemporary fiction, drama, and poetry, selected from among American bestsellers (still the majority of titles, representing approximately 60 percent of the collection's new acquisitions); from small and alternate presses, emphasizing women's and multicultural literature (25 percent); and from foreign literature in English translation (15 percent).

Another collection which has been developed to more adequately serve diverse populations is the newspaper collection. The Purdue Libraries subscribe to numerous newspapers, primarily local and regional selections, with representative titles from across the United States and the world. However, in recognizing that only very limited views may be reported in this selective collection, the Undergraduate Library also coordinates and maintains a collection of international publications donated to the Libraries by campus student organizations. This collection is comprised primarily of newspapers from other countries, although a number of popular magazines are also included, and most are written in the native language.

Title selection of these newspapers is the responsibility of the student organizations, although a balance of representation and perspective is maintained by the library, with the cooperation of the Office of International Programs. Since American ethnic and minority press publications were not well represented in the collection, the library added a subscription to a collection of such publications on a full-text CD-ROM database.[10]

The benefits of the newspaper collection are great. The scope and nature of the collection are such that it is current and dynamic enough to remain a vital source of information, directly relevant to our users, yet administratively, the cost is minimal. It is used primarily as a popular reading collection; however, the educational benefits are apparent as well. These materials provide a variety of differing viewpoints (e.g., the Chinese language publications represent various social and political perspectives) which are useful in illustrating the need for careful evaluation of sources. Additionally, they encourage students to explore other sources of information which may have heretofore gone unnoticed.

The facility, the staff, and the collections are tremendously important indicators of an institution's responsiveness to its users. Developing these resources to consider the values and beliefs, skills and abilities of a diverse, multicultural population provides the foundation for building an effective instruction program. The ability to adapt to changing needs and a willingness to take risks concerning library services can be achieved more easily with an educated and willing staff, knowledgeable of the resources that are available. Instilling an attitude of tolerance and flexibility is critical to fulfilling the mission of the library in today's society in which cultural diversity is so readily apparent.

DEVELOPING THE INSTRUCTION PROGRAM

The design of instructional services for diverse user groups can be a complicated issue, one which requires considerable thought and planning. As with any instructional program, one must first conduct a needs assessment, which involves identifying the audience and determining their information and instructional needs. In a large university setting, the student population is so heterogeneous that to make assumptions and design programs to meet even the majority of the students' needs will invariably still leave significant gaps. However, a basic understanding of learning styles of both the students and the instructors may provide valuable insights into designing effective and relevant bibliographic instruction services.

Learning style generally refers to the patterns of behavior that direct an individual's learning. Each person has a unique learning style composed of several components: their cognitive inclinations, how they perceive and process information; affective aspects, including emotional and personality characteristics; physiological traits and sensory perceptions; and sociological preferences.[11] With the increasing awareness of cultural diversity in American classrooms, numerous studies have been conducted to determine whether different population groups tend to learn differently than others. Some researchers, such as Hale-Benson, Ramirez, Anderson, and Cooper, have posited that African Americans and Hispanic Americans, as a result of their cultural heritage, are more affective and relational, viewing the world more holistically, as connected parts.[12] European Americans, on the other hand, tend to approach learning more analytically and impersonally. Some research indicates that the cognitive styles of some groups are oriented more toward the visual than the oral. Others contend that Asians have a lower preference for warmth, intake, and mobility while learning, are less conforming, and remember better auditorially and visually than Caucasians.[13] Hands-on/real-life experiences may be necessary for some groups, such as nontraditional students, who tend to prefer instruction that incorporates real-life examples, things they can relate to.[14]

While the research to date suggests that cultural and ethnic differences in learning styles do exist among various segments of the population, it also engenders considerable debate. Learning styles are individual *as well as* culturally derived. Generalizations based on cultural styles, without considering individual differences, may indeed have a negative effect on the instruction.[15] As stated by Stodolsky and Lesser in an early study on learning patterns, "...social class and ethnic influences differ not only in degree but in kind, with the consequence that different kinds of intellectual skills are fostered or hindered in different environments."[16] Information about learning styles, then, may be used most effectively in individualizing the learning process for all students, regardless of the composition of the particular audience.

Language is also an important consideration in library instruction, particularly when the class includes students from other countries. The majority of international students who enter American higher education institutions come from countries where English is not utilized as a second or official language, or a language of commerce.[17] For those who have had English language training, it is not uncommon that much of it was restricted to reading and writing and the verbal aspects were not emphasized. They may, therefore, not have achieved the proficiency needed to clearly express their own questions or needs.[18] For others, English may not figure prominently in their previous educational experience at all. Problems with language skills may also be an issue for American minority students.[19] Because of language and cultural differences, as well as physical and hearing impairments, some students may not be able to absorb all the necessary information given in a bibliographic instruction session.

A student's general perception of a library, how it functions, and its role in the general education process may be quite different from that of the instructor. The student may come from a culture where textbooks are so precious they are locked away to prevent loss or are held in faculty offices rather than libraries. Students in some cultures are trained by recitation and thus feel that it is necessary to copy down every word. The material they use may be prescribed to them rather than being given a wide variety of choices as in American academic libraries. Returning adult students may find that the library they left a decade earlier is quite a different place, filled with CD-ROMs, online catalogs and other technological developments.

The issues of learning style, language proficiency, and perceptions about the role of the library are important factors in designing library instruction programs in a multicultural environment. Each has tremendous impact on the individual student's ability and capacity to learn. Understanding the role each of these factors play in the learning process, and relating them to the diversity of needs of the students, will foster more successful and effective learning experiences. The key to addressing these issues in the Purdue University Libraries has been to develop a multi-faceted program of offerings, each reinforcing the others, but presenting the information in a variety of formats, styles, and languages.

Orientation

Orientation is perhaps the most basic level of library instruction: acquainting the patron with the facility and general resources. The Purdue Libraries provide orientation services through a variety of means. To accommodate a large student body, an audio tour on cassette was developed to introduce students to the Undergraduate Library. This method of orientation has proven useful for its availability to large numbers of students, but it is also very effective for students with limited language proficiencies and for those with physical disabilities. While the Library conducts only a very limited number of walk-through tours, there is an oft-cited disadvantage to this method of orientation. Students unfamiliar with the American library philosophy or those with limited English language proficiency are unable to absorb and comprehend quickly enough all that is said before being shepherded off to another area of the library. Similarly, for physically challenged individuals on a group tour, unless the instructor or guide is completely sensitive to the limitations of the facility and the difficulties of access one may encounter, more attention may go in to simply navigating the building rather than learning about the services. The audio tour solves this problem by providing a floor plan and checklist, identifying key resources and service areas, and by allowing users to repeat any portion of the tour at their own convenience. For those patrons who are unwilling or uncomfortable to ask questions, this approach may alleviate some of their fear or trepidation, thus overcoming at least some of the initial barriers that present themselves. We must be careful, however, not to assume that the audiocassette tour can fully take the place of more personal service and contact with the library staff.

An additional approach to orientation of the Purdue Libraries is directed more specifically towards international students. In cooperation with the Office of International Student Services, representatives from the Libraries meet with newly-enrolled international students as part of a week-long orientation program to the campus and the community. A brief introduction to the Libraries is presented and a series of handouts are distributed to each student, including one brochure written in seven different languages explaining basic services, functions, and terminology of the Purdue University Libraries. Conceived and designed by the Instructional Design Librarian, this brochure is one in a series introducing individual libraries and library services. This brochure specifically serves to fulfill the following objectives:

- the need to understand the Western philosophy of libraries, i.e., 'access' to information in all formats, open stacks, etc.;
- an explanation of services available in American university libraries which may not exist in developing countries, that is, database searching, term paper consultation, the reserve materials function, interlibrary loan, photocopying;
- an understanding of the multi-faceted aspects of the 15 libraries of Purdue—their individual focus, scope of resources, services, layout, borrowing privileges, hours of operation, and so forth;
- a familiarity with the kinds of materials available within the libraries which not only provide current linkages with their culture and home countries but also to enhance their educational and cross-cultural experience in this country;

- a working knowledge of the appropriate specialized library terms needed to effectively interface with professional and clerical staff in the search for information.[20]

A follow-up session is offered to explain in more detail the organization of the Libraries and the use of key resources, including the online information system, CD-ROM indexes, and other reference sources. This session is designed to include only key information necessary to get the students started in their academic careers at Purdue.

One additional approach to orientation has been to offer tours in native languages. This supplemental service has been designed to help meet some immediate needs of students new to the country and to provide a "first step" in becoming acquainted with the library system. The tours, offered early in the fall semester, are very general and allow the patrons to learn about basic services without worry of misunderstanding Americanisms or library jargon. The tours are conducted by individuals proficient in the language, either identified from among the library staff or, where a given language is not represented, from appropriate student organizations. Volunteers enlisted from student organizations are first trained by a librarian. A basic introduction to the library and the library system, cursory introductions to the collections and some of the computerized resources, with which many international students are unfamiliar, and rudimentary search techniques for using the online information system are covered in the training.

Instruction

The core of the Purdue Libraries' instructional services is the Undergraduate Library's Research Skills program. The program has been developed into a multimedia, multi-faceted array of offerings accommodating the needs of many learning styles. The components of the program include: (1) a slide presentation which provides a brief orientation to the Purdue library system; (2) a printed guide, *The Savvy Student's Guide to Library Research,* which presents a model research strategy and introduces students to resources primarily available in the Undergraduate Library; (3) *Information Access,* a hypercard tutorial, which is available for use on Macintosh computers in the Instructional Media Center of the Undergraduate

Library, parallels the information presented in the research guide, but includes interactive exercises throughout the program; (4) the Research Project Advisory Service, providing individualized consultations by appointment; and (5) library workshops, usually offered in the evenings, designed to convey general principles about libraries and resources.

Each of the components of the program may be used independently of any of the others, although in many cases several of them used in conjunction with another will be more effective. In addition to these services, class presentations are offered, and a number of handouts and bibliographies are always available, whether to entire classes or for individuals as they come in to the libraries for specific purposes. Because of language and cultural differences, as well as physical and hearing impairments, some students may not be able to absorb all the necessary information given in a lecture; therefore printed materials become increasingly important. Librarians who present bibliographic instruction sessions often know the subject so well or have given the lecture so often that they may not be aware they are not communicating effectively to many students. Jargon, projection, enunciation, and accent may interfere.[21] Instructional handouts and annotated bibliographies can assist these individuals in clarifying and reinforcing key points covered in a class presentation and therefore further their continued educational development. They can also serve as a reminder to the student that the librarian is available for further individual consultation.[22]

The process of developing many of the printed guides and handouts in the Purdue Libraries has been one of cooperation among the instruction librarians. Once a need is identified, a draft of each handout is presented to a committee for review. The committee considers the general content of the handout, the language and tone in relation to the intended audience, and stylistic consistency with other handouts. The very nature of a committee review incorporates a variety of perspectives into the content and limits individual biases, thereby ensuring greater usefulness to a wider range of users.

The services available in the Purdue Libraries are not designed with any single group of users in mind. Rather, they attempt to address larger issues. Individually, the separate components may not be unique, but it is the overall concern with cultural awareness as a theme and guiding principle that serves our patrons well. The slide presentation offers a visual orientation to the library system and its services, which may be better suited to some individuals than a lecture-type presentation. The printed guide is a required or optional text for many of the basic composition classes, but it is also available for sale to anyone who wishes to purchase it. It focuses on the Undergraduate Library, but the information is presented within a context or framework of general concepts which may be applied to any library situation. Being in printed form, it may be retained and referred to time and time again. The hypercard program offers yet another, more interactive format, which some students may find more conducive to their learning style. The entire program may be completed in one sitting; or it may be referred to only for particular sections to refresh one's memory about selecting and refining a topic, developing a research strategy, using the online catalog, or selecting an index appropriate to their topic. The advisory service has been very successful especially for the nontraditional and international students, as well as students enrolled in the General Studies program. The more individualized approach seems to help set them at ease, freeing them to ask questions they may be too timid to ask in a class setting. Students have utilized this service in a number of ways: as reinforcement of concepts discussed in a class presentation but applied to their specific, immediate research needs; independent of any other library instruction, for assistance in formulating a search strategy and identifying relevant sources; or for more in-depth discussion about general library concepts, etc. The workshops present general library concepts, such as basic organization of a library and how its catalogs and indexes relate to that organization, fundamental concepts regarding the differences between card and online catalogs, print, online, and CD-ROM indexes, etc., and basic search techniques and strategies. These, too, have been utilized heavily by international and nontraditional students.

Taken as a whole, the bibliographic instruction program in the Purdue Libraries is very flexible and has proven useful in addressing the needs of a large student body with many different needs. Although each of the components will not necessarily serve all learning styles equally well, address all the differing cultural perceptions, or provide the appropriate level of information for every individual, the hope is that at least most needs can be accommodated in some fashion. Whether it is a greater reliance on visual or oral presentation, rote learning or active learning, print or computerized, group or individual instruction, the program is adaptable to many situations.

The success of the instruction program in the Purdue Libraries is rooted in cultural awareness. Recognizing and responding to the diversity of the campus population has provided library instruction services that are grounded in openness, sensitivity, and innovation, and thereby enhance the educational improvement of students from a wide variety of cultural backgrounds. The multi-faceted approach retains the necessary flexibility to adapt to changing needs so that, as the campus population evolves, so will the instruction program, with a strong foundation on which to build.

CONCLUSION

Cultural awareness stems from a comparative study of cultures. The alien culture of another people is like a mirror without which our own culture cannot be detected. Paul Bohannan, in *We, The Alien,* relates an interesting episode that reveals vividly the mutuality of cultural awareness:

> I was coming home on a streetcar late one August afternoon from the playground where I taught during some summer vacations while I was a college student. White and Negro men who had obviously been digging and...working in the sun boarded the car. They were all dirty and sweaty.... A white woman standing by me complained about the smell of the Negroes; they did smell. I wondered about the white workers and moved next to them; they smelled, too. The blue cotton uniform which I wore as a playground teacher was wet with perspiration from my strenuous day. I then became aware that I smelled. [It] was a discovery—(Hortense Powdermaker 1966).[23]

What then was the discovery? The discovery was, "We are all aliens to each other." Black and white, male and female, Chinese and American, Westerners and Easterners, each with our own specific cultures imbedded in our character, all smell to each other. It behooves each of us to reflect on the nature of our richly multicultural society and to consider how we can most effectively foster cultural awareness through our actions, thoughts and deeds, both professionally within our libraries and personally throughout our lives.

NOTES

1. Mary Alice Ball and Molly Mahony, "Foreign Students, Libraries, and Culture" *College & Research Libraries* 48 (March 1987): 160-165; Patrick Andrew Hall, "The Role of Affectivity in Instructing People of Color: Some Implications for Bibliographic Instruction," *Library Trends* 39 (Winter 1991): 316-326.; Mary M. Huston, "May I Introduce You: Teaching Culturally Diverse End-Users Through Everyday Information Seeking Experiences," *Reference Services Review* 17 (Spring 1989): 7-11; Gina Macdonald and Elizabeth Sarkodie-Mensah, "ESL Students and American Libraries," *College & Research Libraries* 49 (September 1988): 425-431; Terry Ann Mood, "Foreign Students and the Academic Library," *RQ* 22 (Winter 1982): 175-180; Dario J. Villa and Jane Jurgens, "Minority Students in Higher Education: A Challenge for the 90's," *Illinois Libraries* 72 (November 1990): 626-628.

2. A. R. Hagey and Joan Hagey, "Meeting the Needs of Students from Other Cultures," *Improving College and University Teaching* 12 (Winter 1974): 42-44.

3. Elaine P. Adams, "Internationalizing the Learning Resources Center," *College Board Review* 119 (Spring 1981): 19, 27-28; Dick Feldman, "The International Student and Course-Integrated Instruction: The ESL Instructor's Perspective," *Research Strategies* 7 (Fall 1989): 159-166; Sally G. Wayman, "The International Student in the Academic Library" *Journal of Academic Librarianship* 9 (January 1984): 336-341; Ball and Mahony, "Foreign Students, Libraries, and Culture"; Hagey and Hagey, "Meeting the Needs of Students"; Macdonald and Sarkodie-Mensah, "ESL Students"; Villa and Jurgens, "Minority Students."

4. A. L. Kroeber and Clyde Kluckhohn, *Culture: A Critical Review of Concepts and Definitions* (Cambridge, MA: Peabody Museum of American Archeology, 1952), 181.

5. Clifford Geertz, *The Interpretation of Cultures: Selected Essays* (New York: Basic Books, 1973), 5.

6. Huston, "May I Introduce You," 8.

7. Carla J. Stoffle, "A New Library for the New Undergraduate," *Library Journal* 115 (1 October 1990): 50.

8. Manuel D. Lopez, "Chinese Spoken Here: Foreign Language Library Orientation Tours," *College & Research Libraries News* 44 (September 1983): 265, 268-269; Jean Sheridan, "Andragogy: A New Concept for Academic Librarians," *Research Strategies* 4 (Fall 1986): 156-157; Robert G. Trujillo and David C. Weber, "Academic Library Responses to Cultural Diversity: A Position Paper for the 1990's," *Journal of Academic Librarianship* 17 (July 1991): 157-161; Adams, "Internationalizing the Learning Resources Center."

9. Louise Greenfield, Susan Johnston, and Karen Williams, "Educating the World: Training Library Staff to Communicate Effectively with International Students," *Journal of Academic Librarianship* 12 (September 1986): 227-231; Irene Hoffman and Opritsa Popa, "Library Orientation and Instruction for International Students: The University of California-Davis Experience" *RQ* 25 (Spring 1986): 356-360.

10. The CD-ROM product is *Ethnic Newswatch* (Stamford, CT: SoftLine Information, Inc., 1992-).

11. Sonia Bodi, "Teaching Effectiveness and Bibliographic Instruction: The Relevance of Learning Styles," *College & Research Libraries* 51 (March 1990): 113-119; Claudia E. Cornett, *What You Should Know About Learning Styles* (Bloomington, IN: Phi Delta Kappa Educational Foundation, 1983); Rita Dunn and Kenneth Dunn, *Teaching Students Through Their Individual Learning Styles: A Practical Approach* (Reston, VA: Reston Publishing Co., 1990); Rita Dunn, Josephine Gemake, Fatimeh Jalali, and Robert Zenhausern, "Cross-Cultural Differences in Learning Styles of Elementary-Age Students From Four Ethnic Backgrounds," *Journal of Multicultural Counseling and Development* 18 (April 1990): 68-93; Waynne B. James and Michael W. Galbraith, "Perceptual Learning Styles: Implications and Techniques for the Practitioner," *Lifelong Learning* 8 (January 1985): 20-23.

12. Charles S. Claxton, "Learning Styles, Minority Students, and Effective Education," *Journal of Developmental Education* 14 (Fall 1990): 7.

13. Dunn et al, "Cross-Cultural Differences in Learning," 72.

14. Jeanne B. Ewing, Mary E. Ewing, Jack London, and Yolanda Ramirez-Ponce, "Adult Education and Computer Literacy: A New Challenge," *Lifelong Learning 10* (November 1986): 21-23; Barbara Foster, "Hunter Midtown Library: The Closing of an Open Door," *Journal of Academic Librarianship* 2 (November 1976): 235-237; Mood, "Foreign Students."

15. Claxton, "Learning Styles," 6; Luis Baez, *Basic Skills Curriculum for Cultural Inclusiveness and Relevance, 1990-91.* ERIC document ED341816. (Milwaukee, WI: Milwaukee Area Technical College, 1991, microfiche), 15.

16. Baez, *Basic Skills Curriculum,* 15.

17. Macdonald and Sarkodie-Mensah, "ESL Students," 425.

18. Lopez, "Chinese Spoken Here," 268; Mary E. Nilles and Dorothy B. Simon, "New Approaches to the Multi-lingual, Multi-cultural Students in Your Library," *Catholic Library World* 55 (May/June 1984): 438.

19. Villa and Jurgens, "Minority Students," 627.

20. Kovac, Roberta, "Internationalization of the Purdue University Libraries: A Project to Develop Instructional Resources/Programs for International Students Faculty, and Visiting Scholars," Global Initiative Faculty Grant Proposal, Purdue University, 1991, 2.

21. Adams, "Internationalizing the Learning Resources Center," 27; Macdonald and Sarkodie-Mensah, "ESL Students," 426.

22. Hoffman and Popa, "Library Orientation and Instruction for International Students," 358.

23. Paul Bohannan and Martha C. Ward, *We, The Alien* (Prospect Heights, IL: Waveland Press, 1992), 35.

THE INTERNATIONAL STUDENT IN THE U.S. ACADEMIC LIBRARY:

BUILDING BRIDGES TO BETTER BIBLIOGRAPHIC INSTRUCTION

Kwasi Sarkodie-Mensah

INTRODUCTION

The literature available on foreign students and their use of libraries in the United States, scant as it is, is full of difficulties the students encounter in using academic libraries. The difficulties have been attributed, among other things, to the nature of libraries, concept of reference services, notion of closed stacks in other countries, difficulty in expression in English, different educational systems, little familiarity with American library tools, and lack of understanding on the part of American librarians of other cultures. The 1980s and the present time will stand out in library history as an era during which attention was paid to the plight of the foreign student in libraries in academic institutions in the United States (I will be using the terms "foreign students" and "international students" synonymously.)[1] However, in spite of this, until recently no substantial studies have been done involving foreign students themselves.[2]

THE INTERNATIONAL STUDENT AND LIBRARIES:
AN ENCAPSULATION OF THE LITERATURE

The literature on international students and libraries in the United States has been one of the helpful means of determining the nature of library use of international students in this country, as well as the pattern of library use in their home countries. These can be summarized briefly as follows.

Curricula in many foreign countries arc textbook oriented. Thus international students in the United States, foreign to the idea of substituting other books for prescribed materials, tend to encounter problems, even when they could use substitute titles. Lewis describes this problem appropriately:

> Since Asian students have been accustomed to using few books, they usually think only a certain title will do. It does not readily occur to them to substitute if the volume originally sought is unavailable. They are accustomed to single textbooks and rote learning.[3]

True as it is that Lewis was referring to Asian students, much of the work coming after her was built on this observation, with the exception that most of the problems of international students in libraries were examined across the board, rather than by using a specific area of the world.

Another characteristic that can be attributed to international students and libraries in the literature is that libraries in many foreign countries serve as study halls. Thus, international students, rather than seeing the library as a potential locale of research and original work, will conceive of the library as an escape from noise. Many writers on this subject attest to this. In the words of Wayman:

> [L]ibraries are regarded as a place to study, not research, as they are not considered necessary to the educational process. Instead there is a great reliance on the knowledge of the professor, who either hands the students the books they need, often a single text, or uses a reserve book system.[4]

Several writers on the question of international students and U.S. academic libraries contend that foreign students will not ask for assistance in United States academic libraries in time of need. The reasons advanced for such behavior include attitudes carried over from home countries, where not asking for help was an acceptable modus operandi.[5] In many foreign countries, such attitudes are common, and international students, of various ages, status, and academic preparations tend to shy away from reference librarians in the United States, even when they can benefit from asking for assistance.

The nature of library operation in many foreign countries has been seen to be a source of difficulties for international students in their use of libraries in this country. Used to closed stacks, and other differences in library operation, foreign students using U.S. academic libraries may encounter tremendous difficulty.[6] However, there is usually a distinction made between the facility of library use by students from developed countries, especially European nations and those coming from Third World countries.[7]

An area of difficulty that writers are unanimously in agreement on is language. Both verbal and nonverbal communications can pose problems, not only to the international student in the library, but also to the librarian with whom a library transaction is taking place. Coupled with the language problem are cultural differences such as the perception of the woman in society, or the emphasis placed on authority, that may also influence the interaction between librarians and students from other countries.[8]

Several articles have confirmed that the level of difficulty in some areas of library use may not be as acute as has been indicated in the literature. In the words of Hoffman and Popa, "We had assumed that students from Third World countries had not had the technological advantages of their American counterparts. Yet preliminary results seem to indicate that a majority of these students have had experience using computers." A good 61 percent of the students indicated that closed stacks were not new to them.[9] In a recent study done mostly on Asian students, even though the respondents encountered difficulties in most of the areas the literature mentions, it was interesting to note that over 70 percent found using online catalogs in the United States much easier than the traditional card catalog.[10] It is studies like these that make it imperative for us to involve the students themselves as much as possible in any attempt to understand them and to better appreciate their needs and design programs for them.

IDENTIFYING THE ISSUES IN
INTERNATIONAL STUDENTS' LIBRARY USE

In the 1982-83 academic year when I was a library science student and a graduate assistant in a university library which offered superb services to all students, including students from various corners of the world, the late night and wake-up calls I received from international students, asking me to meet them in the library to assist them in using the library convinced me that there was a need to alleviate the problems international students encounter in their use of U.S. academic libraries. It became obvious to me that if any meaningful understanding was to be gained from the subject of foreign students and libraries, there was an urgent need to survey the students about their patterns of library use in this country, the use they made of libraries when they were in their countries, and some of the concerns they had about libraries and librarians in the United States.

As a veteran student in Ghana, the Ivory Coast, Spain, and the United States, and with work and travel experience in France and Nigeria, I became literally obsessed with providing some insight into the question of international students and United States academic libraries. For my doctoral dissertation, I sent a 32-item questionnaire to international students in two universities in New Orleans, Louisiana in the 1986/87 academic year.[11] The questions were structured around patterns of library use by the students, materials used for research and term papers, what international students would do when they encountered difficulties, and what they found difficult about using library and research tools. Other questions were about the type of library orientation programs they had had on their campuses, whether they had to write term papers in their countries, and the extent to which they depended on library materials. Included also were whether the students asked for assistance in the library in times of need, and why they did not, if they never did so.

Students were asked to provide a description of the libraries they used in their countries, to indicate whether or not their grade and/ or high schools had libraries, and to describe them if they did. Students were asked for background information on countries, sex, age, degrees, majors, years on their campuses and in the United States as a whole, native languages and language(s) of instruction in grade school, high school, and university. The students were also asked to indicate what other materials, apart from books and magazines, were available in their high school libraries. The last item asked students to write down any comments they had about their use of libraries or other items they believed the questionnaire did not cover. A list of terms and their definitions were provided to aid respondents who might not be familiar with library terminology.

INTERNATIONAL STUDENTS AND U.S. ACADEMIC LIBRARIES: WHAT THE STUDENTS SAY

My survey of university students in New Orleans was answered by 388 students, of whom 72 percent were male and 27 percent female. One percent did not indicate their sex. The division of the sexes of the respondents follows the pattern indicated in the literature whereby male foreign students have always outnumbered their female counterparts. Most of the students responding to the questionnaire were between 21 and 30 years of age. The percentage of graduate and postgraduate students was higher than that of undergraduates. Fifty-one majors/areas of study were indicated by these 388 students coming from 77 different countries and 116 language groups. Forty-two percent of these students had been on their campuses and in the United States as a whole for between one and three years.

In spite of the emphasis on textbooks in many foreign countries, 80 percent of the respondents in my survey said they would use both books and periodical articles to write term papers, as opposed to the 11 and 7 percent who would use only books and only periodical articles respectively. When they could not locate library materials they were looking for, 68 percent would readily ask for assistance rather than shy away from the library staff. For 31 percent of the respondents, the library was primarily used as a study hall. This was followed by 35 percent who chose research work as the second most important reason for visiting the library. This finding is in consonance with the literature.

When it came to library facilities in the United States that were new to the respondents, the following breakdown, with the exception of interlibrary loan and online searches, presents an interesting contrast to what is portrayed in the literature: Open stacks were new to only 14 percent, while to 17 percent large library collections were a new phenomenon. Interlibrary loan, photocopying machines, and microforms were new to 49, 19, and 39 percent respectively. Online computer searches proved new to 60 percent of the respondents. It should be mentioned that at the time of the study neither of the two library systems had online catalogs.

When the factors of: previous exposure to libraries in the home countries of the respondents, country of origin (developed or underdeveloped), years spent in the United States and on the campuses of the respondents, and language of instruction used at various educational levels in the home countries, were tested against various areas of library use, language of instruction stood out as the factor producing the most significant findings. This buttresses the emphasis placed on language as a major source of difficulty. However, apart from previous exposure to libraries that produced one and the least significant finding, country of origin had only three areas with significant findings. A cross tabulation by country and the areas of library difficulty revealed that there was no difference between the difficulties faced by students from Western countries and other parts of the world. It is fair to say that the three areas where significant findings were found—main way of locating books in the library, asking for assistance in times of need, and not thinking that asking for assistance would make librarians think the student was stupid—may indicate that students from developed countries felt a little more comfortable using U.S. libraries.

Another major revelation from the survey is that international students may not be experiencing as much difficulty as the literature portrays. This may not be surprising, since many of the studies have been based on speculations and observations about libraries in other parts of the world and have excluded students. On the other hand, people used to foreign students can attest to the concept of saving face. Many of the respondents may have answered in a positive manner to create an impression that their countries may not be as backward as the library community in the United States may want to believe. For those of us familiar with the double standards portrayed by some patriotic international students, and the likelihood of being regarded as a "CIA agent" when pertinent questions are asked, some responses may indicate the mistrust many foreign students have in us.

Student Perceptions of Library Service

The survey produced about 100 comments reflecting on library services in the United States and in the home countries of the respondents, as well as the behavior of U.S. academic librarians toward foreign students. Many positive comments commended librarians in the United States and their assistance to library patrons from other countries. However, in addition to comments on the inadequate resources on other countries, many respondents perceived U.S. academic librarians as rude, uncaring, snobbish, and not making any effort to understand the needs and concerns of international students in libraries. A few such examples on which we can build are:

A.   Sometimes it is useless to ask the library personnel for help.
B.   Sometimes the people in the library are not helpful.
C.   You should have asked about the behavior of the librarians. Some of them treat foreign students badly. I feel that sometimes they ignore foreign students when we ask for help. They are also sometimes impatient and snobbish.
D.   You should visit the library in my school. It is just a market place. The boss, the librarian, and other workers, and even some of the students misbehave. There is too much noise coming from the intercoms, and fire alarms. I use it because I have no alternative. Please visit it one day.[12]

IMPROVING LIBRARY SERVICE TO INTERNATIONAL STUDENTS: STAFF TRAINING AND STUDENT INSTRUCTION

The comments from the respondents provide some interesting insight into the perception of librarians by international students. It is clear to me that both librarians and international students have to examine the implications of this state of affairs. What constitutes "snobbish" behavior in the eyes of the foreign students? Do American librarians actually ignore students from other cultures? Or do these students generalize matters from a single experience? Is it possible that when a reference librarian has to provide divided attention to several patrons when traffic is heavy at the desk, foreign students feel that they are being neglected just because they are not Americans? These are some of the issues that need to be investigated to achieve any meaningful approach of service to foreign students. Understanding problems of foreign students entails to a large extent acquiring a knowledge about their natural and adopted behaviors.

In any effort to educate American librarians about foreign students, the involvement of the entire library staff—professional, nonprofessional, and even student workers—cannot be overemphasized. Students coming to the library do not always go to professional librarians. Making every person on the staff aware of and familiar with behavior patterns and cultural differences of people from other nations, and how these can affect their use of the library as well as their approach to library personnel, can be beneficial to the library staff as a whole when it comes to dealing with foreign students.

Politeness, diplomacy, mistrust and face-saving prevent some international students from making any specific requests. From my experience in dealing with international students, I can say with positive certainty that many international students prefer help coming from staff members who are "foreign" or have experience in dealing with international students. Thus, whenever possible, such people should be made an integral part of any programs organized for international students.

Many of the students in the survey advocated for library instruction sessions held solely for international students. In the words of one of the respondents:

> How to use the library is part of an academic education. Instruction to library use should not be optional. A minimum of six hours should be devoted to proper orientation. I firmly believe that it is necessary to take a course in bibliography. In my country they do not offer it as far as I know.[13]

REACHING INTERNATIONAL STUDENTS: TAPPING INTO MARKETS FOR BIBLIOGRAPHIC INSTRUCTION

In the light of the findings and from my dealing with foreign students, I believe that any program designed to assist international students in the library must involve both the students and the other units on campus which serve them. On many college campuses, foreign students can be found in various groups. They may be enrolled in specific programs such as English as a Second Language, or other accelerated language programs. They may be transfer students, or fresh incoming students from their countries. On many campuses, the majority of foreign students go through an international students office before they make any contact with the rest of the campus. Such offices should be the initial points of contact between the library and these students. Libraries should establish cordial links with international student offices, language centers, and other similar offices serving people from other nations, including visiting scholars.

A welcoming note from the library to new foreign students mentioning available library services is always a welcome addition to the orientation week package. A need analysis survey based on students' past and current use of libraries will provide the library with the basis on which to plan library programs for international students. As mentioned above, a good number of students will be found in courses that may be well established on campus. However, there are bound to be other pockets of groups of users who may not fall within the established programs on campus. Those that come to mind include transfer students, international students coming from U.S. institutions to pursue graduate studies, students on permanent resident visas, and visiting scholars. On many campuses, student organizations attract foreign students. Organizations may be grouped by countries, regions of the world, or even by religious orientations. If libraries are to cover all bases in serving students, these groups must be incorporated in the aggressive library instruction marketing program. Through their meetings, and sometimes even during social events, these students can be reached if only to be told that the library is willing to assist them in their use of the resources, as well as to educate them to develop a logical strategy of locating information.

Reaching visiting scholars may entail a lot of diplomacy and tactfulness. Some of the visiting scholars may be the cream of the crop in their countries, yet the labyrinthine nature of library operations and facilities in the United States may be an obstacle in their research unless someone takes the time to assist them.

The above may sound complex and tedious, but if libraries are to achieve the optimum in their service to users from other nations, such aggressive and time-consuming techniques must be applied.

USING THE INTERNATIONAL STUDENT OFFICE TO BUILD A BRIDGE OF ALLIANCE AND UNDERSTANDING

The library and the International Student Office (ISO) at Northeastern University in Boston enjoy a healthy relationship that works in the long run for the benefit of the students served.[14] One of the many programs the office organizes for new students is called

OASIS (Orientation Assistance for International Students), a mandatory program for all new undergraduate international students. It is a three-day affair during which students are introduced to American values, higher education in the U.S., and Northeastern University in particular. Students are also provided with the opportunity to open a bank account, complete university registration, take English and Mathematics placement tests, and have campus tours. Students are also given assistance in finding shopping places and locating apartments in the Boston area.[15] The library is invited to participate in all the events, which culminate in a dinner at a local restaurant.

One of the most gratifying components of the program is the library tours given to these students in groups of 10 after an afternoon picnic lunch. Students and staff from the ISO come into the library for an hour-long tour of the library facilities. The purpose of these tours is to introduce the students to services in the library, but more especially to familiarize them with the physical locations of such services and other components of the library. The usefulness of the library involvement in the entire orientation program is that throughout the program, the presence of the librarian gives the students an indication that the library is a vital component in their studies in the United States. Also, the face of the librarian in their presence becomes a familiar one, and when tours begin in the library, the shyness, uncertainty, and anxiety that often characterize the initial tour period have been erased.

At the graduate student level, the library participates in the general orientation of new graduate students, during which representatives from various campus units address all new graduate students. The library joins the second, and special orientation for international students, during which other campus representatives provide further information about the university. For the library, this is an opportunity to invite the students to take advantage of special tours for international graduate students held several times a day during the orientation period. The second orientation meeting also provides us with a forum to address certain issues. Many international students are of the impression that librarians are clerical staff, and thus may bypass the person at the desk, in the hope of speaking to a person of a higher authority. Informing the students that reference librarians have at least a Master's degree, and thus have been in the shoes the students are just about to wear creates an atmosphere of trust and respect. Various topics such as interlibrary loans, CD-ROM databases, and consortium libraries, as they relate to their research work are emphasized. Once again, the familiarity of a face, and the presence of the librarian at these programs are favorably received by the students. Interaction with the students also makes it possible for the librarian to inquire into the background of many of the students: their previous exposure to libraries, and the nature of library services in their countries, library services they are used or not used to, and how many of them are transfer students from other U.S. institutions. Those who fall in the latter group, and thus have been exposed to U.S. libraries, often provide assistance during the tours, explaining briefly some of the topics touched on. The library components of the orientation program has always been among the top-rated sessions.

Another joint effort between the international student office and the library has been the introduction of visiting scholars to the library staff. Such an alliance makes it possible for the library to reach out to such scholars on a one-to-one basis, and make them feel comfortable with being offered assistance in the library. The ISO also maintains a list of all individual international student organizations on campus. As part of our aggressive marketing programs, we attend meetings of these organizations to announce the availability of various library services, including individualized instruction sessions for students who need them. This word-of-mouth communication, and the spread of it by the students assists us in reaching a larger percentage of international students.

INTEGRATING LIBRARY INSTRUCTION INTO ENGLISH AS A SECOND LANGUAGE PROGRAMS

While the University libraries work with other units on campus to provide better library services to as many international students as possible, the instruction program with English as a Second Language classes (ESL) through the English Department has been one of the most successful. After one of the ESL instructors specifically asked the library to do two library sessions for his students, as opposed to the regular one-shot lecture, the idea of the need for more BI time for international students was adopted by several of his colleagues. The objectives of one course, English for International Students, include mastering skills "necessary to integrate research materials into expository and discursive academic papers"; enhancing "the skills necessary to plan and produce academic research papers," and becoming "thoroughly familiar with the research resources of the library and the data-gathering and organization techniques necessary to capture important information."[16] Since students are strictly forbidden to plagiarize, mastering the MLA Handbook is another objective of the course.

The library visit for most of these ESL classes comes in the sixth or seventh week of the semester, when the students have been introduced to the major concepts of writing and research: grammar review, paraphrasing/summarizing, outlines, drafts, and thesis statements, thus when the students come to the library, they have something to work on to make the visit applicable to their topics. A three-page paper is required after the first library visit, in addition to the required library assignment after each visit. At the end of the course, a five-page-minimum research paper based on the library research is required.

What is Covered

Findings of my survey were the guiding light in the development of the instructional program. The first library session begins with a 15-20 minute tour of the floor where most public service points and access catalogs are located. The instructors prefer that the first class cover the online catalog, finding books in general, and becoming familiar with reference tools. Since many of the students in these classes may have been on tours given through the International Student Office, going over some of the areas serves as a reinforcement. Students who may be new to the tours are also helped out by their peers on the tours. Back in the library bibliographic instruction room, equipped with state of the art technology and providing remote access to most of the online services in the building, after a brief 10-item pretest of students' library knowledge, students are introduced to the first part of the Arp and Wilson Three-Step Research Strategy.[17] Classification systems, arrangement of books by subject, general information sources, and using the online catalog to locate books are covered. Media and government documents are mentioned, and depending on the slant of the class, they are incorporated into the presentations. General information sources, such as encyclopedias—which usually contain signed articles by experts in the field, definitions of jargon and other technical terms, and bibliographies at the end of the articles—are stressed. In addition to using the online catalog to find books, reading the information on each book record is emphasized so that students learn how to authenticate their citations and give credit to sources they may be using.

The library exercise that is given to students is due back to their instructor at the next class meeting. It consists of two parts: the first part asks the students to find two books on their topic, using the online catalog. They are required to provide the following information: author/editor/compiler of the source, title, place of publication, publisher, date, call number, and the level in the library where each source will be located. They are also asked to indicate whether the items are on the shelf or checked out.

The second component of the library exercise requires the students to locate a general information source on their topics. These can be encyclopedias, dictionaries, or handbooks. They are to look up their topic by subject and to indicate the title of the article or entry in the general information source, whether or not the article is signed, whether technicalities or jargon are defined or explained, and whether there is a bibliography at the end of the entry. If there is, and there is a book among the list, students are required to search in the online catalog to see if the library owns the source. Students are required to write down the titles of other types of materials listed in the bibliography for the second library session.

The second library session concentrates on finding current information. Thus in addition to touring the print indexes and abstracts and the CD-ROM workstation locations, time is spent in the microform and government documents sections; and the major public services areas, the current periodicals room, as well as the location of bound journals are shown. The classroom session includes the explanation of indexes and abstracts, their proliferation according to their general, subject-specific, or cross-disciplinary nature. A very popular handout students are exposed to, and equally embraced by their teachers is the Subject Guide to Indexes and Abstracts. Not only does this handout introduce students to these tools, but it also alerts students to the myriad of indexes they are likely to encounter in other classes or other research projects.

The library assignment given after the second session requires the students to use a print index and a CD-ROM database appropriate to their topics to locate two articles on their topics. Those who are unable to locate appropriate information via the CD-ROM databases must indicate so on their assignment sheets. They are requested to provide the citations to their articles: author(s); title of article; journal name; volume number; issue number, if any; date and page numbers. The importance of being able to read these are emphasized throughout the sessions and also during the period they are working on the exercises. It must be mentioned that several teachers have given the students five points towards their final grade for completing the library assignments.

Assessing the Benefits

The above may sound commonplace and nothing unique. I would like to argue for the uniqueness of these sessions by saying that the work that goes into getting to know as many of these students as possible pays off tremendously. Through working with several departments on campus, the library is able to gain a better understanding of the needs of the students in terms of library use. The willingness of many teachers to take a step-by-step approach to introducing students to the library at the appropriate times makes the library experience a relevant one for the students. The requirement that students turn in the library assignments to their teachers places a high value on the entire exercise. The fact that several teachers award students points makes the students willing and anxious to go through both exercises, asking for help in the library as the need arises. And finally, the contents of the instruction is grounded in research on student needs.

CONCLUSION

Even though the past decade will stand out in library history as a time when the best of efforts were made to understand the plight of the international student in U.S. academic libraries, the exclusion of students in the vast majority of the research work makes it hard to gain better knowledge on the topic. More energy should be expended on using international students in any such studies. A survey conducted by this author revealed that international students may not be experiencing as much difficulty in their use of libraries as the literature portrays. Although language was an area where problems in library use were concentrated, factors such as previous exposure to libraries, country of origin, and length of time spent in the United States did not present themselves as having any significant influence on the level of difficulty in using the library. While it may be possible that many respondents answered the survey in the most positive manner in order to save face, as is the case with many foreign students, many of the respondents also indicated snobbishness, uncaring attitude, and lack of etiquette on the part of American academic librarians. There is a glaring need for both librarians and students to address their differences to ensure the best of service. Building relationships between the library and existing campus resources, such as international student offices, will go a long way in understanding the needs of this special group of users. By participating in the programs of these offices, the library can open up opportunities to provide both tours and informal bibliographic instruction to help these students make the best use of the library.

ACKNOWLEDGMENTS

I would like to thank the instructors of the English as a Second Language program at Northeastern University, Boston, for allowing me to use their material in this article. I am especially indebted to Carey Reid, through whose vision the need for special attention to the needs of international students was widely received among his colleagues. I am also grateful to the staff of the International Student Office for making the University Libraries an integral part of their programs for international students.

NOTES

1.   I am aware that many people feel "international students" is a better term. I tend to disagree with this notion, especially since the U.S. Immigration and Naturalization Service continues to use the term "foreign students." "International students" may be the politically correct term, but many students from other countries have no trouble being labeled as "foreign students."

2.   For example, Dania M. Bilal, "Library Knowledge of International Students from developing countries: A Comparison of Their Perceptions With Those of

Reference Librarians." Ph.D. diss., Florida State University, 1988; and Hassan Ahmadi, "Reactions of International Students to Academic Library Services and Resources: Problems and Difficulties encountered by International Students in Terms of Using Library Services and Resources at Two Sample American Universities (USC and UCLA)" Ph.D. diss., University of Southern California, 1989.

3.   Mary G. Lewis, "Library Orientation for Asian College Students," *College and Research Libraries* 30 (May 1969): 268.

4.   Sally G. Wayman, "The International Student in the Academic Library," *Journal of Academic Librarianship* 9 (January 1984): 339.

5.   Terry Ann Mood, Foreign Students and the Academic Library," *RQ* 22 (Winter 1982): 175-180.

6.   Laura S. Kline and Catherine M. Rod, "Library Orientation Programs for Foreign Students: A Survey," *RQ* (Winter 1984): 212.

7.   Molly O'Hara, "Bibliographic Instruction for Foreign Students," (Paper delivered at ACRL Third International Conference, Seattle, April 4-7, 1984): 231.

8.   Wayman, "International Student," 337.

9.   Irene Hoffman and Opritsa Popa, "Library Orientation and Instruction for International Students: The University of California-Davis Experience," *RQ* (Spring 1986): 358.

10.   Ziming Liu, "Difficulties and Characteristics of Students from Developing Countries in Using American Libraries," *College and Research Libraries* 54 (January 1993): 28-29.

11.   Kwasi Sarkodie-Mensah, "Foreign Students and U.S. Academic Libraries: A Case Study of Foreign Students and Libraries in Two Universities in New Orleans, Louisiana" (Ph.D. diss., University of Illinois at Urbana-Champaign, 1988).

12.   Sarkodie-Mensah, 105-106.

13.   Ibid., 105.

14.   Author was the Bibliographic Instruction Coordinator at Northeastern University Libraries from September 1989 to September 1992.

15.   Letter sent by the International Student Office, Northeastern University, to incoming international students, May 1992.

16.   Carey P. Reid, "English for International Students," Northeastern University (Winter 1993): 2.

17.   Lori Arp and Lizabeth A. Wilson, "Library Instructor's View—Theoretical [and Practical]," *Research Strategies* 2 (Winter 1984): 16-32.

LIBRARY SERVICES IN AN ASIAN AMERICAN CONTEXT

Julie Tao Su

INTRODUCTION

The rapid growth of the Asian population, along with other ethnic minority groups in the United States, has ushered this country into a multiethnic and multicultural society. The growing dependency of the U.S. economy on foreign trade has placed American society in a global community where intercultural understanding is imperative. The library profession has been serving the ethnic and cultural minority groups since the mid-sixties, and therefore a large body of literature has been published addressing various issues concerning cultural diversity and library services. However, the majority of the literature either deals with general principles or focuses on issues relevant to the African American or Hispanic American groups, with very little emphasis placed on the Asian community. This paper attempts to provide a brief overview of public and academic library service with specific relevance to Asian Americans.

Demographic Change

The 1990 United States census reveals that the combined population of the major four ethnic minority groups (African

Americans, Hispanic Americans, Asian and Pacific Islanders, and American Indians) comprises 61.5 million, or close to 25 percent of the U.S. total population, up from 46 million or 20 percent of the total population in 1980. It is projected that in the year 2000, these minorities will comprise 30 percent of the nation's total population, and the figure will approach 47 percent in the year 2050.[1]

While the Asian and Pacific Islanders group ranks third in population among the four minority groups, it has had the fastest growing rate, followed by the Hispanic Americans and the African Americans. The Asian population in America grew from 1.4 million in 1970 to 3.5 million in 1980, with a phenomenal 141 percent increase,[2] and it expanded to 7.3 million in 1990, reflecting another 107.8 percent increase. The Census Bureau now projects that by the year 2000, Asian Americans could approach 12 million, or 4.5 percent of the U.S. population, and the number would increase to 41 million or 11 percent of the total population by 2025.[3]

The growth of the Asian population in America is closely tied to the U.S. immigration and refugee policies for Asians. Although Asians came to the United States as early as the 1840s, due to a series of restrictive immigration laws, Asian immigration virtually came to a halt in the late 1920s. The Immigration Act of 1965, effective in 1968, reopened the door for Asian immigration and thus dramatically increased the number of Asians entering the United States. Since 1975, a large number of Indo-Chinese refugees from Vietnam and other Southeast Asian countries were admitted into this country. By 1980-84 Asians had already exceeded Hispanics to become the largest group of annual legal immigrants.[4]

Future projection depends largely on U.S. immigration policy and Asian political developments. If the current immigration policy that favors family unification remains unchanged, the Asian population will continue to grow at a rapid rate. The concern for Hong Kong's political climate after it is returned to the People's Republic of China in 1997 may also cause an increase in Asian immigration. In addition, the new Chinese Student Protection Act of 1992 (Pub. L. No. 102-404, 106 Stat. 1969) will soon allow an estimated 80,000 nationals of the People's Republic of China to adjust to permanent resident status in the U.S.

Diversity in the Asian Population

Before 1970 the major components of Asians in the United States were Chinese, Japanese, Korean, and Filipino; however, since 1970 the group has expanded to include Asian Indians, Vietnamese, Cambodians, Laotians, and others from Southeast Asia. Asian Americans now represent a group of people with diverse linguistic, cultural, political, economic, and educational backgrounds. At one end of the spectrum, there are second or third generation American-born Asians who are well-assimilated into the mainstream society, and there are first generation immigrants who are highly educated professionals or successful businessmen and have achieved middle class status. At the other end, there are recent refugees or "boat people" from Southeast Asia who are ill-prepared for the new environment, have no English language proficiency or transferable working skills, and are living below poverty level.

Another segment of recent Asian newcomers are temporary residents who are here for business. Since the 1980s, a growing number of Asian companies, especially Japanese-owned, have set up offices or plants in the United States. As a result, Japanese top management staff and their families are moving into communities all over the country—over 200,000 at last count.[5] However, there have been tensions or misperceptions between the Japanese and the Americans, especially within highly conservative, homogeneous communities. Some community members have had mixed feelings about the Japanese, which is a result of their long-held resentment towards the minority group, or from their personal resistance to the cultural changes that the Japanese business might bring in.[6] However, with proper cultivation and knowledge, hostility can be changed into hospitality, and mutual understanding can be built between the newcomers and the local residents.[7] The Tecumseh Public Library (Michigan) has been successful in bridging the gap between the conservative host community and the incoming Japanese community by sponsoring Japanese cultural programs, music performances, business seminars, and even a reception for the newcomers.[8]

Rising Public Interest in Asia

Although the American public has long been interested in the political changes in Asia, a growing interest in the area's economic development has recently surfaced, especially within the business community. As a result of dynamic economic growth in the past two decades, the Pacific Rim countries have become major participants in international trade, and Japan's economy now ranks as the second largest in the world. In fact, the Pacific Rim has surpassed Western Europe to become the largest regional trading partner of the United States.[9] Many U.S. corporations as well as individual businesses are seeking opportunities to establish business in Asia. These, among other factors, have generated an increasing need for economic and cultural information about Asia and its people.

THE LIBRARY ORGANIZATION AND THE ASIAN POPULATION

The American Library Association (ALA) has been active in addressing issues concerning library services to the four major minority groups. Between 1986 and 1992 the association conducted more than 56 pre-conference and conference programs relevant to ethnic and cultural diversity, and among the 56 programs, more than 17 had direct relevance to the Asian American population.[10]

Within the American Library Association units, there are two affiliated organizations which focus mainly on Asian American librarianship: the Asian/Pacific American Librarians Association (APLA) and the Chinese-American Librarians Association (CALA). The Asian /Pacific American Librarians Association was first founded and affiliated with ALA in 1982. The Chinese-American Librarians Association was formed in 1983 as the result of the merger of the Midwest Chinese-American Librarians Association (established in 1973 in Chicago) and the Chinese Librarians Association (established in 1974 at Stanford). Both organizations have been active in addressing various issues regarding library services to Asian Americans in their annual programs. Since 1989 the Chinese-American Librarians Association has encouraged its members to compile a series of local or regional Chinese American resources directories. As of 1992, four directories had been published covering the metropolitan areas of Chicago, New York, the state of Indiana, and the Midwest region.

THE PUBLIC LIBRARY AND THE ASIAN POPULATION

Diversity in Library Services

Since Asian Americans include a number of groups who differ enormously in their educational levels, socioeconomic characteristics, cultural backgrounds and degrees of assimilation, their information needs are also widely varied. In order to provide service that best meets the needs of the specific community groups, it is important for librarians to first identify the ethnic groups in their community and then to conduct an information needs assessment with a strong community input.[11] This paper delineates some basic library and information needs of the following groups within the Asian American population.

Native-born Asian Americans

The information needs of second or third generation Asians whose primary language is English and who consider themselves Americans first, then Asians are basically the same as those of their white peers. A growing number of public libraries serving large Asian American communities have recognized the need to maintain a collection reflective of Asian American heritage. Such a collection will not only provide a sense of identity for Asian Americans, but also provide information about the minority group for the larger community, thus promoting intercultural and interracial understanding between Asian Americans and the members of other ethnic groups, including those in the majority population.

Foreign-born Asian Americans

Since the basic information needs of well-established, foreign-born Asian Americans are similar to that of their white peers, they do not require specialized library service. However, this group greatly desires materials in their native language. In addition, those who have civic concerns require information on political, social, and economic issues affecting the ethnic group.[12] Their children also need materials for native language training or retention. A public library serving the community where Asian languages are taught either at community-organized language schools or at secondary or post-secondary institutions should consider building a collection to support the curriculum at various levels. Such a collection would serve all students in Asian language programs disregarding age or ethnic background.

New Immigrants

As new immigrants or refugees are most concerned about learning English, finding a job, and making life adjustments, they need information on language classes, citizenship, health services, employment opportunities, etc. that will assist them in their fundamental daily lives.[13] American public libraries have made significant efforts in the past two decades to meet these survival needs of new immigrants through bilingual/bicultural resources, programs, and staff. Although there are several innovative and successful programs, the Queens Borough Public Library's New American Project (NAP) offers the most comprehensive and multifaceted services for new immigrants. The project has several components:

- English as Second Language (ESL) classes
- Foreign language collections in thirteen languages including Chinese, Hindi and Korean
- Mail-A-Book service for seven foreign languages, including Chinese and Korean
- Cultural and coping skills programs
- Information referral services.

Particularly noteworthy are the ESL program and the Mail-A-Book service. In response to an overwhelming demand for ESL classes, the Queens Borough Public Library not only operates one of the largest ESL programs in New York but also provides computer assisted instruction(CAI) for individual students to practice their language skills. The free Mail-A-Book service provides descriptive lists of books in seven foreign languages and allows Queens residents to borrow these books without coming to the library. This service has resulted in a large volume of circulation, especially for the Chinese materials.[14]

Recognizing the need for providing survival information in the immigrants' native languages, the Canton Public Library (Michigan) developed the *Wayne County Newcomers Resource Guide,* customized and produced in Chinese, Japanese, Hindi, and English versions to serve a large Asian immigrant community. The guide identifies various service agencies, ethnic community organizations, and the ESL classes in the community. It also provides information on citizenship, local government, income tax, library service, and so forth. Published in 1991, the guide was widely distributed and has been very well received. Many other public libraries have since requested sample copies and perceived it as a model that can be adapted in other locations with a large concentration of non-English-speaking immigrants.[15]

The Youth

Due to their lack of English proficiency, many new immigrant children have problems at school and need assistance for class assignments. The problem is especially serious among Southeast Asian refugees. In fact, there have been reports of disturbing high school dropout rates among the Khmer, Hmong, and Laotian students in some urban areas.[16] In response to this type of concern in the Cambodian community, the Mark Twain Branch of the Long Beach Library System (California) recently developed an After-School Study Center Program, known as Mark Twain "ASSC," to help a large number of Cambodian youth with their school assignments. Featuring a bilingual staff, trained volunteer tutors, and even basic school supplies and free photocopies of homework related materials, the program helped a total of 882 students in one year.[17]

The Elderly

Library services to the elderly in the Asian community are incidental and rare. Mathis notes in her article on the Los Angeles Public Library's bookmobile service that one of the regular bookmobile stops includes a senior citizen center where most of the elderly speak and read Japanese.[18]

Communication and transportation are the most commonly recognized problems unique to Asian elderly immigrants. Library resources and programs in native languages should serve the Asian elderly well if transportation is provided. Services such as the Queens Borough Public Library's Mail-A-Book program would be an excellent model for serving the homebound and the elderly. Library programs presented in native languages and held at senior citizen centers or retirement homes with a large Asian population would receive positive response. It is suggested that implementing services and programs as such would be most cost efficient if libraries could develop a strong partnership or coalition with the government agencies or community organizations who share the same concern for the Asian elderly.[19]

Diversity in the Collection

The library's service goals as well as the Asian community's information needs must be well defined and identified prior to collection building. Furthermore, the library's mission should include promoting intercultural and interracial awareness as well as providing information about Asia for the majority population. A well-developed Asian collection should include Asian language materials and translated works covering a wide array of subjects relevant to the types of community served as well as Western language materials on Asia and Asian Americans.

Asian Language Collections

The rapid growth of the Asian American population has generated an increasing demand for Asian language collections in public libraries. In addition, due to the influx of newer immigrants from Southeast Asia, language collections in public libraries have expanded from the traditional Chinese, Japanese and Korean languages to include Vietnamese and other Southeast Asian languages. Asian language collections not only provide information for the new immigrants who have limited English reading abilities, but also meet the needs of the well-established Asian Americans who have been here for many years. The hunger for Asian materials is evidenced by the abundance of Asian bookstores in major ethnic neighborhoods across the nation. Although Asians are traditionally more accustomed to browsing in bookstores and purchasing or even renting personal copies rather than using public libraries, given a well-developed Asian language collection and adequate publicity, libraries have not had difficulty in attracting new Asian patrons. A large number of libraries have consistently reported high circulation figures for their Asian language collections. When the Los Angeles Chinatown branch library first opened in 1977, every Chinese book in the initial collection of 500 volumes was checked out on the first day.[20] In 1991, a year after its move to a new building, Chicago Chinatown Branch reported the highest circulation among 82 branch libraries in the system.[21]

Asian Community-based Collections

A growing number of libraries have been established by a variety of Asian community organizations to provide materials for Asian language readers. The size of these libraries ranges from small, bilingual Christian literature collections housed in Chinese or Korean churches to large libraries such as the Hinomoto Library in Los Angeles and the Chinese Information and Cultural Center (CICC) Library in New York City.

The Hinomoto Library in Los Angeles is an example of an early attempt to provide Asian language materials to the public. Established in 1934 by a Japanese religious organization, it maintains a large Japanese language collection (55,000 volumes as reported in 1972), including fiction and non-fiction of all subjects, some of which are hard-to-find reference works. The library serves a large Japanese reading population as well as students in Japanese studies in the Greater Los Angeles area.[22]

The CICC library was opened in 1991 as a research library for both traditional and contemporary Chinese studies. It maintains a bilingual circulating collection (30,000 volumes in 1991) on humanities and social sciences and an extensive Republic of China (Taiwan) government document collection. It also provides an unique bilingual same-day-news service from Taiwan, available to the media and academic institutions free of charge. The library is open to the public, and materials are also available through interlibrary loan.

Another very recent development is the emergence of Chinese culture center libraries in a number of U.S. metropolitan areas with large Chinese populations. These libraries, operated by the Chinese Cultural Service Centers and funded by the government of the Republic of China (Taiwan), aim to provide a circulating collection of Chinese books (both fiction and non-fiction), magazines, newspapers and media for the Chinese communities. In general, these libraries are heavily used by a large Chinese readership. The Chinese Cultural Services Center of Chicago reported that one third of its library's collection is constantly in circulation.[23]

Diversity in Service Approaches

Three types of approaches have been used by public libraries in providing service to the Asian American population.

Asian Neighborhood Libraries

In the 1970s, with the support of Library Services and Construction Act (LSCA) funds, several public library systems began to open branch libraries in predominantly Asian neighborhoods and to develop Asian language collections.[24] Examples of these early establishments include Chinatown branches in Los Angeles, San Francisco, Chicago, New York, and the Oakland Public Library's Asian Community Library. While the Chinatown branches mainly serve the Chinese communities, the Asian Community Library in Oakland provides materials in five Asian languages (Chinese, Japanese, Korean, Pilipino, and Vietnamese) for a diverse Asian community in Oakland.

Today, many of these early libraries continue to grow and serve as major providers for the Asian communities. The Chicago Chinatown Branch, first established in 1970, outgrew its original location and moved into a new building in 1990. The library now holds the largest public library collection of Chinese materials in the Midwest and is equipped with microcomputers and Chinese software for patron use.[25]

The Little Tokyo Branch of the Los Angeles County Public Library system, on the other hand, is one of the newest Asian neighborhood libraries, opened in 1989. The library maintains a collection of 60 percent Japanese materials and 40 percent English materials, of which the Japanese materials are the most heavily used, making up 90 percent of the library's total circulation.[26]

Foreign Language Collections

Although the old Asian neighborhoods have continued to expand and a few new Asian towns have been established by new immigrants, the majority of Asian Americans are widely dispersed in metropolitan areas as well as suburban communities all over the United States. In fact, some of the new Asian towns are commercial districts or shopping strips rather than residential neighborhoods.

In response to the increase of the Asian American population or the settlement of Asian refugees in their communities, many public libraries have begun to develop, expand, or re-orient their foreign language collections. In 1988 the St. Louis Public Library began building English as a second language and foreign language collections at the Barr and Carpenter branches to serve the newly settled Asian and Hispanic communities in these two neighborhoods.[27] In the same year, the Denver Public Library expanded its Vietnamese collection and recruited a full-time Vietnamese staff member to serve the Vietnamese refugees.[28] When Elmhurst, New York changed from an old German and Italian neighborhood to a Chinese and Korean community in the 1980s, the Elmhurst Branch Library of the Queens Borough Public Library shifted its collection orientation from traditional Western European languages to Asian language materials. As of 1991, 25 percent of the library's holdings was in Chinese or Korean, and eight out of 10 library users were Asians.[29]

Mobile Library Services

Bookmobile service to the Asian community is poorly documented in library literature. However, in 1978 bookmobile service was cited in use by the Oakland Public Library's Asian Community Library, and a number of now successful Asian branch libraries such as the Los Angeles Chinatown Branch, Little Tokyo Branch, and the Chicago Chinatown Branch were originally bookmobile stops.

The Los Angeles Public Library's Inner City Bookmobile Service presents an excellent program in serving a culturally and linguistically diverse population. The bookmobile reaches several ethnic neighborhoods and provides materials and programs on a regular basis for people who speak Spanish, Japanese, Korean, Chinese, and Vietnamese. The success of this program is largely attributed to its ability in delivering MLS (multilingual service), which includes multilingual resources, programs, and staff.[30]

Success Factors

Key factors for a successful multicultural library program as suggested in the library literature include: community needs assessment, bilingual staff, community partnership, effective library awareness programs, and administrative and financial support. Among these, the factor of bilingual/bicultural staff has been suggested as extremely important in serving patrons having limited English proficiency, in acquiring and processing Asian materials, and in establishing and maintaining contact with ethnic community organizations to gain their cooperation and to promote potential library use.

Yet, community cooperation has been cited as the key factor by many successful projects such as the Mark Twain's ASSC program and the Queens Borough Public Library's New America Project. Involving ethnic community representatives in the total process of program planning and participation can provide the type of service that best meets the community's information needs. It can also assist the library in identifying the available talents, expertise, and resources within the community to present quality cultural programs. A partnership between the library and other community-based organizations can best utilize the experience and expertise of the community-based organizations and the resources, facilities, and equipment of the library.[31]

The benefit of strong support from the ethnic community is also evidenced by the Houston Public Library's foreign language collection project. Through community contact, the library was successful in obtaining gifts of Chinese books from the Chinese consulate in Houston.[32]

THE ACADEMIC LIBRARY AND THE ASIAN POPULATION

American colleges and universities have become increasingly multicultural and pluralistic in nature. The phenomenon is largely due to demographic changes in the student body, the continual growth of the international student enrollment, and the increasing demand for multicultural and international focus in general education.

Asian Students on the College Campus

The U.S. Department of Education reported in 1990 that ethnic minorities comprised 19 percent of the total enrollment in higher education institutions, and students of the Asian or Pacific Islander group comprised 4 percent of the enrollment.[33] The number of Asian

American college students grew from 286,000, or 2.38 percent of the total enrollment in 1980, to 554,000, or 4 percent of the total in 1990, reflecting a dramatic 93 percent increase in a decade. The presence of Asian American students was particularly noticeable in some highly selective institutions. By 1990 the percentage of Asian undergraduate enrollment reached 17.1 percent at Harvard, 18 percent at the Massachusetts Institute of Technology, and 27.3 percent at the University of California at Berkeley.[34] Asian Americans' heavy investment in higher education, as evidenced by these statistics, can be attributed to their cultural tradition that holds high value and respect for education, and the strong belief that educational attainment is the gateway to socioeconomic success.[35]

In addition to the influx of Asian American students on campuses, the increase of Asian international students also contributes to the changing racial and cultural makeup of the student body. The number of students from South and East Asia showed a steady increase in the last decade, from 94,640 or 30 percent of the total foreign student enrollment in 1980 to 229,830 or 56.4 percent in 1990. In other words, more than half of the foreign students were from Asia. Within the group, the number of students from the People's Republic of China had the most dramatic increase from merely 2,770 in 1980 to 39,600 in 1990.[36]

Asian Focus in Higher Education and in Library Collections

Asian American Ethnic Studies

As the demographic components of student bodies change, the demand for greater diversity in curriculum and in library resources grows. Asian American courses and programs, along with other ethnic studies, have been developed gradually in colleges and universities. In recent years, Asian American studies has gained renewed interest and acceptance in the academic community since first beginning in the late 1960s. According to a list compiled by August Espiritu in 1989, there were 21 established Asian American programs in the United States.[37] As a result, demand is growing for Asian American materials to support the teaching and research in academic libraries. Among the few major Asian American collections in the country, the Asian American Studies Library of the University of California at Berkeley has the largest and most comprehensive research collection. In addition to collecting materials on various aspects of Asian American experiences, it maintains a file of Asian American community newsletters and a comprehensive collection of Asian American community newspapers from the late nineteenth-century to the present. The library also has the only archival collection for Chinese American documents in the nation.[38] Poon in her book *A Guide for Establishing Asian American Core Collections* suggests that a strong research collection on Asian Americans not only serves as curriculum support for the Asian American studies program but also provides resources for students and faculty in other disciplines as well.[39]

Asian Area Studies

The development of Asian studies traces its history back to the 1950s, long before the emergence of the latest Asian immigration wave. In fact, it was the dramatic political changes in East Asia immediately following the second World War that led to the establishment of Asian studies and East Asian library collections in major universities.[40] Asian studies has since become a well established and respected discipline on campuses, and East Asian librarianship has also made significant progress in the areas of collection development, bibliographic control, and document dissemination, and has been highly recognized for its contributions to the research community. A survey published in 1992 revealed that the total holdings of East Asian language materials held in 60 large North American libraries exceeded 10 million volumes.[41]

Because of the growing awareness of the economic and strategic importance of the Pacific Rim in recent years, there is a renewed interest in Asia among students and scholars. For instance, the latest student enrollment in college-level Japanese language courses reached 35,000 nationwide in 1991, and the number continues to rise.[42] At the same time, as American higher education begins to infuse the curriculum with global dimensions and international perspectives, a number of courses with a strong Asian focus have also been developed across various disciplines. As a result, there is an increasing demand for library materials (primarily in English) on Asia across all subject areas to support these programs.

Diversity in Academic Library Service

Since Asian Americans are the fastest growing population group in the nation as well as in colleges and universities, academic libraries can expect an increasing number of Asians as patrons. In addition, because Asian American students generally study hard and strive to excel, they are heavy library users.[43] The impact will be particularly noticeable to the libraries serving students in the fields of mathematics, science and technology, as these are the most popular subject majors for Asian Americans as well as Asian international students.[44]

As potential library clientele, there are three distinct groups in the Asian American academic community on campus: native-born Asian American students, Asian international students and Asian American faculty and visiting scholars. As each group has different backgrounds and library experiences, their information needs are different.

American-born Asian Students

Although the information needs of native-born Asian American students are very similar to that of their white peers, many of them are interested in information about their ethnic heritage. According to a survey conducted by the Association of Research Libraries (ARL), Asian American resources are the second most in demand ethnic collection, following African American materials.[45] It is imperative for academic libraries to recognize the need, when developing a culturally diverse collection including materials on Asian cultures and works by Asian Americans and about their experiences, to reflect the campus demographic makeup and to take leadership in supporting multicultural perspectives in higher education.

Asian International Students

For the purpose of this paper, the term "Asian international students" is also used to describe new immigrant students. Asian international students are highly motivated for academic success, and they recognize that library and research skills are directly correlated to their performance. However, as they face the challenges of mastering a second language and adjusting to a new cultural and learning environment, they need special assistance in developing library and research skills in order to become self-sufficient and effective library users.

Library orientation and instruction.   Many Asian students arrive on campus with at least minor, and often severe deficiencies in English, particularly in terms of language comprehension and oral communication.[46] In addition, the American library system and its terminology are completely foreign to them, since many students come from countries where libraries have closed stacks, offer very limited reference assistance, and are used mainly as study halls.[47] Effective library orientations for Asian international students should be held separately from the general orientations for all students and presented in the students' native languages as needed. This approach not only ensures that students understand the presentations, but it also encourages questions from them, as they generally feel more at ease asking questions in small groups and in their own languages. Orientations could be guided by a bilingual staff member, by a trained volunteer, or by using other devices such as a self-guided library tour or video presentation with bilingual audio tapes.[48]

Wayman suggests applying the "big brother" system by using international students who are experienced library users as guides.[49] A similar approach was implemented at the Lockwood Memorial Library of the State University of New York at Buffalo (SUNY-Buffalo). As reported in 1983, the library trained the returning international students as volunteers to guide library orientations in the students' native languages. A librarian was present during the session as a resource person. The program, given in several foreign languages including Chinese (both Mandarin and Cantonese), Japanese, and Thai, was widely publicized with flyers in the relevant languages, and received overwhelming positive response from the international students.[50]

Like other international students, Asians come from a different educational background in which very little independent research is required, and learning is heavily dependent on memorization of lectures and textbooks.[51] Effective bibliographic instruction will familiarize students with basic research tools and skills and prepare them for effective library use. The function of the reference librarian should be strongly emphasized to Asian students, as they are not accustomed to the services available to them. Otherwise, Asian international students may continue to use the library as a study hall only. Much has been written on bibliographic instruction for international students and the importance of understanding their cultural backgrounds, learning styles, and previous library experiences. Principles, strategies, and techniques suggested in library literature for international students are generally applicable to Asian students.

In addition to structured bibliographic instruction, some libraries have offered personalized library consultation service for international students. As a component of the Library Orientation and Instruction for International Students (LOHS) program developed in 1984, the University of California-Davis Library formed a core group of librarian volunteers to serve as library contacts for international students. Their names, phone numbers and areas of specialization were listed in the library brochure, and international students were encouraged to contact the librarians for library assistance.[52] Purdue University (Indiana) since 1992 has also offered such personalized service by enlisting library faculty and staff with foreign language expertise as library consultants for international students.[53]

Collections for international students.   As the number of Asian students increase, so does the need for Asian language materials and newspapers. Asian language newspapers reporting news from home countries and from an Asian perspective are particularly in demand not only by Asian students but by faculty as well. Academic libraries that are under severe budget constraints may consider the possibility of obtaining a gift subscription from other campus service agencies, Asian student organizations, or the local ethnic community.

As a service to a very large number of Chinese students on the Purdue University campus, the University's Humanities, Social Sciences and Education Library (HSSE) maintains a Chinese reading room to house a collection of approximately 1,000 volumes of Chinese books. The collection was developed as a result of a cooperative effort of various Chinese student organizations and is not a formal part of the library's holdings. The arrangement was made in response to the students' request in the 1960s for housing Chinese books, and the collection by 1993 had outgrown the shelving capacity and was desperately in need of a larger room. In the meantime, the library administration recognized that needs for Asian language materials existed not only among the Chinese students but also among a growing number of Korean and Asian Indian students at Purdue. The library was planning to expand the collection to include Korean and Hindi materials and was seeking better arrangements for housing and management.[54]

Library outreach. Academic libraries need to be aggressive in reaching out to Asian international students. Close communication and coordination with campus international student service units and Asian student organizations are the keys to a successful outreach program. Library services and programs need to be widely publicized through a variety of channels; promotional flyers printed in multiple languages generally attract the international students, as they deliver a welcoming message and reflect the library's commitment in serving them.

A library brochure for international students, faculty, and visiting scholars was developed in seven languages (including English, German, French, Spanish, Swahili, Chinese, and Japanese) by the Purdue University Libraries in 1992. The multilingual brochure, entitled *Welcome,* was prepared in order to support a campus-wide internationalization effort and was very well received by international students as well as the university administration. It has been used not only as a library guide but as a campus promotional publication by the academic units in recruiting international students and faculty. The brochure is regarded as a model for other academic libraries in producing library publications for the international community on campus.[55]

Asian Faculty and Visiting Scholars

Since the majority of Asian faculty members received advanced degrees from American institutions, they are often familiar with the library system and research methods in their fields of specialty, and their information needs are not different from their colleagues'. However, many Asian faculty members maintain personal or professional interest in their countries of origin and are in need of current information. Academic libraries need to identify the information needs of Asian faculty and provide materials to support their research interests.

Library service for visiting scholars is rarely documented in library literature. In fact, these scholars are an often neglected group for libraries, partly because they are not permanent members of the campus communities, and partly because libraries are not aware or informed of their arrival. Since many of them are on campus for special research projects and are in need of library support, academic libraries should coordinate with campus international offices to provide library orientations as part of their campus orientations and to provide library resources and services to meet their research needs.

CONCLUSION

We have witnessed the development of Asian Studies and East Asian libraries in the 1950s and the 1960s, the beginning of library services and materials for Asian minority groups in public libraries and the birth of Asian American ethnic studies and collections in academic libraries in the 1970s, and the expansion of bilingual Asian collections on all subjects in both public and academic libraries since the 1980s. These isolated movements, each driven by a different set of social, political, economic, or academic changes which have taken place in the United States or in Asia, have created a mosaic of multilingual, multicultural, and multiethnic library services and materials relevant to Asia or Asian Americans, not only for the Asian population but for all people of all U.S. population groups.

Future development calls for library cooperation at all levels and in all areas among various types of libraries. Although there are some ongoing cooperative projects among public libraries, such as the Ethnic Resource Centers in California and the Newark Public Library's Multilingual Materials Acquisition Center in New Jersey,[56] there is virtually no evidence of cooperation between public and academic libraries in serving the Asian American population. The recent successful collaboration between the Mark Twain Branch of the Long Beach Public Library and a local university library in developing Khmer materials to serve the Cambodian community hopefully will inspire future coalitions between public and academic libraries.[57]

Future direction also points toward the development of electronic databases of bibliographic (including the library catalog) and non-bibliographic information (including community information) in all languages including non-Roman characters. These databases would utilize the computing networks at local, state, national, or international levels as electronic highways and superhighways to deliver a wide array of information in all languages including non-Roman characters. Such is the model recently proposed by Patricia Tarin as "the support service hub" for the proposed ethnic resource centers in California.[58] An interactive system like this will have the capability of providing direct user service for the non-English speaking Asian population to access bibliographic as well as non-bibliographic information. In such an electronic environment, the library profession will play a new and important role as providers of information, not just materials or resources, to link together the multilingual/multicultural community and information through telecomputing networks.

NOTES

1. Jennifer Cheeseman Day, *Population Projections of the United States, by Age, Sex, Race, and Hispanic Origin: 1992-2050* (Washington: Bureau of the Census, 1992), xviii-xix.

2. Robert W. Gardner, Bryant Robey, and Peter C. Smith, *Asian Americans: Growth, Change and Diversity* (Washington:Population Reference Bureau,1985).

3. Day, *Population Projections of the United States,* xix.

4. Gardner, *Asian Americans,* 4.

5. Stratford P. Sherman, "Japan's Influence on American Life," *Fortune 123* (June 1991): 115.

6. Marney Nordstrom, "The Library as Welcome Wagon," *American Libraries* 20 (November 1989): 955.

7. Harold Wiley, "Members of the Japan-America Society of Indiana are Working to Change Heartless Hostility into Hoosier Hospitality," *Indianapolis Star,* 19 February 1992.

8. Nordstrom, "Library as Welcome Wagon," 955-7.

9. "Gist: U. S. Economic Relations with East Asia and the Pacific," *U.S. Department. of State Dispatch* 3, Suppl. no. 5 (August 1992): 31.

10. *Addressing Ethnic and Cultural Diversity: a Report on Activities of the American Library Association 1986-1989 (Chicago: ALA, 1990) and ALA Annual Conference Programs,* 1990-1992.

11. Lubomyr R. Wynar, "Library Services to Ethnic Communities," *Catholic Library World* 49 (November 1977): 159.

12. Stephen Stern, "Ethnic Libraries and Librarianship in the United States: Models and Prospects." in *Advances in Librarianship,* vol. 15, ed. Irene P. Godden (San Diego: Academic Press, 1991), 95-96.

13. Henry C. Wang, and Suzine Har-Nicolescu, "Needs Assessment Study of Library Information Service for Asian American Community Members in the United States" in *Report of the Task Force on Library and Information Services to Cultural Minorities, National Commission on Library and Information Science* (Washington, NCLIS, 1983), 81.

14. Renee Tjoumas, "Giving New Americans a Green Light in Life: a Paradigm for Serving Immigrant Communities," *Public Libraries* 26 (Fall 1987): 104.

15. Mrs. Ophelia Lo, Adult Services Librarian, interview with author, February 1993. For more information, contact Canton Public Library, 1200 South Canton Center Road, Canton, MI 48188.

16. Jayjia Hsia and Marsha Hirano-Nakanishi, "The Demographics of Diversity: Asian Americans and Higher Education," *Change* 21 (November/ December 1989): 28.

17. Nancy Messineo, "ASSC" [After-School Study Center Program] and You Shall Receive: Community Partnership in California," *School Library Journal* 37 (July 1991): 19-22.

18. Marie Mathis, "Bookmobile Service in an Urban Area," in *The Book Stops Here: New Directions in Bookmobile Service,* ed. Catherine Suyak Alloway (Metuchen, N.J.: Scarecrow, 1990), 279.

19. Kathleen Falcigno and Polly Guynup, "U.S. Population Characteristics: Implications for Libraries," *Wilson Library Bulletin* 59 (September 1984): 25.

20. Ruby Ling Louie, "Los Angeles Chinatown Branch: a Working Model for a Library/School Joint Venture," *Illinois Libraries* 67 (January 1985): 26.

21. Walter Wu, "Library is Where East Meets West," *Chicago Tribune,* 19 January 1993.

22. Keum Chu Halpin, "The Hinomoto Library of Los Angeles," *California Librarian* 33 (October 1972): 217.

23. Mr. Ting Chang, Chinese Cultural Services Center of Chicago, telephone interview with author, 22 January 1993.

24. Roberto G. Trujillo and Yolanda J. Cuesta, "Service to Diverse Populations," in *ALA Yearbook of Library and Information Services,* vol. 14 (Chicago: ALA, 1989), 8.

25. Wu, "Library is Where East Meets West."

26. Ms. Susan Thompson, Senior Librarian, Los Angeles County Public Libraries, Little Tokyo Branch, telephone conversation with author, 24 February 1993.

27. Mary Mulroy, "Library Outreach to the Non-English Speaking in St. Louis," *Show-Me Libraries* 41 (Summer 1990): 9.

28. "Denver PL Reaches Out to Vietnamese Community," *Library Journal* 113 (December 1988): 29.

29. "62 Queens Libraries Await Deep Cuts," *New York Times,* 13 June 1991, Metropolitan edition.

30. Mathis, "Bookmobile Service," 276-283.

31. Margaret King Van Duyne and Debra Jacobs, "Embracing Diversity: One with One's Bold New Partnerships," *Wilson Library Bulletin* 55 (February 1992): 42-44.

32.   Elaine P. Goley, "Developing Library Collections to Serve New Immigrants," *School Library Journal* 32 (October 1985): 95.

33.   "Table 193.—Total Fall Enrollment in Institutions of Higher Education...1976 to 1990," *Digest of Education Statistics 1992* (Washington,: U.S. Dept. of Health, Education, and Welfare, Education Division, National Center for Education Statistics, 1992), 203.

34.   Fox Butterfield, "Why They Excel," in *Race and Ethnics Relations* (Guilford, CT: Dushkin, 1991/1992), 92.

35.   Jayjia Hsia and Marsha Hirano-Nakanishi, "The Demographics of Diversity, Asian Americans and Higher Education," *Change* 21 (November/December 1989): 25.

36.   "Table 398.—Foreign Students Enrolled in Institutions of Higher Education in the United States and Outlying Areas...1980-81 to 1990-91," *Digest of Education Statistics 1992,* 421.

37.   Shirley Hune, "Opening the American Mind and Body, the Role of Asian American Studies," *Change* 21 (November/December 1989): 61.

38.   Wei Chi Poon, *A Guide for Establishing Asian American Core Collections* (Berkeley, CA: Asian American Studies Library, University of California, 1989), 10.

39.   Ibid., 11.

40.   Karl K. Lo, "Area Studies in United States Libraries: IV. East Asian Collections," in *Advances in Librarianship,* vol. 15, ed. Irene P. Godden (San Diego, CA: Academic Press, 1991), 268.

41.   CEAL Task Force for Annual Review and Survey of Library Resources, "Current status of East Asian collections in American libraries, 1991/1992," *Committee on East Asian Libraries Bulletin* no. 98 (1993): 35-36.

42.   Sherman, "Japan's Influence on American life," 118.

43.   Jay Mathews, "Asian-American Students Creating New Mainstream," *Race and Ethnic Relations* (Guilford, CT: Dushkin 1991/1992), 109.

44.   Hsia, Jayjia, *Asian Americans in Higher Education and at Work* (Hillsdale, NJ: Lawrence Erlbaum, 1988), 128.

45.   Otis A. Chadley, "Addressing Cultural Diversity in Academic and Research Libraries," *College and Research Libraries* 53 (May 1992): 210-211.

46.   Mary Genevieve Lewis, "Library Orientation for Asian College Students," *College and Research Libraries* 30 (May 1969): 271.

47.   Terry Ann Mood, "Foreign Students and the Academic Library," *RQ* (Winter 1982): 177.

48.   Laura S. Kline and Catherine M. Rod, "Library Orientation Programs for Foreign Students: a Survey," *RQ* 24 (Winter 1984): 213.

49.   Sally G. Wayman, "The International Student in the Academic Library," *The Journal of Academic Librarianship* 9 (January 1984): 340.

50.   Manuel D. Lopez, "Chinese Spoken Here: Foreign Language Library Orientation Tours," *College and Research Libraries News* 44 (September 1983): 268.

51.   Gina Macdonald and Elizabeth Sarkodie-Mensah, "ESL Students and American Libraries," *College and Research Libraries* 49 (September 1988): 426.

52.   Irene Hoffman and Opritsa Popa, "Library Orientation and Instruction for International Students: The University of California-Davis Experience," *RQ* 25 (Spring 1986): 356-60.

53. "Purdue Libraries Internationalize with New Multi-lingual Brochure," *Focus on Indiana Libraries,* March 1992, 5.

54. Mr. Jeffrey Garrett, Foreign Literature Bibliographer, Purdue University Libraries, telephone conversation with author, January 1993.

55. "Purdue Libraries Internationalize," 5.

56. For information on the Newark Public Library's multilingual materials acquisition program, contact: Ingrid Betanourt, Newark Public Library, P.O. Box 630, Newark, N.J. 07101-0630.

57. Messineo, "ASSC" and You Shall Receive," 21.

58. Patricia Tarin, *Ethnic Resource Centers: Proposed Models* (Sacramento: California State Library, 1991), 17-19.

LA LECTURA ES UN PLACER/READING IS FUN

Adán Griego

INTRODUCTION

During the 1992 presidential campaign the concept of "reinvesting in America" became part of the political debate. In the following pages we will visit two very different places that have been doing just that long before the term entered the political discourse of presidential politics.

In a 1992 Library Journal article, two Spanish-language publishers lamented the poor reading habits of the Spanish-speaking population. In the same article the ethnic materials evaluator for the County of Los Angeles Public Library offered advice to these publishers on the growing demand for Spanish-language books in the United States.[1]

The two institutions under discussion below are bearing witness to this growing demand for Spanish-language reading materials. They provide library services along with an array of other community services to the Latino communities in two different parts of the country.

WHAT'S IN A NAME?

Inevitably, before beginning to address library-related issues of the Latino community, defining nomenclature becomes essential. There are the cries of "Latino si, Hispanic, no."[2] But so as not to get lost in the details, we agree with Salvador Güereña in using "the term LATINO as a more or less generic and inclusive descriptor which encompasses subgroups of various Latin American origins."[3] In this essay, the term "Hispanic" will be used only when quoting others, as we prefer the use of "Latino."

WHAT DO THE NUMBERS SAY?

It is no secret that the Latino population in the United States is already an emerging minority-majority in some parts of the country. Data from the 1990 census indicates a Latino population of more than 21 million (13 million of Mexican ancestry; 2.7 million of Puerto Rican heritage; 1 million of Cuban roots; and 5 million encompassing those of Caribbean, Central and South American provenance).[4] As this population continues to increase, "the total number of Hispanics is expected to grow by nearly 40 percent over the next 10 years from 21.4 million to 29.7 million. By 2010, U.S.-resident Hispanics should number 38.5 million...."[5]

YES, THEY ARE READING IN EAST HARLEM!

February is not the ideal time to vacation in New York. I had come to visit friends from graduate school, and they mentioned a non-traditional library and learning center in East Harlem. Perhaps I could offer some ideas, they thought.

On a cold winter morning, as the bus approached the last stop, Lianne Werlein-Jaen, executive director of The Friendly Place/El Sitio Simpático (TFP/ESS), told me with great enthusiasm what her community-based organization was all about. "The mission of TFP/ESS is to provide a culturally rich learning environment that encourages members of the community of all ages to become avid readers, active learners and critical thinkers."

Certainly TFP/ESS is a very alternative source of library services, one of its goals being "to operate a multicultural library that meets and adapts to the needs of residents and serves as the ideal site for literacy work," added Ms. Werlein-Jaen. It is located in East Harlem, home to a population of more than 100,000, evenly divided between Latinos and African Americans. According to the 1990 census, the residents of East Harlem are primarily low and moderate income. The Latino population is mostly first and second generation Puerto Ricans, and a small but growing population of Mexicans (not from the United States Southwest), Dominicans and Central American immigrants. This area is roughly bounded on the south by 96th Street, on the north by 141st Street, on the east by the Harlem and East Rivers and on the west by Fifth Avenue. East Harlem is one of the poorest communities of New York City, as the following statistics can attest:[6]

- Approximately one-fifth of all births are from young mothers (about one-third of the population is under 18 years).
- It has the third highest infant mortality rate in Manhattan.
- About one-third of all youth are unemployed (more than three times greater than the City's unemployment rate).
- Only one-third of the total population has a high school education (less than 10 percent are college graduates).
- An estimated 26 percent of all arrests in the area are persons under age 21.
- Well over 100 storefronts or street locations are used as distribution points for controlled substances in areas adjacent to schools.
- About 3,000 youngsters are homeless due to drugs.

The Friendly Place/El Sitio Simpático was started here in 1981 under the auspices of the American Reading Council.[7] It has gone through its ups and downs in terms of finances, but according to its executive director, a more financially stable situation has now enabled this community-based, non-profit organization to attract new sources of financial support.

The building was cold, since the heating had been turned off over the weekend. Ms. Werlein-Jaen introduced me to her staff, and they were enthusiastic about my visit and my plans to write about the successes and challenges of TFP/ESS.

As we began the tour, Ms. Werlein-Jaen added that theirs was one of the few community-based literacy and educational programs in the city that "operates out of its own well-stocked library and bookstore." She showed me the two book shelves that served as their "bookstore," with approximately 20 titles. I offered to buy Sandra Cisneros' *The House on Mango Street*. Their "bookstore" offers new and used books for sale at reduced prices. In an effort to encourage readers to begin at-home collections, TFP/ESS sells books to patrons at prices they can afford. "Ours is the only bookstore in the area, and one of the few outlets city-wide that stocks children's books in Spanish," said Ms. Werlein-Jaen.

Almost all books are received as donations, and a strong campaign has brought in contributions from commercial booksellers, publishers, libraries and individuals. Every week the staff places several used materials, both books and periodicals, on the free book table, "along with donated clothing and household items," added one of the staff.

The library's lending systems are set up to make the borrowing of books easy and natural for people who may not feel comfortable in a more formal library setting. It is open to everyone throughout the week. Books are loaned for one week, and renewals are made on request with no overdue fines. Ms. Werlein-Jaen added, "We are more interested in making sure that books get into people's hands."

While we were moving from the "bookstore" section to the library area, there was some noise by the window that distracted and alarmed the staff. It seemed that a group of drug pushers which we had seen around the corner as we entered the building was now taking refuge from the cold as they leaned against the window that showed a book display. After the staff knocked on the window, the group moved away. "As you can see, this place serves children as a refuge from the dangers of the street," noted Ms. Werlein-Jaen.

We continued the library tour. Departing from the traditional library arrangement, the children's and adult sections have been combined so that any person in need of remedial reading material will feel more at ease when searching for a book. In order to make materials more attractive to readers, books are shelved with covers face-out, even if this means using more space.

As we finished our tour Ms. Werlein-Jaen noted that in some instances they are lacking reading materials. A middle-aged Puerto-Rican man seemed to have read almost every Spanish-language title in the library. I offered to donate several paperback Latin American novels. A few weeks after my visit, I received a note thanking me for my in-kind contribution.

It is interesting to note that The Friendly Place/El Sitio Simpático functions not only as a library/bookstore but also as a source of literacy services for children and their families, offering a Family

Learning Program, a Group Visits Program, an After School Program and a Career Awareness/Work Experience Program.

The Family Learning Program is an integrated literacy program whose philosophy is based on four key elements which Ms. Werlein-Jaen lists:

(a) Learning to read is a social activity—children develop emergent-literacy skills when read to by adults with whom they have a significant relationship.

(b) Given the proper support, all parents can take an active and caring role in their child's development.

(c) Early exposure to a nurturing environment helps children learn to love, not fear, reading and writing.

(d) Parents' literacy skills can be improved as a by-product of their work with their children.

The Group Visits Program aims to establish linkages with neighboring agencies and to extend library and literacy services to day care centers, Head Start programs and day camps. On any given day TFP/ESS offers its library and other services to both children and adults of the surrounding community.

The After School Program hopes to fill a gap between home and school. In breaking with the traditional after-school program which concentrates on homework help and recreational activities, this program is language based. "We believe that a whole-language approach to literacy will serve as an alternative arena to stimulate a child's full learning potential," Ms. Werlein-Jaen explained. A new program coordinator had been hired within the last six months to carry out this non-traditional approach to the After School Program, focusing on activities as a means of acquiring literacy skills as opposed to the traditional method of learning through grammar, phonics, and so forth.

In addition to the Family Learning, After School and Group Visits programs, there is the Career Awareness/Work Experience Program, which is almost as old as the library. It aims to give teenagers and young adults the opportunity to gain work experience through internships and volunteer work opportunities in several agencies throughout the city and in the TFP/ESS itself.

Before leaving The Friendly Place/El Sitio Simpático, Ms. Werlein-Jaen pointed to the African American Heritage Month exhibit on The Living Wall. "We believe that by making art and cultural activities accessible to our people, we fulfill an important part of our obligation to the community. The Living Wall is a community art gallery, regularly maintained, which gives both emerging and established local artists and children an opportunity to exhibit their work."

Since the following day was the beginning of Women's History Month, the staff had asked the mothers and daughters who use the center to bring in their own photographs to mount an exhibit on The Living Wall.

"We believe that literacy work must be based in the use of appealing literature and that libraries must be accessible to the non-reader. Most public schools are still using traditional methods to teach reading and writing; they rely on grammar and spelling lessons. Public libraries are totally inaccessible to the non-reader. The Friendly Place fills in these gaps," said Ms. Werlein-Jaen as I concluded my visit.

SOUTHERN CALIFORNIA: SUN, SUN AND BOOKS TOO!

I arrived back in Santa Barbara, glad to be home and to have escaped the frigid temperatures of the East coast. As I tried to catch up with my reading I noticed a brief article in the *Los Angeles Times Magazine* about the Center for the Study of Books in Spanish for Children and Adolescents at the California State University, San Marcos Campus.[8] Our own Chicano Studies Library Collection, the *Colección* Tloque Nahuaque, was able to supply me with a telephone number for the Center.

The Center for the Study of Books in Spanish for Children and Adolescents/Centro para el Estudio de Libros Infantiles y Juveniles en Español (Center/Centro) opened in 1989 as a part of the newest campus of the California State University System. It could not be farther away from East Harlem, not only in terms of distance and physical environment but also in terms of focus. It is located in arid and sunny Southern California, between Los Angeles and San Diego. "It is truly typical Southern California suburbia," said Dr. Isabel Schon, the Center/Centro's founder and director, as we talked over the telephone.[9]

We began our conversation in English and then turned to Spanish as Schon said, "¡Ah, usted habla español!" (You speak Spanish!).

I asked her to tell me about the Center/Centro. "It is an interdisciplinary university unit. It endeavors to serve the university community and the public, and to maintain strong ties with organizations interested in meeting the needs of young Hispanic readers."

As I asked about the origins of the Center/Centro, Dr. Schon took me back to her growing up in Mexico. "Libraries were really a luxury," she added. Coming to this country to do her studies in library media at the University of Colorado, she pursued her interests in Mexican children's literature and the effects of books and reading on Latino children. "I began to ask myself, 'Why do our [Hispanic] children, not read? What impact does not reading have on their personal and academic self-esteem?'" That became her field of academic research.[10]

Since its beginnings, Dr. Schon envisioned the Center/Centro as a way of fostering reading. As such, it serves as a resource for teachers, parents, librarians and other professionals. As the only collection of its kind not only in this country, but perhaps in the world, the Center/Centro has the goal of gathering from around the globe every currently published book in Spanish for young readers. The director not only has made its more than 6,000 books a reference library but she also publishes a list of recommended books, which she happily shares with any one who requests it. As a reviewer for *Booklist, Hornbook, Journal of Reading,* and others, Schon shares her findings with a broad audience of educators and librarians.

It is worth noting that in following a librarian's philosophy of collecting materials that represent various viewpoints, the Center/Centro's collection stocks "recommended," "marginal" and "not recommended" titles. Schon pointed out that the field of children's and young adult literature in Spanish-speaking countries is just developing, unlike those in England and the United States. Thus, many of the "not recommended" titles are those that instruct youngsters on how to behave or to be "good." "These are mostly dull books, and our young readers agree. They, like most adults, take an instant dislike to books that they consider boring," added Schon.

The Center/Centro has sponsored two conferences to make its resources widely known. For the first one she invited the Mexican writer, Martin Luis Guzman, and at the second such gathering, in October of 1992, she invited the noted Harvard sociologist Nathan Glazer. Dr. Schon was especially pleased that Glazer accepted her invitation to speak. "As you know, he is an opponent of bilingual education, but I wanted to show him that bilingualism and politics don't necessarily have to mix," she noted. Judging from the 47 vendors and publishers from Mexico, Spain, Argentina and the United States that exhibited books and other materials from young readers, Schon's efforts are becoming successful.

The Center/Centro's collection is open to the public Monday through Friday when University classes are in session. It also sponsors "Cafés Literarios," informal discussions about books in Spanish and books in English about Hispanics/Latinos for children and adolescents. In these "Cafés Literarios" participants are asked to bring a book, or books, to share and discuss, noted the director.

Dr. Schon enthusiastically pointed out that during the Summer of 1993, in cooperation with the College of Education, the Center/Centro will offer three one-week Summer Workshops/Talleres de Verano as an "introduction to an analysis of current practices and problems in selecting and using books in Spanish for children and adolescents."

Toward the end of our telephone conversation we talked about the importance of reaching educators and librarians early in their academic careers. Dr. Schon, an idea person, quickly mentioned her next task, to influence the library school curriculum of the institutions in the area.

Schon maintains a hectic schedule. When she is not at the Center/Centro, she is at another campus office, with her beeper. She seems to find time for several tasks, including publishing and maintaining the Center/Centro's collection and yet remains optimistic, as she was during our telephone conversation.

ACTIONS, ACTIONS, ACTIONS

These two institutions provide outstanding models for offering service to the Latino community. While they serve different groups in very distinct milieus, they share the common goal of making reading materials more available to the Latino community.

As the political discourse of "reinvesting in America" begins to move from the level of rhetoric to one of concrete action, both of these libraries provide arenas where ideas are being tested and are yielding positive results.

The Friendly Place/El Sitio Simpático, with the array of services that it provides to a community plagued with crime and drugs, has shown that "reinvesting" in the community has had tangible results: the children whose interest in reading has been sparked early on; the teenagers who have acquired job skills; the parents who have become involved in their children's education. The collective result of these community-based solutions has been to help alleviate the increasing rate of high school dropouts in the Latino community. Ms. Werlein-Jaen's assessment is quite telling: "Poor education and a lack of educational opportunities go hand in hand with poverty and high unemployment, feeding a cycle of economic despair.... Of the Latino community here, only eight out of 10 finish high school."

Schon's more recently established Center/Centro is living up to its goal of creating and maintaining strong ties with community organizations. It helps meet the needs of young Latino readers through its "Cafés Literarios," where on any given Thursday evening parents, community leaders, educators and librarians meet to discuss reading materials for young Latino readers. With its Summer Workshops/Talleres de Verano, the Center/Centro is attempting to reach professionals during their academic preparation as they get ready to serve the Latino community.

CONCLUSION

In conclusion, we can only ask, where are the "reinvestments in America" with Friendly Places in East Los Angeles and the barrios of San Antonio? Where are Dr. Schon's ideas in other public academic institutions where the Latino population is already an emerging minority-majority?

ACKNOWLEDGMENTS

The author wishes to thank Cheryl LaGuardia, Patrick Dawson, Cecily Johns, and Christine Oka, all of the University of California, Santa Barbara Library, for their comments and suggestions in the preparation of this manuscript.

NOTES

1.   Hoffert, Barbara. "¡Se Lea Español Aqui!" *Library Journal* 117 (July 15, 1992): 34.

2.   Shorris, Earl. "Latino, Si, Hispanic No," *New York Times,* 28 October 1992.

3.   Güereña, Salvador, ed. *Latino Librarianship: A Handbook for Professionals* (Jefferson, North Carolina: McFarland, 1990), xiii.

4.   U.S. Bureau of the Census, *Statistical Abstract of the United States, 1992* (Washington, 1992), 41.

5.   Exter, Thomas, "One Million Hispanic Club," *American Demographics* 12 (February 1991): 59.

6.   City of New York, Community Board No. 11, Borough of Manhattan, *Statement of District Needs: Fiscal Year 1994* (El Barrio, New York, 1993).

7.   The Friendly Place/El Sitio Simpático is located at 1948 First Avenue, New York, New York 10029, telephone (212) 410-3020; fax (212) 831-5955.

8.   Erkham, Mark. "Separating the *Trigo* from the Chaff," *Los Angeles Times Magazine,* 7 March 1993, 10.

9.   The Center for the Study of Books in Spanish for Children and Adolescents is at California State University, San Marcos, California 92096-0001; telephone (619) 752-4070, fax (619) 752-4030. Upon request, the Center provides an annotated list of recommended and not recommended titles as well as copies of the proceedings of its Conferences on Books in Spanish for Young Readers.

10.   Dr.Schon was the recipient of the 1992 Denali Press Award by the Reference and Adult Services division of the American Library Association for "achievement in creating reference works that are outstanding in quality and significance and provide information specifically about ethnic and minority groups in the U.S." (e.g., *Books in Spanish for Children and Young Adults: An Annotated Guide, Series I-V* (Metuchen, N.J.: The Scarecrow Press, 1978-1989.)

PROVIDING LIBRARY SERVICES TO THE LATINO COMMUNITY: SUGGESTIONS FOR FURTHER READING

Beaudin, Janice et al. "Recruiting the Underrepresented to Academic Libraries: Challenges and Opportunities." *College & Research Libraries News* 51 (December, 1990): 1016-1022+. Final report of the Association of College and Research Libraries (ACRL) Task Force on Recruitment of Underrepresented Minorities.

Carlon, David B. et al. *Adrift in a Sea of Change: California's Public Libraries Struggle to Meet the Information Needs of Multicultural Communities.* Berkeley: Center for Policy Development, 1990. Considers and proposes ways for California's public libraries to provide quality services to the state's increasingly multicultural communities.

Echavarria, Tammy. "Minority Recruitment: A Success Story." *College & Research Libraries News* 51 (November, 1990): 962-964. Discusses the Undergraduate Student Internship Program (USIP) at the University of California, San

Diego, "which brings minority students into the pipeline of training to become professional MLS-degree librarians."

Güereña, Salvador, ed. *Latino Librarianship: A Handbook for Professionals.* Jefferson, North Carolina: McFarland, 1990. A guide for librarians and administrators interested in serving Latino constituencies better; describes issues and resources for this population.

Janes, Phoebe and Ellen Meltzer. "Origins and Attitudes: Training Reference Librarians for a Pluralistic World." *The Reference Librarian* 30 (1990): 145-155. Addresses the need for "multicultural training for reference librarians in the face of demographic changes to serve a changing and diverse clientele."

LaGuardia, Cheryl, et al. "Instruction and Identity: Diversity in Library Classes and Collections." *The Reference Librarian.* Forthcoming special issue on "Reference Services and Sources Related to Racial and Ethnic Diversity." Discusses development of credit-bearing library classes and single-session subject-oriented instruction in an academic library serving a culturally diverse user population plus the impact in collection development.

Librarians Association of the University of California. "The Many Voices of Diversity; Report of the Ad Hoc Committee on LAUC Regional Workshops on Cultural Diversity in Libraries," Oakland: University of California, 1992. Photocopy. Addresses and makes recommendations on: Developing and Accessing Culturally Diverse Collections; Reference Service and Bibliographic Instruction to Multicultural Users; and Recruitment, Advancement and Retention of racially and ethnically diverse librarians within the University of California System.

Metoyer-Duran, Cheryl. The Information and Referral Process in Culturally Diverse Communities." *RQ* 32 (Spring, 1993): 359-371. Discusses the Gatekeeper Study, conducted in 1990 by the California State Libary, which examined the information-seeking behavior of ethnolinguistic gatekeepers in several American Indian, Asian American and Latino communities of Southern California.

Scarborough, Katherine. "Collections for the Emerging Majority." *Library Journal* 116 (July 15, 1991): 44-47 Discusses the conference "Developing Library Collections for California's Emerging Majority," which dealt with theoretical and practical aspects of collections for racial, ethnic and linguistic minorities.

————. *Developing Library Collections for California's Emerging Majority: A Manual of Resources for Ethnic Collection Development.* Oakland: Bay Area Library Information System, 1990. Manual intended to aid public, academic and school librarians in formulating policies and adopting practices that will offer relevant library services for California's culturally diverse population.

Schon, Isabel. "Outstanding Children's Books in Spanish." *Hispania* 75 (May 1992): 413-416. Annotated list of children's fiction and non-fiction titles from Latin America, Great Britain and the United States.

————. "Recent Noteworthy Books in Spanish for Young Readers." *School Library Media Activities Monthly* 8 (March 1992): 32-33, 39. Annotated bibliography, for school library media specialists and teachers, of recent books that encourage reading by Spanish-speaking students and others wishing to learn Spanish.

————. "Contrasts in Quality: Recommended and not Recommended Books in Spanish for Children and Adolescents." *Teacher Education Quarterly* 18 (Fall 1991): 73-83. Annotated bibliography presenting a selection of outstanding books in Spanish for young readers, including a list of "not recommended" titles.

Trujillo, Roberto G. and David C. Weber, "Academic Library Responses to Cultural Diversity: A Position Paper for the 1990s," *Journal of Academic Librarianship* 17 (July 1991): 157-161. Considers successes and failures of academic library responses to multiculturalism and discusses the critical role of the library director in implementing changes.

TRANSFORMING ACADEMIC LIBRARIES FOR EMPLOYEES AND STUDENTS WITH DISABILITIES

Donna Z. Pontau

The world is evolving into a "society of organizations" where knowledge is the primary resource for individuals and for the economy overall.[1] Consequently, the most essential resource for retaining an organization's competitive advantage is its "qualified, knowledgeable people," and organizations will have to "market membership as much as they market products and services—and perhaps more. They have to attract people, hold people, recognize and reward people, motivate people, and serve and satisfy people."[2] Who will these "qualified, knowledgeable people" be? Studies such as *Workforce 2000* and other U. S. Labor Department reports indicate demographic changes in the workforce plus declines and shortages of skills in those people entering it as the twenty-first century approaches.[3]

There is a segment of America's workforce which has been heretofore underutilized, but for whom an information or knowledge society offers great opportunities: persons with disabilities. Adaptive equipment and computers allow this segment of the workforce to transcend or circumvent barriers in order to utilize their mind power in the work world. "According to the U.S. Bureau of Labor Statistics, more then 90 percent of the net new job openings through the year 2000 will be in information-intensive and service-intensive occupations. In these positions, brain power, not physical dexterity, will be the prime requirement."[4]

Persons with disabilities cannot simply bound into the workforce; numerous attitudinal, facilities, and service barriers exist. Academic library administrators have a unique opportunity to remove these barriers and to hasten the integration of persons with disabilities into the American economy which needs their talents and expertise. First, library administrators who develop truly accessible institutions enhance their functioning in the new knowledge society of organizations. The Library expands its candidate pool when openings occur, and is in a much better position to retain those qualified staff who later develop disabling conditions—whether temporarily, permanently, or through the aging process. Also, accessible libraries benefit from the competitive advantages of having a diverse employee base. Second, academic library administrators' commitment to providing accessible libraries in facilities, services, materials, and staff enhances the educational, professional, and personal goals of individuals with disabilities. This discussion documents the advantages of such commitments by academic libraries both as employers and as service providers. Examples for attaining accessibility for persons with disabilities in light of the Americans with Disabilities Act legislation and regulations will also be addressed.

BACKGROUND: TERMINOLOGY, STATISTICS, AND THE AMERICANS WITH DISABILITIES ACT

Before proceeding much further, it is important to provide some definitions and background. Numerous definitions abound for the word "disability"; one prominently used now is that provided in the Americans with Disabilities Act of 1990 (Public Law 101-336): "The term 'disability' means, with respect to an individual—(a) a physical or mental impairment that substantially limits one or more of the major life activities of such individual; (b) a record of such an impairment; or (c) being regarded as having such an impairment." This definition seems vague and confusing to many persons, but the intent of the definition was flexibility. Rather than provide a checklist of what disabilities were covered by the law, it was intentionally written to be applicable in particular circumstances and in the future when certain conditions might exist which were not present when the law was drafted. There are approximately 43 million Americans with disabilities who benefit from this legislation.

"Work disability" is a less inclusive term. The Census Bureau defines a work disability based on the following criteria: (a) the individual has a disability which prohibits him or her from working at all or at a particular line of work, (b) the individual has retired or left a job for health reasons, (c) the individual has a long term physical or mental illness or disability which prevents any type of work performance, or (d) an individual did not work at all in the previous year because of a disability or illness.[5] Data from the 1990 Census reveal that 8.2 percent of the total U.S. population aged 16 to 64 has a work disability.[6] The unemployment rate for men and women with a work disability in 1988 was 14.2 percent compared to 6.2 percent and 5.2 percent respectively for males and females who did not have work disabilities.[7] These people can be put to work!

Disability types have been traditionally classified in four groups; these groups and definitions are clearly explained in an article in *Adult Learning*:

Cognitive disabilities: disorders or impairments in the ability or rate of accepting, processing, storing, and recalling information. Examples are learning disabilities and developmental disabilities such as mental retardation. It is important to note that a person with a learning disability is *not* mentally retarded. The person's intelligence is not in question; but rather, the information acquired through the senses is scrambled like a "radio that is not quite on the station or a TV slightly out of focus."

Physical disabilities: interference or inability to initiate certain physical or muscular movements that others take for granted.

Sensory disabilities: significant impairments of one or more of the major senses, such as sight or hearing, that for others provide important channels for receiving information.

Mental or emotional disabilities: problems coping with the stresses of life or distinguishing the real from the imagined. This disability is not related to intelligence level.[8]

While disability types can be categorized, persons with disabilities are individuals. Two people with visual difficulties will have differing levels of severity in their disabilities, and identical strategies or equipment for overcoming the sight barriers may not be appropriate. Likewise, their skills and competencies will differ. Leonardo da Vinci had superior artistic skills even though he had epilepsy. Bruce Jenner, Greg Louganis, and Jim Abbott are all superior athletes even though the first two gentlemen have learning disabilities and Mr. Abbott has an orthopedic impairment. Cher, Whoopi Goldberg, and Marlee Matlin have excelled in the performing arts despite difficulties caused respectively by dyslexia, learning disabilities, and deafness. Persons with disabilities have made notable contributions to science as well: Alfred Nobel had epilepsy, Albert Einstein had a learning disability, and Alexander Graham Bell had a hearing loss. It is the *individual* who is of foremost importance—not the disability.

It is this spirit that brought passage of the Americans with Disabilities Act (ADA) in 1990. The legislation and its regulations have far-reaching impacts on employment and accessibility of facilities, transportation, communication, and services. While this law represents another landmark in United States civil rights legislation, the ADA *is not* an affirmative action directive. It does attempt to open society more fully to persons with disabilities so they might compete more equitably in the job market and use and participate in those services and institutions enjoyed by others.

Section 504 of the Rehabilitation Act of 1973 and its regulations have been in effect for almost 20 years, but many universities and colleges covered by that legislation have not operated in complete compliance. The ADA used Section 504 as its foundation and expanded the coverage to other areas and state and local jurisdictions. Consequently, most academic libraries have a lot of work to do in order to meet requirements for facilities, accessibility of collections and services, and equitable employment practices.

The ADA has three main titles: Title I—Employment, Title II—Public Services, and Title III—Public Accommodations and Services provided by Private Entities. Much material has been published on ADA requirements. Two excellent sources with which to begin an examination are *The Americans with Disabilities Handbook* by the

U.S. Equal Employment Opportunity Commission and the U.S. Justice Department and *How Libraries Must Comply with the Americans with Disabilities Act* by Donald Foos and Nancy Pack.[9] Numerous articles have appeared in a variety of journals and newspapers. Help is also available from the American Library Association (ALA). The Association of Specialized and Cooperative Library Agencies, a division of the ALA, established the Americans with Disabilities Act Assembly. This group met for the first time at the 1993 Midwinter meeting and will hold open, question-answer sessions at every midwinter and annual conference for years to come. The intent of this Assembly is to provide information and suggestions—but not legal advice—concerning the numerous aspects of this civil rights legislation. While it is easy to get bogged down in the specifics, the spirit of the law can assist library decision-making and compliance efforts.

THE ACADEMIC LIBRARY AS AN EMPLOYER

Recruiting Competent Staff

No successful organization can ignore the workforce trends and still hope to attract the best workers. According to the U.S. Labor Department report *Workforce 2000,* the traditional member of the American labor force—white males—will constitute only 15 percent of the total between 1985 and 2000, while women and other ethnic and racial groups will constitute the remainder.[10] The number of working age people with disabilities is presently projected to be between 13 and 16 million by the year 2000.[11] This segment of the population represents an untapped source of labor and talent. In many instances, it is the *attitudinal* barriers which are more powerful deterrents to success in the job market rather than the disabilities themselves.

Many administrators, department heads, and human resources personnel are unfamiliar, misinformed, or have misconceptions about persons with disabilities. Persons with disabilities "are separate and distinct individuals, not a homogeneous category labeled 'the disabled'."[12] Some employees with disabilities will be stellar while others are abysmal and still others will perform their duties adequately. People with disabilities are not necessarily tragic, brave, heroic or inspirational. Persons with disabilities desire financial independence like most people. It cannot be assumed that more on-the-job accidents will occur, an organization's insurance rates will rise, or absentee rates will skyrocket if individuals with disabilities are integrated into an organization's workforce.[13] Actually, persons with disabilities, in general, often have lower absentee rates, less turnover, and are every bit as conscientious as their "able-bodied" counterparts.[14] Corporations such as Pizza Hut, DuPont, Marriott, and McDonald's—companies with proven track-records in hiring persons with disabilities—have demonstrated the successful integration of persons with disabilities into their workforces. DuPont, in fact, has employee data covering 30 years which demonstrates that workers with disabilities "rank equal to or better than fully abled employees on key job performance measures."[15]

Academic libraries hire people at a variety of levels—professional, support staff, and student assistants; the activities of these employees are wide-ranging: public service, technical service, clerical, and even manual labor. Many opportunities exist to match qualified individuals with disabilities to specific jobs. The ADA does not specifically require employers to revise job descriptions, but libraries may wish to do so in order to determine what the "essential functions" of each job type are. Knowing this, library personnel doing the hiring might be able to see more clearly how the *capabilities* of a particular applicant with a disability match a particular job opening. The individual's qualifications and capabilities—based on "reasonable accommodations"—then serve as the measure with which to judge the individual among other applicants.[16]

The ADA does require that employers make "reasonable accommodations" for otherwise qualified applicants with disabilities unless the accommodations represent an "undue hardship." The cost of modifications for persons with disabilities is often misconstrued to be a major hiring stumbling block. Actually, the costs are generally not exorbitant, and in fact most job accommodations cost little or nothing. Data compiled by the U.S. Department of Labor and the Government Accounting Office in 1989 indicated that modifications of less than $50 are all that is needed for half of all workers with disabilities to perform their jobs. Twenty percent of modifications cost between $50 and $500, and another twenty percent cost between $500 and $1000.[17]

No specific cost studies have highlighted the library environment. Since many library positions require office or desk work, the numerous adaptations appropriate for the business world workstation or office would be applicable to the library environment. It would be unreasonable to modify miles of book stacks, but products for reaching and retrieving items from shelving do exist. Catalogs of products such as *The First Whole Rehab Catalog: A Comprehensive Guide to Products and Services for the Physically Disadvantaged* by A. Jay and Margaret Ann Abrams can be consulted for ideas.[18] The ABLEDATA database, sponsored by the National Rehabilitation Information Center (NARIC) lists 18,000 assistive devices.[19] JAN—the Job Accommodation Network is based at West Virginia University and offers free assistance on the modification of worksites. Numerous local, county, and state rehabilitation organizations can offer suggestions, also.[20]

One of the largest unnecessary hurdles in workplace accommodations can be library technology; the use of online catalogs, automated circulation systems, CD-Rom workstations, or systems such as Lexis/Nexis permeates into almost every library job. Such automated library resources have not been designed to interface easily with adaptive equipment. Adaptation is possible, however; and there are signs that vendors are paying more attention to the issue. For example, Dynix has linked with the adaptive technology company Telesensory Systems to offer an adaptive OPAC package, with the Lee County Library System in Fort Myers, Florida serving as the first test site.

What exactly is adaptive equipment? A magnifying glass could be considered adaptive equipment, but it usually refers to a piece of equipment which modifies a procedure or process in order for a person with a disability to do something independently. For computers, more specifically, "adaptive technology" refers to any "software or hardware addition to the computer that renders it accessible to a person with special needs."[21] Examples include voice synthesizers which "speak" the contents of the computer screen or a page of text and text enlarging programs which allow the text on the computer screen to be magnified and read in large print. These types of adaptive technology aid employees with blindness, low vision, or other print impairments such as dyslexia. Other types of adaptive technology focus on the keyboard. Many people with dexterity difficulties due to arthritis or paralysis, for example, cannot easily type or execute various keystroke requirements in order to operate a computer. The "heaviness" of their fingerstrokes may cause duplicate characters to print on the screen or they may not be physically capable of performing simultaneous keystroking to generate boots, execute various commands, or cease erroneous printing. Adaptive technology, in these instances, modifies traditional parameters in order for sequential keystroking to occur or for the printing of extra characters to be inhibited.

More and more adaptive technology from numerous companies for various purposes is appearing on the market; again, not all these products will necessarily work with a particular CD-Rom or OPAC system. Help is available when investigating what adaptation might benefit an employee—or library user. Two recent books on the topic are Barbara Mates' *Library Technology for Visually and Physically Impaired Patrons;* and *Access to Information: Materials, Technologies, and Services for Print-Impaired Readers* by Tom McNulty and Dawn M. Suvino.[22] The IBM Special Needs/ Independence Series Information Center in Boca Raton, Florida will send free materials upon request concerning adaptive technology compatible with IBM products for mobility impairments, hearing impairments, speech or language impairments, learning impairments, or vision impairments. Apple Computer's Worldwide Disability Solutions Group is also active.[23] The two journals *Library Hi Tech* and *Computers in Libraries* provide product information: the November 1992 issue of *Computers in Libraries* focused on library equipment and furniture for persons with disabilities, while the first 1993 issue of *Library Hi Tech* focused on the theme "Adaptive Technologies for Accommodating Persons with Disabilities."[24]

One of the newest options for researching adaptive technology and other issues concerning the accessibility of libraries for persons with disabilities is the electronic discussion group. As this chapter was being written, the listserv for the LITA Adaptive Technology Interest Group was in its infancy; this listserv, ADAPT-L, is based at American University in Washington, D.C.[25] Another new listserv is AXSLIB-L, originally sponsored by the Interuniversity Communication Council, better known as EDUCOM. EDUCOM's Project EASI (Equal Access to Software and Information) started this e-mail list early in 1993 to answer questions about technology issues, to lobby vendors to make their products internally highly accessible, and to encourage network accessibility.[26] The project is now affiliated with the American Association for Higher Education.

Information on adaptations and workplace modifications is increasingly easy to find, but the best source of information concerning adaptations is the individual with the disability. The individual functions with the disability in many other life activities. No workplace adaptations can be made without input from the individual; he or she may well discuss applicable accommodations during the employment interview. Recruiting employees with disabilities need not be a Herculean challenge; in fact, it is simply good business.

Retaining Employees Who Become Disabled

As mentioned earlier, approximately 43 million Americans have disabilities. While many of those persons were born with their disabilities, others have acquired disabilities at various stages in life due to aging, illness, or injury. Five out of six people were *not* born with their disability.[27] The 1992 edition of the National Safety Council's annual report *Accident Facts* states that 8,600,000 disabling injuries occurred in 1991. Of those, 310,000 resulted in permanent impairments.[28] Also, new causes of disabilities appear through time. Lyme disease, carpal tunnel syndrome, and chronic fatigue syndrome are relatively new maladies, yet they all can have an impact on a person's performance of life's major activities and influence work capabilities.[29] In short, current employees may acquire disabilities at any time. It can be in the organization's best interest to retain these employees.

Employees are an organization's most expensive investment today. An accessible institution plus a supportive, accepting, and welcoming organizational climate will encourage a newly disabled employee to return to work. As discussed earlier, workplace adaptations are not the huge expenses managers fear. Employees who became disabled and *do not* return to work cost an organization money on two accounts. First, the employee's valuable work experience is no longer paying dividends. Further, if a replacement is hired, additional training dollars must be expended. These costs are not insignificant to corporations. A survey in 1988 of subscriber organizations of a major business journal concluded that $5.3 billion dollars was spent that year on training and development. Keeping an experienced employee when a disability occurs saves dollars.[30]

Operational Benefits

Research in the social and administrative sciences indicates that organizations having diverse, multicultural work forces develop competitive advantages over organizations which do not. Diversity may favorably impact the marketing of services and products and the creativity and innovation of the staff.[31]

Libraries continually assess their user communities—their "markets." As the markets for libraries diversify, some researchers believe it is prudent to diversify the staff as well. The rationale is that the "insights and cultural sensitivities" that members from various diverse groups or subpopulations have can be invaluable in planning for and attracting clients in the same groups. For example, academic libraries recognized the demographic shift on campuses and have initiated transformations of their institutions accordingly. Collections were scrutinized for their coverage, language, formats, and reflections of the American experience in all its hues and perspectives. Many libraries created the position of Multicultural Librarian and expanded efforts to actively encourage library use among underrepresented students.[32] In the process, many academic libraries established higher visibility on their campuses and forged links with campus departments such as EOP or Admissions and Records with whom they had little contact before. Hiring staff with disabilities should have a similar impact on students with disabilities on campus; as they see themselves reflected in library staff, they may well be more receptive to the services and collections developed for them.

The experiences and cultures of traditionally underrepresented groups cannot help altering the organizational climate and environment of the workplace. Further, their diffusion into the work climate can encourage creativity and innovation. As stated in the article, "Managing Cultural Diversity: the Challenge of the '90s,"

[A] diverse workforce brings a broad spectrum of backgrounds, interests, point of view, and ways of doing things to a firm. The rich mixture of ideas they can provide should bring fresh perspectives to the solution of problems and encourage the emergence and growth of creativity. Companies which view their employees as a homogenous mass will lose the added value that a multicultural workforce provides.[33]

Persons with disabilities have daily life experiences dealing with obstacles requiring problem-solving skills. Because their "reality" will differ from that of their colleagues, their solutions to a problem may differ. Take the development of an informational library handout or locally designed online catalog screen. If the Library's goal is simplicity and clarity of the message, a librarian with a disability may have different assumptions about what basic library literacy "average" users possess; he or she may also have had experiences which focus his or her attention not just on the message content, but on the format and presentation as well. Such attention, in the end, improves the product for *all* users.

THE ACADEMIC LIBRARY AS AN EDUCATIONAL INSTITUTION AND SERVICE PROVIDER

Academic libraries can directly impact the educational success of the growing number of students with disabilities. This segment of the library's user population, however, cannot benefit from the information housed in their campus libraries if the building is not accessible, if library materials or services are not usable, or if the library staff cannot communicate with them!

Students with disabilities do exist now on college campuses—and their numbers are growing. First, Fall 1986 statistics (still the statistics cited in government reports) indicate that 1,319,229 students at post-secondary institutions declared a disability—10 percent of all students enrolled.[34] The American Council of Education has published two reports: *The American Freshman: National Norms for Fall 1992* and *College Freshmen with Disabilities*. The estimated first-time freshmen enrollment was 1.7 million. Almost 1 percent of entering freshmen had a hearing loss, 0.3 percent had a speech difficulty, 1.1 percent had an orthopedic or physical disability, 2.1 percent had a learning disability, 1.5 percent had a health or medical problem, 2.2 percent had a visual disability, and 1.5 percent had various other disabilities.[35] Today, one in every 11 freshmen reports a disability; only one in 38 freshmen reported a disability in 1978. The number of students having "invisible" disabilities such as hearing losses, learning disabilities, or dyslexia is growing rapidly. In 1985, 14.8 percent of freshmen reported learning disabilities; in 1991 the figure was 25 percent.[36] Many students did not divulge their disabilities in the past. The passage of the ADA, a growing sense of pride in the disabled community, and earlier diagnosis of learning disabilities contribute to the growth in the statistics.

What can academic libraries do to improve their effectiveness and usefulness to students with disabilities? Administrators can examine their institutions using applicable ADA regulations pertaining to facilities, collections, communications, and services. The ADA does not mandate many specifics for libraries, but a few examples of necessary changes based on the law's content follow. Braille signs must be posted, and informational handouts must be available in alternative formats such as audiocassette or large print. If a class attending a bibliographic instruction lecture has a hearing impaired student, then that student must be able to understand the presentation; consequently, the Library should arrange for a sign language interpreter or have an FM amplification system in place. Library technology was addressed earlier in this discussion. Adaptations applicable for employees might also be applicable for public service points based on a survey of a campus' students, faculty, and staff having disabilities. Among the academic libraries which already have made great strides in this area are the University of Texas-Austin, Texas Woman's University in Denton, and Wright State University, Dayton, Ohio.

Collection development policies may need revision to include the acquisition of materials in large print or audiocassette formats. Instead of buying two copies in the traditional print format, libraries may begin to purchase one in paper and one in audiocassette. Commuting students, for example, would also benefit from the audiocassette version—not just those students with vision or learning disabilities. A certain percentage of the collection development budget could be set aside for such alternative format purchases.

Academic libraries have a responsibility as educational institutions to provide adequate accessibility for students with disabilities— regardless of ADA mandates. A college education develops a student's mind as well as preparing him or her for the workplace; consequently, the student population with disabilities requires the same opportunities for discovery and preparation. Accessibility efforts, therefore, are not special favors, but rather means to accomplish the same goals desired for nondisabled students. Just as there are unsubstantiated fears concerning costs and impacts of hiring persons with disabilities, there are frequently administrative concerns about costs and impacts on other students and staff if services for students with disabilities are expanded, especially in tight budget times. Not all accessibility efforts are costly or adversely affect current services. Appointing a Library Liaison to Patrons with Disabilities, developing a policy statement for services, and planning staff workshops are all activities which improve library use for students with disabilities with minimal costs.[37]

The appointment of a particular librarian with job responsibilities for assisting and advocating the library and information needs of students with disabilities is a step toward enhancing their academic achievement. This person need not be the official library ADA Coordinator—the library staff member designated to implement and monitor ADA compliance.[38] At many universities, such as San Jose State University, University of Oregon, and Northern Illinois University, the Liaison is a member of the public services staff—frequently the Reference Department—and spends approximately 25 percent of the work week engaged in Liaison activities. Liaison activities include individualized research assistance, instruction, problem resolution, policy development, collection development, interaction with Disabled Students Office personnel and any campus students with disabilities clubs or associations, public relations and marketing of library services, staff awareness and training, and continuing education.

The Liaison, as a contact person among the library staff, helps students with disabilities feel less estranged from the "mysteries" of library policies and organization. After all, many college students with disabilities possess little library experience and/or limited library literacy skills due to the historical inaccessibility of these institutions. Roberto G. Trujillo and David C. Weber, in their article "Academic Library Responses to Cultural Diversity: A Position Paper for the 1990's," encourage academic librarians to "develop the skills and cultural competencies needed to reach the less visible, less assertive, less prepared students. Some individuals must be reached outside the library, shown the usefulness of library services, and convinced that the library can and will be responsive to their needs. Some students simply do not know how to take advantage of resources that librarians may consider are there for the taking."[39] The Library Liaison to Patrons with Disabilities attempts to fulfill the needs and strategy espoused by Trujillo and Weber.

The ADA requires libraries to conduct self-studies of their institutions and to involve members of the Library's clientele with disabilities.[40] A written policy statement on services, collections, and so forth can easily be derived from such a study. A written policy on services for patrons with disabilities represents a "commitment to such services and insures uniformity and conformity in all Library departments."[41] Further, the policy statement can be edited to create promotional brochures or new student orientation handouts.

What is the respectful terminology to use when assisting library patrons with disabilities? How is a TDD answered? What are some signs which might alert a reference librarian that a patron has a learning disability? An understanding of issues such as these by all levels of library staff improves library services for students with disabilities. Language impacts people profoundly, and is one important way persons with disabilities will measure the sincerity of a library and its services. People-first terminology such as "user with a wheelchair" rather than "wheelchair-bound user" is important to hear because it reflects the focus on the individual rather than the disability. Knowing that struggling to find the "right word," frequently returning for the same instructions or directions, or getting flustered when trying to explain or focus a reference question or term paper topic are possible signs that the patron may have a learning disability enables staff to utilize techniques which minimize or circumvent the disability. Such staff skills, like TDD operation and etiquette, are easily relayed during staff workshops or brown-bag lunches. While these skills may seem trivial, they contribute a great deal in raising the comfort level of both the students with disabilities *and* of the library staff. With increased comfort comes a reduction in fear, and consequently, a reduction in attitudinal barriers on both sides.

Academic libraries can contribute to the academic success of all students; but accessible facilities, services and collections are required for such benefits to students with disabilities. Again, students are not requesting special favors but rather means to circumvent or eradicate present barriers. A student once explained it with this analogy. A wide river can present a "natural" barrier for a car interested in driving in a certain direction; similarly, a disability can be a "natural" barrier to an individual's pursuit of information in libraries. A bridge constructed over the river eliminates the barrier for the car; similarly, library services for the disabled eradicate barriers to information and library resources.

CONCLUDING COMMENTS

Who will be the "qualified, knowledgeable" employees whose expertise is increasingly essential to successful organizations and institutions in the next century? Individuals with disabilities are poised to fill the void. However, institutions and organizations seeking the talents of the disabled must first recognize and appreciate their skills, reward their capabilities and demonstrate an interest in modifying their environment. Institutions and organizations must first attract and then retain employees with disabilities by transforming organizational attitudes, facilities, services, and policies into a welcoming and accessible culture.

Academic library administrators now have the opportunity to transform their institutions into places where the disabled will desire to work, and where future members of the workforce with disabilities will receive education and training for the ever-expanding Information Age. The impetus for such a transformation is two-fold. First, some transformations are now mandated by the ADA. Attitudes and sincerity, however, cannot be legislated. Transformations generated by a sense of responsibility both for the vitality of the library and its staff as well as the educational success and aspirations of students with disabilities will be those of greater value and longer duration.

NOTES

1. Peter F. Drucker, "The New Society of Organizations," *Harvard Business Review* 70 (September-October 1992): 95.

2. Drucker, "The New Society," 100.

3. Kevin R. Hopkins and Susan L. Nestleroth, "Willing and Able" (Special Advertising Supplement), *Business Week* no. 3237 (October 28, 1991), 66.

4. Ibid., 72.

5. Robert C. Ficke, *Digest of Data on Persons with Disabilities* (Washington, D.C.: National Institute on Disability and Rehabilitation Research, 1991), 32.

6. U.S. Bureau of the Census, *1990 Census of Population and Housing: Summary Social, Economic, and Housing Characteristics: United States* (Washington, D.C., 1992), 185.

7. Ficke, *Digest of Data,* 33.

8. Sylvester Pues, "Adults with Special Learning Needs: An Overview," *Adult Learning 2* (October 1990): 18.

9. Equal Employment Opportunity Commission and the U. S. Department of Justice, Americans with Disabilities Act Handbook (Washington: EEOC, October

1991); and Donald D. Foos and Nancy C. Pack, comps. and eds., *How Libraries Must Comply with the Americans with Disabilities Act* (ADA) (Phoenix, AZ: Oryx Press, 1992).

10.   Sami M. Abbasi and Kenneth W. Hollman, "Managing Cultural Diversity: the Challenge of the '90s," *Records Management Quarterly* 25 (July 1991): 25.

11.   Hopkins, "Willing and Able," 70.

12.   Hugh H. McDonough, "Hiring People with Disabilities," Supervisory Management 37 (February 1992): 11.

13.   Ibid., 11-12.

14.   Patricia M. Buhler, "Hiring the Disabled—The Solution to Our Problem," *Supervision* 52 (June 1991): 17.

15.   Judith Waldrop, "The Cost of Hiring the Disabled," *American Demographics* 13 (March 1991): 12.

16.   Peter Manheimer, "The Americans With Disabilities Act: the Legal Implications," in *How Libraries Must Comply With the Americans with Disabilities Act,* ed. Donald D. Foos and Nancy C. Pack. (Phoenix, AZ: Oryx Press, 1992), 89-111.

17.   Waldrop, "Cost of Hiring," 12.

18.   A. Jay and Margaret Ann Abrams, *The First Whole Rehab Catalog: A Comprehensive Guide to Products and Services for the Physically Disadvantaged* (White Hall, VA: Betterway Publications, 1990).

19.   Mr. Dan Wendling, NARIC Media Specialist, e-mail message to the author via AXSLIB-L discussion group, 12 February 1993. Contact Mr. Wendling via e-mail at danlw@well.sf.ca.us for more details.

20.   Ruth O'Donnell, "Planning to Implement the ADA in the Library," in *How Libraries Must Comply,* 68.

21.   Tom McNulty and Dawn M. Suvino, Access to Information: *Materials, Technologies, and Services for Print-Impaired Readers* (Chicago: American Library Association, 1993), 6.

22.   McNulty and Suvino, *Access to Information;* Barbara Mates, *Library Technology for Visually and Physically Impaired Patrons* (Westport, CT: Meckler, 1991).

23.   IBM Special Needs/Independence Series Information Center can be reached by mail at P. O. Box 1328, Boca Raton, FL 34429; the toll-free telephone number is 1-800-426-4832. Apple Computer Worldwide Disabilities Solutions Group can be contacted by telephone at (408) 974-7910; Apple Computer's Corporate Office is at 26525 Mariani Avenue, Cupertino, CA 95014.

24. *Computers in Libraries 12,* no. 10 (November 1992); *Library Hi Tech* 11, no. 1 (1993).

25.   Mr. Christopher Lewis, Media Services Librarian, American University, Washington, D.C., e-mail message to the author, 24 February 1993. Contact Mr. Lewis at clewis@american.edu for more details about the ADAPT-L listserv.

26.   Mr. Dick Banks, Library Learning Center, University of Wisconsin-Stout, e-mail message to the author, 11 February 1993. Contact Mr. Banks at rbanks@uwstout.edu for more details on AXSLIB-L.

27.   Richard Nelson Bolles, *Job Hunting Tips for the So-Called Handicapped or Persons Who Have Disabilities* (Berkeley, CA: Ten Speed Press, 1991), 10.

28. National Safety Council, *Accident Facts* (Itasca, IL: National Safety Council, 1992), 1.

29. Bolles, *Job Hunting, 10.*

30. Morton E. Grossman and Margaret Magnus, "The $5.3 Billion Tab for Training," *Personnel Journal* 68 (July 1989): 54.

31. Taylor H. Cox and Stacy Blake, "Managing Cultural Diversity: Implications for Organizational Competitiveness," *Academy of Management Executive* 5 (1991): 45.

32. Otis A. Chadley, "Addressing Cultural Diversity in Academic and Research Libraries," *College & Research Libraries* 53 (May 1992): 206-214.

33. Abbasi and Hollman, "Managing Cultural Diversity," 30.

34. U. S. Department of Education, National Center for Education Statistics, *Digest of Education Statistics* (Washington, D.C.: Government Printing Office, 1992), 207.

35. "This Year's Freshmen: A Statistical Profile," *Chronicle of Higher Education,* January 13, 1993, A30.

36. "Note Book," *Chronicle of Higher Education,* 4 November 1992, A27.

37. Donna Pontau, "Elimination of Handicapping Barriers in Academic Libraries," *Urban Academic Librarian* 8 (Winter 1991/1992): 3-12.

38. O'Donnell, "Planning to Implement the ADA," 35.

39. Roberto G. Trujillo and David C. Weber, "Academic Library Responses to Cultural Diversity: A Position Paper for the 1990s," *Journal of Academic Librarianship* 17 (July 1991): 159.

40. O'Donnell, "Planning to Implement the ADA," 36.

41. Pontau, "Elimination of Handicapping Barriers," 8.

LIBRARY SERVICES FOR OLDER ADULTS

Linda Lou Wiler and Linda Marie Golian

INTRODUCTION

The future of libraries hinges partially upon their ability to meet the information needs of our rapidly aging society. Who are the older adults, and how can libraries support their needs? These questions foster some of today's major discussions.[1] A broad definition of the older adult includes those aged 50 and older. Dynamic librarians answer the challenge to bolster this growing segment of our population through developing comprehensive programs and services.[2]

OLDER ADULT LIBRARY PATRONS

A passive, non-voting, widowed woman, living alone on social security typically describes the average American's view of an older library patron.[3] She visits her public library infrequently, and her reading interests are cookbooks, best selling non-fiction and novels.[4]

Research consistently proves this damaging stereotype false. All people respond to the aging process in a way that is unique, but consistent with their cultural background, health situation, and psychological make-up.[5] Patron personalities stay virtually the same during the aging process.[6] Demanding and difficult young patrons usually become demanding and difficult older patrons.[7] Flexible young adults who can change and develop become older individuals who continually demonstrate their capacity to adapt.[8]

These older patrons are an influential part of our society. As voters they decide the outcome of many community referendums, including pressing library-related issues.[9]

Informed librarians diligently plan library services to support a positive concept of aging. In developing beneficial programs for older adults, they use a well-defined planning process. These nine interrelated steps form a continuous cycle for designing older patron services:

1. Create an older library patron advisory group
2. Review resources
3. Conduct a community profile and needs assessment
4. Review staffing, collections and building facilities
5. Review laws and funding sources
6. Set goals and priorities
7. Design and implement programs
8. Promote library programs and services
9. Evaluate progress[10]

ADVISORY GROUPS

To meet the needs of a library's complex population, library administrators often create advisory groups. The hard-working group members provide suggestions, feedback, positive criticism and at times, the physical labor to accomplish necessary projects.

Many libraries already have established broad-based circles which include older adult members who advise and support the administrators about issues of concern to them. Sometimes, however, the library administrators recognize the need to create a separate committee that focuses specifically upon older adult needs.[11] Promoting both alternatives provides added ideas and insights.[12]

NEEDS ASSESSMENT

When assessing older patron needs, inquiring librarians interview these community members:

1. Older adults using the library
2. Residents living in senior centers and nursing homes
3. Health care and other professionals
4. Representatives from other agencies working with older adults
5. Older adult family members and care providers
6. Community leaders and politicians
7. Directors of elderly studies in educational institutions

The complete older adult needs assessment includes the concerns of retired residents, nursing home patients, homebound patrons, and adults in senior day care centers. It also reviews and studies the reading habits of the older adult community. Most current surveys conclude:

1. Reading is one of the top five leisure activities for older adults.
2. Older adults enjoy reading magazines and newspapers more than other library materials.
3. Older readers are less likely to use their public library. They like to borrow books from friends or relatives because of transportation difficulties.
4. Older library users borrow more materials than other patrons.
5. Older adults prefer subjects related to the past such as history and biographies.
6. Older patrons prefer reading light materials such as mysteries and short stories.
7. Active older adults are more likely to use libraries.
8. Older readers prefer materials with few sexually explicit references.
9. Today's older adults are different from those of earlier years. Future generations of older patrons will want different materials.[13]

OLDER ADULT SERVICES COORDINATOR AND LIBRARY STAFFING

A highly motivated, well-trained professional staff is the primary factor in sustained library services for older adults.[14] When providing services and materials for older patrons, sensitive library administrators need to appoint a talented staff member to direct the program. This individual can work full- or part-time, depending upon the library's staffing needs. As a dynamic, knowledgeable leader of older patron services, the coordinator possesses:

1. A wide knowledge of library materials, both print and non-print
2. An ability to relate instructional materials to staff, volunteers and library patrons
3. A compassionate, realistic, respectful, and professional style
4. A common-sense attitude
5. An awareness of resources available in other libraries or agencies
6. The ability to plan library services cooperatively, set goals and conduct continuous and rigorous evaluation
7. Experience in conducting large and small group activities
8. An understanding of bibliotherapy, its techniques, potentials and dangers
9. Knowledge of special characteristics of older adults
10. Ability to research, organize and maintain records concerning programs and materials designed to serve older adults
11. An awareness of intergenerational dynamics
12. Good writing skills for developing program and informational articles and materials
13. Good communication skills for educating and training staff, patrons and families[15]

Volunteers

The use of volunteers in older adult services fosters good public and community relations. Volunteer programs provide essential workers that allow many libraries to develop, test or expand programs and services for older patrons.[16] Acting as community conduits, the older volunteers help librarians learn what elderly patrons want and need.[17]

COLLECTION ASSESSMENT

Astute librarians base collections upon the characteristics of the user community, while considering the proximity of other libraries in the region. They gather materials other than books when developing libraries for older patrons. A comprehensive collection includes materials in a combination of formats including:

1. Standard library materials
2. Large print books, magazines, newspapers
3. Specialized magazines on aging and older adult issues
4. Books on audiocassettes
5. Braille materials
6. Captioned materials for deaf and hearing impaired
7. Film and video
8. Materials for information and referral packets
9. Multi-media kits
10. Genealogy and local history resources[18]

Audio-Visual Materials

One frailty associated with aging is visual impairment. Librarians should consider purchasing equipment that allows viewing videotapes in the same large format as 16mm or 35mm films. This action allows libraries to sponsor presentations that provide increased enjoyment for older adults with visual problems. The resulting satisfaction turns a simple program into a festive occasion allowing older adults to relax and reminisce.[19]

Large Print Materials

Libraries serving older adults should collect large print books and periodicals such as *New York Times Large Type Weekly* and *Reader's Digest.*[20] Publishers reacting to the growing demand for large print materials often provide these items simultaneously with regular editions.[21]

Accommodating this growing interest in large type books, some libraries sponsor large print discussion groups. They also pay special attention to the physical location of large print materials. Understanding librarians realize that older patrons benefit from large print materials shelved in well lighted areas, with large lettering on the shelf labels.[22]

Multi-Media Kits

Multi-media kits include materials especially designed to stimulate the sensory and intellectual faculties of older adults. Created for use in senior centers, retirement homes and libraries, these kits contain an assortment of instructional aids.[23] The materials include slides, cassettes, song booklets, poems, photographs and materials for other activities such as crossword puzzles.[24] Bi-Folkal Productions produces multi-media kits known for their exceptional quality and variety of subject matter.[25]

Specialized Periodicals

Currently there exists an explosion of periodicals in subject areas related to a positive aging attitude. These publications primarily target the active older adult. They include profiles of famous seniors and upbeat news on subjects such as travel, health, finances, dining, and entertainment.[26]

EQUIPMENT

Insightful librarians purchase equipment that helps older adults with hearing and visual impairments to use traditional and computerized library collections. The considerate librarian purchases reading tables and audio-visual carrels especially designed for wheelchair access. Other equipment considerations include:

1. Push carts to help carry books and materials
2. Copy machines with enlarging capacity
3. Microform reader/printers with a variety of magnification lenses
4. Word synthesizers that transfer printed words into audio sounds
5. TDD equipment
6. Sound modifiers for audio equipment and public access phones
7. User aids, such as magnifiers and small book lights, to circulate with library materials[27]

PHYSICAL ENVIRONMENT AND BUILDING FACILITIES

Federal and state construction laws now lead library architects to address barriers affecting older patrons. Many older libraries, however, host an assortment of barriers that limit access and participation by many older adults. The concerned librarian conducts routine ergonomic building reviews of both exterior and interior features and strives to rectify the problems found.

Exterior Considerations

1. Adequate number of handicapped parking spaces
2. Easily identified handicapped parking areas
3. Well-lighted parking lots
4. Identifiable and safe paths leading to the library
5. Ramps built with a rise no greater than one foot within a twelve foot range
6. Covered walkways that provide protection from foul weather elements
7. Non-skid traction on all walkways
8. Signs posted with large and clear lettering
9. Doors opening inward, away from patron

Interior Considerations

1. Braille lettering available on internal signs, room plates and elevators
2. Kiosks and information centers designed for comfortable access by all patrons including those restricted to a wheel chair
3. One public service counter less than thirty-six inches in height
4. Doors and exits clearly marked in colors that contrast with those of walls and flooring
5. Carpeting colors that are distinctly different from those of walls and furniture
6. Brightly colored textured strips installed on floors where a change in grade occurs
7. Staircases designed with resting areas between short flights
8. Enclosed steps at back and sides
9. Sturdy handrails in contrasting colors installed in stairways[28]

LAWS

A complete review of available resources includes researching and understanding all significant local, state and federal regulations. Laws covering library programs for older adults generally fall into three groups: acts on the elderly, acts on persons with disabilities, and acts on libraries.[29] The following federal laws constitute a few of the ever-changing regulations that try to bring dignity and fulfillment to this diverse segment of our society:

Elderly

AGE DISCRIMINATION EMPLOYMENT ACT (ADEA) followed by the *AGE DISCRIMINATION ACT (ADA)*[30]

OLDER AMERICAN ACT authorizes grants for the training and counseling of family care-givers.[31] The Administration on Aging (AoA) carries out these provisions.[32] More than nine programs promote employment and volunteer activities among the aged: Age Discrimination in Employment (ADE), Community Based Manpower problems, Community Service Employment Program for Older Americans, Employment Programs for Special Groups, Foster Grandparent Program, Retired Senior Volunteer Program (RSVP), Senior Companion Program, Service Corps of Retired Executives (SCORE), and Volunteers in Service to America (VISTA). On the local level each state has its own Area Agency on the Aging.[33]

Disabilities

AMERICAN WITH DISABILITIES ACT (ADA) broadens the Rehabilitation Act's definition of people with disabilities.

ARCHITECTURAL BARRIERS ACT affirms the right of all people with physical disabilities to have access to and use of public buildings. This act allows older adults with disabilities to maneuver in public and academic libraries.[34]

CAPTION FILMS ACT provides captions for the hearing-impaired.

PRATT-SMOOT ACT made large-print materials available.

REHABILITATION ACT became the "Bill of Rights" for the person with disabilities. The law addresses employment, access, education, transportation and a variety of other items that affect both the elderly and libraries.[35]

Libraries

HIGHER EDUCATION ACT funded workshops and research programs for specialized training in serving older adults.

LIBRARY SERVICES AND CONSTRUCTION ACT (LSCA). The National Commission on Libraries and Information Science (NCLIS) is the major advisory agency to the president and Congress on American library needs. Since the elderly's tax dollars go to support public libraries, libraries should plan programs for this constituency. Local taxes continue to support these special older adult programs; therefore they must be realistic and unique.[36]

FUNDING

Libraries represent only one resource among several offering educational and informational services for older adults. It is crucial that librarians work with other agencies to avoid a duplication of effort and unwanted competition for limited program funding.[37] Sometimes this requires that librarians assume a leadership role in the community. They should bring together the various agencies for joint planning and discussion.[38]

Programs serving older adults are an expensive proposition for libraries and other agencies because of the need to increase staff and purchase special materials.[39] Major funding constraints cramp abilities to add staff, provide training in new program areas, broaden program services, and expand non-traditional library materials. A knowledgeable and resourceful project director persists until a mix of funding sources is found to support these areas. Grants and donations from various federal, state and local governments, foundations and other private sources help fill this need.[40]

Despite the availability of special funding sources for older adult programs, library administrators should not separate these services from the traditional library budget. Developing non-restrictive programs aids library administrators in requesting additional community support and federal/state funding. If outside funding disappears, the perceptive librarian continues these diverse programs with available funds.[41]

GOALS AND PRIORITIES

In consultation with library administration and advisory groups, the older adult service coordinator sets program goals and priorities. These consultations draw upon data collected on available staff, library materials and collections, building considerations and equipment needs. Wise administrators and advisory members realize libraries cannot try to serve all the needs of every patron. They try to balance limited budgets, staffing considerations and the needs of the entire library community. This is not easy, and sometimes libraries must place an emphasis on services that support the majority of older patrons.[42]

PROGRAMS

For older adults, the library is a combination recreational reading center, consumer information resource, learning facility, information and referral distributor, and a job training facility. Libraries are also resource centers for professional caregivers and family members. They play a crucial role in providing information and services for homebound patrons, institutionalized adults, and adult day care center participants.

Libraries support the special needs of older adult patrons by educating society about ageism and designing programs for their unique needs. When creating services for older patrons, the program coordinator must address the psychological/sociological environment and physical conditions. Through the resulting programs librarians:

1. Empower older people to learn how to meet their own needs
2. Teach older adults how to use existing programs whenever possible
3. Provide information in easy to understand language and multiple formats
4. Relate program subject to current situations
5. Make programs intergenerational, stressing the positive potential of older persons as contributors to our society
6. Create a positive environment
7. Support programs and informational statements with research

8. Consider fatigue and include rest breaks
9. Provide programs in nontraditional settings, for example a library program at an adult day care center
10. Provide programs on nontraditional topics
11. Schedule programs in the morning or afternoon[43]

PSYCHOLOGICAL, PHYSIOLOGICAL AND SOCIOLOGICAL CONSIDERATIONS

For older adults, a library is more than a building that houses books.[44] It is an intellectual community center for people hungry for culture and social contact.[45]

Older patrons may suffer from low self-confidence and self-esteem as a direct result of discrimination or negative events. They may require additional coaxing, praise and positive reinforcements for trying new library programs.[46]

Although better educated than previous generations, today's older patrons still include many illiterate individuals. Enterprising libraries sponsor special literacy programs for these patrons.[47]

Philosophy Of Caring

Libraries producing quality services supply accurate information in an atmosphere of genuine concern and respect for the older library patron. Patience and good listening skills are essential in helping many older patrons who have concentration, hearing, visual, and physical disabilities. Regardless of patron age, all librarians should adopt an earnest philosophy of patron caring, and follow these guidelines:

1. Treat patrons with respect and dignity
2. Treat patrons as intelligent human beings; do not talk down to them or treat them like children
3. Realize that a loss of hearing, vision, or bladder control does not indicate a loss of intelligence
4. Smile
5. Adopt a positive attitude
6. Listen thoughtfully to the informational request

7. Ask older adults for service suggestions
8. Maintain eye contact
9. Make sure the person understands the information communicated
10. Do not rush older patrons; allow them to proceed at their own pace
11. Realize self-concept problems associated with aging
12. Encourage and coach older patrons
13. Highlight the positive by reiterating the patrons' accomplishments[48]

When working with older adults or any patron with auditory, visual or physical limitations, the following suggestions are also very helpful:

Auditory Tips

1. Avoid monotone voice quality
2. Repeat important points
3. Reemphasize important facts with visual aids
4. Speak directly to lip reading patrons
5. Encourage use of hearing aids
6. Try to create an environment free of distracting outside noise
7. Speak clearly
8. Consider equipping auditoriums with amplifiers and microphones
9. Advertise that the library provides signers for programs if requested in advance
10. Use static eliminating carpet to reduce noise[49]

Visual Tips

1. Prepare all handouts on non-glare/non-glossy paper
2. Create reading areas with good, non-glare lighting
3. Consider preparing audio tapes for library information
4. Double space and use large print and boldface type on all handouts
5. Encourage use of glasses and magnifying lenses to aid reading
6. Fix flickering lights promptly

7. Place posters and signs at eye level for easier viewing by people wearing bifocal lenses
8. Use pictures and large diagrams with sharp color contrasts[50]

Physical Tips

1. When designing informational programs, include rest breaks to aid fighting physical fatigue
2. Encourage stretching and movement during presentations to offset fatigue
3. Purchase chairs with arms to make it easier for adults to push themselves up and out of sitting position
4. Seat older patrons away from air conditioning vents and drafts
5. Prepare handouts and work sheets with extra large write-in areas for patrons with arthritis
6. Try to provide basic services on the first floor for easier physical access
7. Install ramps and grip bars[51]

DESIGNING SPECIAL INFORMATIONAL PROGRAMS

Librarians have designed several innovative programs of special value to older adults. Bibliotherapy, extension services, information and retrieval programs, multigenerational and multicultural programs and self-directed and lifelong learning programs particularly benefit the elderly.

Bibliotherapy Programs

Bibliotherapy programs support the healthy progressive aspects of an individual's life.[52] Before beginning a bibliotherapy program outside the library, librarians should inform care facility administrators of the librarian's role.[53] Librarians are not entertainers, who come to do a show or performance. Librarians lead, stimulate and direct patrons in using their untapped capabilities. The following guidelines help librarians in producing successful bibliotherapy programs:

1. Create a calm and relaxed atmosphere
2. Choose a comfortable area with good lighting and adequate space for physical movement
3. Intervene when one member is monopolizing the conversation
4. Start procedures to lessen the chance of several people talking at once
5. Identify the speaker, and repeat questions and statements for all members to hear
6. Stay in control by being authoritative and firm, but understanding and gentle

Economic Programs

Older patrons have unique economic problems associated with limited incomes and learning how to become or remain solvent.[54] They benefit from programs designed to help them become better consumers. They need special help in managing finances, reviewing medical programs, and preparing for retirement.[55]

Older adults also need help in job related issues. They consider libraries primary job resource facilities for all workers searching for employment, training for new careers or upgrading current job skills. As society ages, the older library patron becomes an increasingly important part of the work force that requires these services.[56]

Extension Services

Older adults are more security conscious than younger adults. They prefer to stay inside their own neighborhoods for everything other than essential medical care.[57] Transportation difficulties and fatigue problems often limit their ability to travel to local libraries.[58]

Extension services such as books-by-mail and bookmobiles provide opportunities for many older adults requiring recreational and informational materials. Innovative programs add non-book materials to these delivery services.[59]

Institutionalized adults have additional extension service concerns. Nursing homes are just one example of the wide range of institutionalized living options for older adults. Many of these places provide unattended collections of reading materials for their residents. Such collections have minimal impact and benefit for the older adult residents.[60] To help these patrons, many libraries develop and deliver informational materials and programs to these locations.[61]

Information And Referral Programs

Information and referral programs began in the 1960s with increased federal funding for social programs.[62] This service provides older adults and their care-givers with links to opportunities, services and resources that can help their particular situation.[63]

Public agencies on aging typically run information and referral programs. Libraries have a special role in supporting these programs by acting as a referral service to the agency for aging.[64] Some libraries also compile informational packets for distribution on a local level. Creative librarians prepare attractive packets with large type printing. Typical information includes:

1. Complete addresses and phone numbers of other local area information and referral services
2. Listing of self-help and support groups
3. Referral directory for medical, legal, and social concerns
4. Bibliographies
5. Copies and descriptions of laws[65]

Multigenerational/Multicultural Programs

Today, housing developments for young families, families with children, families with no children, or retirement communities replace the traditional multi-generational neighborhoods. This separation of family units reinforces age segregation. Many children grow-up without the benefit of direct contact with older adults.[66] Discerning librarians realize older adults are not the only target of ageism. Children are very often the subject of age-biased attitudes. Designing multi-generational programs provides librarians a wonderful opportunity to serve two special populations with very similar needs and problems.[67]

Imaginative librarians also include multicultural concerns within intergenerational programs to help unite disparate communities. These activities help foster an understanding of the ethnic differences and similarities in the treatment of older adults in various cultures.[68]

Self-Directed And Lifelong Learning Programs

Traditionally, libraries are places of independent, self-planned, self-directed, and self-paced education. Older adults appreciate a librarian's enthusiastic assistance in jointly designing their learning activities. However, older adults want to initiate the planning and proceed at their own pace.[69]

Additional Program Suggestions

Besides these highlighted programs, the library administration may want to consider the following programs:

1. Informational lecture series such as retirement planning[70]
2. Audiovisual film series
3. Creative writing/poetry workshops[71]
4. Local history/autobiography/genealogy groups
5. Programs explaining Medicare benefits
6. Community information fairs
7. Discussion programs for family care-givers
8. Read-aloud programs[72]
9. Oral history programs
10. Recreational lectures series
11. Special monthly activities; for example, Scotland days in March[73]

PROMOTION

When promoting the library's programs and services for older patrons, librarians need to follow a two-part process. Different approaches are needed for attracting users and community support. The complete promotional package aids libraries in attracting new users. It also gathers community support and identifies additional funding sources.

Libraries beginning new programs and services for older patrons need to begin the promotional process by first supporting existing programs. Later librarians can gradually add information about the new programs. By listening and responding to older adults' needs libraries keep existing patrons and attract new ones.[74]

Before going out into the community, the entire staff should understand the goals and priorities of the older patron program. Library staff needs to prepare materials highlighting services. Several promotional activities the library may consider include:

1. Supplying a wish list of books and materials needed for older patron programs to local civic groups
2. Providing information concerning older adult services at voter registration stations
3. Delivering books to shut-ins through Meals-on-Wheels
4. Displaying library posters in senior citizen centers, nursing homes, doctors' offices
5. Providing extra copies of large print reading materials and library promotional handouts in eye doctors' offices
6. Producing a monthly calendar of library events for older patrons and distributing it to nursing homes, senior centers, and local media resources[75]

EVALUATIONS

All comprehensive library programs and services require some form of regularly scheduled evaluation review. This review can be as simple as an annual report, written by the older adult services coordinator, or a formalized survey. In either case the evaluation should provide library administrators with highlights of successful activities, and information and recommendations concerning opportunities for improvements. Several questions to address during the evaluation include:

1. Is the program accomplishing its goals?
2. Do these goals need updating?
3. Is the library satisfied with the results?
4. What can be done more effectively and efficiently?
5. Is the library receiving support, including financial aid, from local community leaders? [76]

As part of the evaluation process, the library should resurvey members contacted during the needs assessment.

CONCLUSION

Successful library involvement with older adults combines thoughtful consideration of the older generational needs and values, and a well-organized plan. With enthusiastic staff and volunteers supporting an older adult services coordinator's activities, an effective schedule of programs will evolve. Determination and caring will motivate continuing plans for the ever-changing older population.

NOTES

1. Mary Ellen Kennedy Collins, "Attitudes of Public Service Academic Librarians toward the Elderly," *RQ* 27, no. 3 (Spring 1987): 360.

2. Jean Ann Tevis and Brenda Crawley, "Reaching Out to Older Adults," *Library Journal* 113, no. 8 (May 1, 1988): 37.

3. Betty J. Turock, *Serving the Older Adult: A Guide to Library Programs and Information Sources* (New York: Bowker, 1982), vii-viii.

4. Jacquelyne Johnson Jackson, *Minorities & Aging* (Belmont, California: Wadsworth Publishing Company, 1980), 152.

5. Donald E. Gelfand and Charles M. Barresi, *Ethnic Dimensions of Aging* (New York: Springer, 1987), 258-259.

6. Donald E. Gelfand and Alfred J. Kutzik, *Ethnicity and Aging: Theory, Research and Policy* (New York: Springer, 1979), 357.

7. Betty J. Turock, *Information and Aging* (Jefferson, North Carolina: McFarland, 1988), 13.

8. Leo Ip Ling-nam, "Public Library Services to Older People in Pennsylvania: A Survey" (Master's Thesis, Indiana University of Pennsylvania, 1989), 32; Connie Van Fleet, Paul Ardion and Monique Franklin, *Silver Editions II: Advancing the Concept of Library-Centered Humanities Programs for Older Adults. An Evaluation* (Washington, DC: National Council on the Aging, 1991), 13.

9. Elizabeth A. Hudson, *Libraries for a Lifetime* (Oklahoma City: Oklahoma State Department of Libraries, 1989), 50.

10. Phyllis I. Dalton, Library Service to the Deaf and Hearing impaired (Phoenix: Oryx Press, 1985), 242; Library Services to an Aging Population Committee, Reference and Adult Services Division, American Library Association, *Guidelines for Library Service to Older Adults* (Chicago: American Library Association, 1987); Library Services to an Aging Population Committee, Reference and Adult Services Division, American Library Association, *The Library's Responsibility to the Aging* (Chicago: American Library Association, 1981); Turock, Serving the Older Adult, 13.

11. Dalton, *Library Service to the Deaf,* 61.

12. Ron Gross and Barbara Krampiz, *Lively Minds Manual: How to Serve Seniors in Your Community by Meeting Their Needs for Mental Stimulation, Delight, and Empowerment* (Albany, New York: New York State Library, 1990), 15.

13. Judith Kamin, "How Older Adults Use Books and the Public Library: A Review of the Literature," *Occasional Papers, University of Illinois Graduate School of Library and Information Science Number 165* (September 1984), 3-23; Hudson, *Libraries for a Lifetime,* 5-19, 49.

14. Genevieve M. Casey, *Library Services for the Aging* (Hamden, Connecticut: Shoe String Press, 1984), 53, 99.

15. Casey, *Library Services for the Aging,* 77-79, 121; Gross, *Lively Minds Manual,* 13-15.

16. Tevis and Crawley, "Reaching Out to Older Adults," 37-39.

17. Andrew W. Dobelstein and Ann Bilas Johnson, *Serving Older Adults: Policy, Programs, and Professional Activities* (Englewood Cliffs, New Jersey: Prentice-Hall, 1985), 181.

18. Dalton, *Library Service to the Deaf,* 152-166.

19. Hudson, *Libraries for a Lifetime,* 62.

20. Ken Dychtwald, *Age Wave: The Challenges and Opportunities of an Aging America* (Los Angeles: Jeremy P. Tarcher, 1989), 52-53.

21. Shirley E. Havens, "Large Print in Focus," *Library Journal* 112, no. 12 (July 1987): 32-34.

22. Judith Lee Palmer, "Large-Print Book: Public Library Services to Older Adults," *Educational Gerontology 14,* no. 3 (1988): 211-214,

23. Turock, *Serving the Older Adult, 14.*

24. Kate Saunders, "Expanding Outreach Service to Seniors," *American Libraries* 23, no. 2 (February 1992): 176, 178.

25. BiFolkal Productions, 809 Williamson Street, Madison, WI 53703.

26. Dychtwald, *Age Wave,* 52-53.

27. Dalton, *Library Service to the Deaf,* 63-64.

28. William L. Needham and Gerald Jahoda, *Improving Library Service to Physically Disabled Persons: A Self-Evaluation Checklist* (Littleton, Colorado: Libraries Unlimited, 1983), 13-34; Hudson, *Libraries for a Lifetime,* 47-48; Dalton, *Library Service to the Deaf,* 203-205.

29. Havens, "Large Print in Focus," 14.

30. Ling-nam, *Public Library Services to Older People, 33.*

31. Donald E. Gelfand, *The Aging Network: Programs and Services,* 3rd ed. (New York: Springer, 1988), 9-11.

32. Bessie B. Moore and Carol Fraser Fisk, "Improving Library Services to the Aging," *Library Journal* 113, no. 7 (April 15, 1988): 46-47.

33. Jackson, *Minorities & Aging,* 173; Van Fleet, *Silver Editions II,* 38-39.

34. Dalton, *Library Service to the Deaf,* 15; Needham, *Improving Library Service,* 104-107.

35. Dalton, *Library Service to the Deaf,* 16.

36. Needham, *Improving Library Service,* 104-107; Tevis, "Reaching Out to Older Adults," 38; Dalton, *Library Service to the Deaf,* 15-16.

37. Turock, *Information and Aging, 14.*

38. Casey, *Library Services for the Aging,* xii, 19, 53.

39. Turock, *Information and Aging, 14.*

40. Van Fleet, *Silver Editions II, 14.*

41. Ibid., 49-51.

194   LINDA LOU WILER and LINDA MARIE GOLIAN

42. Ibid., 13.
43. Casey, *Library Services for the Aging,* 31-37.
44. Tevis, "Reaching Out to Older Adults," 37-38.
45. Casey, *Library Services for the Aging,* 7; Allan Kleiman, "Brooklyn's SAGE Program: Providing Library Service to All the Elderly," *Library Journal 108,* no. 6 (March 15, 1983): 557.
46. Jackson, *Minorities & Aging,* 3-4.
47. Albert J. Kingston, "Does Literacy Really Enhance the Lives of the Elderly?," *Reading World 20,* no. 3 (March 1981): 169-172; Van Fleet, *Silver Editions II,* 43-44; Turock, *Information and Aging,* 43.
48. Dobelstein, *Serving Older Adults,* 171; Hudson, *Libraries for a Lifetime,* 49.
49. Hudson, *Libraries for a Lifetime,* 51.
50. Needham, *Improving Library Service,* 12-13.
51. Hudson, *Libraries for a Lifetime,* 47-48.
52. Rhea Joyce Rubin, *Bibliotherapy Sourcebook* (Phoenix: Oryx Press, 1978), 179-184.
53. Rhea Joyce Rubin, *Using Bibliotherapy: A Guide to Theory and Practice* (Phoenix: Oryx Press, 1978), 1-10.
54. Ellie Brubaker, *Working with the Elderly: A Social Systems Approach* (Newberry Park, California: Sage Publications, 1978), 52.
55. Kleiman, "Brooklyn's SAGE Program," 557.
56. Alex Comfort, *Say Yes to Old Age: Developing a Positive Attitude toward Aging* (New York: Crown Publishers, 1976), 69; Jean Cornn, "Libraries and the Graying of America," *Southeastern Librarian* 38, no. 1 (Spring 1988): 19.
57. Kleiman, "Brooklyn's SAGE Program," 557.
58. Casey, *Library Services for the Aging,* 7.
59. Harriet L. Eisman, "Public Library Programs for the Elderly," *Wilson Library Bulletin 53,* no. 8 (April 1979): 568.
60. Casey, *Library Services for the Aging,* 71-76.
61. Van Fleet, *Silver Editions II,* 5-14.
62. Gelfand, *The Aging Network,* 63-71.
63. Celia Hales-Mabry, "How Should the Informational Needs of the Aging Be Met?" (Paper presented at the Annual Meeting of the American Library Association, San Francisco, 1987), 3.
64. Brubaker, *Working with the Elderly,* 156-157.
65. Dalton, *Library Service to the Deaf,* 163.
66. Jane Angelis, *Intergenerational Service-Learning* (Washington, D.C.: American Association of Retired Persons, 1990), 32.
67. Bryce Allen and Margaret Ann Wilkinson, "What Do Our 'Senior Citizens' Want from Public Libraries?," *Canadian Library Association* 47, no. 2 (April 1990): 109-110; Hudson, *Libraries for a Lifetime,* 20, 60.
68. Gelfand, *Ethnicity and Aging,* 357-361.
69. Casey, *Library Services for the Aging,* 20; Turock, *Serving the Older Adult,* 17-18.
70. Allen, "What Do Our Senior Citizens Want," 107.

71. Barbara B. Dreher, "Directing a Writing Program for Retirees," *English Journal* 69, no. 7 (October 1980): 54-56.

72. Jim Trelease, *The New Read-Aloud Handbook,* 2nd rev. ed. (New York: Penguin Books, 1989); Gloria Leonard, Judy Evans and Nancy Hoebelheinrich, *Read Aloud Programs for the Elderly Project. Instructional Manual* (Washington, D.C.: Office of Libraries and Learning Technologies, 1987), 1-7.

73. Hudson, *Libraries for a Lifetime,* 64.

74. Kingston, "Does Literacy Really Enhance," 170.

75. Turock, *Serving the Older Adult,* iii, 1-24.

76. Rhea Joyce Rubin and Gail McGovern, *Working with Older Adults: A Handbook for Libraries.* 3rd ed. (Sacramento: California State Library Foundation, 1990), Section III, 11-14.

GAY AND LESBIAN LIBRARY USERS:
OVERCOMING BARRIERS TO SERVICE

Ellen Greenblatt and Cal Gough

Historians may well view the 1990s as the decade of gay and lesbian civil rights in much the same way as the 1960s are often associated with African-American civil rights. Homosexuality is currently a focal point of heated political, social, and religious debate throughout the United States. Issues such as integrating lesbian and gay information into school curricula, ordaining gay and lesbian clergy, lifting the ban on gays and lesbians in military service, and legalizing same-sex marriages and domestic partnerships fill news reports daily. Citizens' groups have initiated anti-gay voter referenda in a least a dozen states and even more municipalities after the passage in November 1992 of Colorado's controversial "Amendment Two,"[1] while local governments have enacted over 130 anti-discrimination laws.[2] Between 300,000[3] and 1.1 million[4] people participated in the April 25, 1993 March on Washington for Lesbian, Gay, and Bi Equal Rights and Liberation, making it one of the largest civil rights demonstrations in U.S. history.

The modern-day gay and lesbian civil rights movement in the United States began 25 years ago on June 27, 1969, when police raided the Stonewall Inn, a gay and lesbian bar in New York City's Greenwich Village. The bar's customers rioted when the police tried to arrest some of them, and the disturbance lasted for four nights.[5] Since the Stonewall

Uprising, lesbians and gay men have become an increasingly more visible and articulate minority. One index to the increasing self-consciousness of gays and lesbians as a social force is the proliferation of media targeted to their information needs. Currently there are over 300 gay and lesbian magazines and newspapers published nationally and 9,000 gay- and lesbian-related books in print.[6] There are also dozens of films and videos with gay and lesbian characters and hundreds of musical recordings made by lesbian and gay performers.

Through professional organizations, librarians have acknowledged the unique information needs of gay men and lesbians. The first caucus of any professional organization in the country to advocate on behalf of gay and lesbian citizens was formed in 1970 as part of the American Library Association (ALA).[7] One year later, ALA passed the following resolution:

> The American Library Association recognizes that there exist minorities which are not ethnic in nature but which suffer oppression. The Association recommends that libraries and members strenuously combat discrimination in services to, and employment of, individuals from all minority groups, whether the distinguishing characteristics of the minority be ethnic, sexual, religious, or any kind.[8]

At its Midwinter Meeting in 1993, ALA's tradition of support for the principle of equal rights of all citizens continued in the political wake of Colorado's Amendment Two when the organization's executive council directed its Intellectual Freedom Committee to review the *Library Bill of Rights* with the express purpose of proposing new language covering gender and sexual orientation as related to library users, staff, materials, and services. The association also canceled a future meeting scheduled for Denver and passed a resolution against contracting for future conferences with any cities legalizing discrimination. ALA upheld this resolution in November, 1993, when the voters of Cincinnati, Ohio passed Issue 3, which bars the City Council from enforcing laws that give legal protection to lesbian, gay or biosexual citizens. The ALA Executive Board canceled plans to hold ALA's 1995 Midwinter Meeting in Cincinnati despite liability for an estimated $200,000 in hotel contracts.

However, two decades of gay-supportive organizational pronouncements from ALA and the determined work of its gay and lesbian caucus have not been enough to secure adequate collections and quality service for lesbian and gay library users in the United States. Few libraries have pursued or even articulated their obligation to provide a reasonable sampling of relevant materials to their gay and lesbian library users. In the 1990s as in the 1970s and before, often the only information about sexual orientation issues that gays and lesbians can find in libraries is written by heterosexual authors. Many of these materials are outdated. Some are written by "authorities" who are gravely misinformed about the available facts. Much of this information ignores the unique concerns of gay men and lesbians or dismisses these concerns as less important than those of heterosexuals. Some materials disparage or condemn lesbians and gay men.

Even though the range of easily-available materials by and about lesbians and gay men is broad, much remains absent from many libraries. This chapter will examine various barriers which interfere with gay and lesbian library patrons' access to library collections and services and will offer suggestions for overcoming these barriers. The authors feel qualified to speak only about gay men and lesbians, although much of the chapter may pertain to other non-heterosexual orientations as well.

THE BARRIER OF PREJUDICE

The most significant factor limiting quality library service to lesbians and gays is heterosexism, the belief in the inherent superiority of heterosexuality and its right to unquestioned cultural dominance.[9] Heterosexism pervades American culture, dictating attitudes, behavior, social opportunity, legal rights, and the allocation of resources. Individuals leading openly gay and lesbian lives frequently suffer from various forms of discrimination, ranging from social ostracism to lethal physical attacks.

Many librarians have never examined the effects of heterosexist assumptions on their work. Such assumptions can influence decisions about materials, library programming, and staffing. Job discrimination against gay and lesbian library employees, or the fear of it, may exist in any workplace and has direct ramifications for patron service. For example, in many libraries, gay or lesbian librarians are hesitant to lend their familiarity with gay and lesbian materials to a collection-strengthening effort; to suggest or volunteer to help lead a staff sensitivity training workshop; or to compile a booklist of exceptionally good gay or lesbian novels to distribute to library patrons who would benefit from such a list. This results in poor service to the library's current gay and lesbian patrons, and the perpetuation of the heterosexist status quo.

While heterosexism may be difficult for even diversity-conscious, service-minded librarians to detect, it is painfully obvious to the gay and lesbian library *users* of most libraries. Though not every librarian personally contributes to the widespread prejudice against the gay and lesbian citizens in our society, many have not examined with any seriousness the extent to which this prejudice unconsciously influences library-related decisions and attitudes. Every librarian can explore ways to minimize the effects of heterosexist prejudice on library users. Individually and in organized groups, many librarians have already begun the painful work of examining internalized and institutionalized racism, sexism, classism, ageism, ableism, and nationalism. The systematic dismantling of the heterosexist aspects of library service should be the next frontier.

THE BARRIER OF MISINFORMATION

Misinformation can be one of the greatest barriers to service as librarians themselves often perpetuate myths and stereotypes concerning lesbian and gay people. For example, many otherwise well-informed librarians may believe that they personally do not know any lesbians or gay men or that no lesbians or gay men use their library. But homosexuality, like heterosexuality, is represented in all segments of the population, throughout all the various racial, socioeconomic, religious, ethnic, age, and ability groups which comprise American society. The gay political slogan, "We are everywhere," is literally accurate. Until U.S. politicians permit the Census Bureau or some other agency to determine the facts concerning the sexual orientation of American citizens and until *all* gays and lesbians feel safe enough to disclose their sexual identity to census workers, there will be no way of reliably estimating the number of gays or lesbians using a specific library in a particular community.

Partly because sexual orientation—unlike skin tone or native language—is an *invisible* patron characteristic, librarians are unlikely to recognize which or how many of their patrons are lesbians or gay men. Unless an individual chooses to disclose that he or she is gay, no one, not even other lesbian and gay people, can know for sure what a particular person's sexual identity may be.[10] To infer otherwise is to stereotype.

Furthermore, librarians should not assume that lesbians and gay men are groups who have identical information needs. Though both lesbians and gay men have historically suffered from heterosexist oppression, lesbians, as women, have been doubly oppressed.[11] Aside from this fact, the actual interests, sensibilities, common experiences, cultural backgrounds, and problems of lesbians differ in many respects from those of gay men. The complexity of specialized information needs does not end there. The gay and lesbian community is a microcosm of society as a whole and the reading interests of its members represent the full spectrum of human diversity.

While providing AIDS information should be a priority in libraries, it is not a substitute for maintaining a well-balanced collection of gay and lesbian materials. Though AIDS has indeed had a disproportionate impact on the gay male community, it is just one issue among many of interest to lesbians and gays.

Finally, librarians should recognize that the constituency for gay and lesbian library materials is much broader than simply gay and lesbian library users themselves. Family members, including the children, parents, siblings, and heterosexual spouses of lesbians and gay men, have a keen interest in such materials. Other likely users include the friends, co-workers, and acquaintances of gay men and lesbians. Teachers, counselors, attorneys, physicians, social workers, members of the clergy, and other professionals working with gays, lesbians, and their families also want to consult these materials, as do students doing school papers and scholars doing historical, sociological, and literary research. Even the intractable opponents of gay and lesbian rights should have the opportunity to discover more about the needs, hopes, and achievements of gays and lesbians. Librarians need to keep this broader constituency in mind in determining the appropriate quantity and breadth of lesbian and gay materials to provide and the kinds of gay- and lesbian-related programs to offer.

THE BARRIER OF CENSORSHIP

Censorship is an obvious barrier confronting many gay and lesbian library users. Current news accounts are filled with reports of censorship threats emanating from both government agencies and organized citizens' groups. Censorship attempts of lesbian and gay materials by pressure groups have been particularly pervasive lately. Some groups have even tried to legislate the systematic censorship of lesbian and gay library materials. One such effort, the Idaho Citizens Alliance's Anti-Gay initiative, included the proposal that libraries limit access to these books to adults only. Idaho Attorney General Larry Echohawk pronounced that such measures would require librarians to be censors and would intimidate Idahoans with the threat of criminal penalties.[12]

Other groups around the country have tried to get libraries to remove particular publications such as *The Advocate,*[13] Madonna's *Sex,*[14] and the children's books *Heather Has Two Mommies* and *Daddy's Roommate.*[15] And while Banned Books Week is observed by many libraries to promote awareness about the dangers of this type of censorship, other forms of censorship are not so widely publicized or recognized. Vandalism can at times also be considered a form of censorship when so-called "library terrorists" mutilate, destroy, or hide items they find offensive.

Unfortunately, not all library censorship is generated from outside the library. Some librarians refuse to include certain books, magazines, recordings, or videos in the library's collection because their contents conflict with their personal moral beliefs. Such a viewpoint is illustrated in a letter to the editor of *American Libraries* about *Daddy's Roommate,* a children's book about a gay father and his lover written from the perspective of the father's young son. The author of the letter, "a practicing Christian librarian," states: "The book supports a life-style that is against traditional Christian family values....My personal opinion is that the book be banned or circulated only with parental consent....Censorship or parental guidelines have a place in American society."[16] Some librarians may feel that buying a book on a controversial subject, such as homosexuality, constitutes an endorsement of that book's point of view. But buying gay and lesbian books does not endorse homosexuality any more than buying *Mein Kampf* endorses Nazism or buying murder mysteries endorses murder.

Other types of internal censorship are even more subtle, such as restricting access to lesbian and gay library materials by instituting parental consent requirements and locating "sensitive" materials in closed stacks or refusing to authorize or obstructing attempts to promote the *use* of lesbian and gay materials with displays, bibliographies, and bookmarks. An example of this type of censorship is Los Angeles Public Library's controversial decision to withdraw materials referring to African American poet Langston Hughes from the materials issued for the library's celebration of Lesbian and Gay History Month in June of 1991 at the request of members of the African American community who objected to Hughes being identified as gay.[17] However, these types of internal censorship can be overcome through examining selection policies and procedures for arbitrary biases which compromise the ability of the library to meet the information needs of any identifiable segment of a library's constituency and evaluating the appropriateness of access and use restrictions.

THE CONFIDENTIALITY BARRIER

Privacy is a major concern of many gay and lesbian library users. Since sexual orientation is a profoundly personal affair, many lesbian or gay library users—especially those just beginning to explore their sexual identity—would feel uncomfortable asking library staff to help them locate gay- or lesbian-related information without some evidence that the library values the privacy of all its users.

The issue of privacy is especially acute in school libraries, rural libraries, and local neighborhood libraries, where library staff are often personally acquainted with library users, their families, friends, and employers. In such instances, many lesbian and gay users feel too inhibited or threatened to borrow materials or ask reference questions of an explicitly gay or lesbian nature. In some of these libraries, such self-disclosure may indeed be risky.

While librarians are not totally responsible for easing the various anxieties library users bring with them into the library, developing a sensitivity to the particular apprehension felt by lesbians and gays will definitely result in better service. Librarians can also reassure users of the confidentiality of their requests by alerting the public of the library's formal policy protecting the confidentiality of library borrowing records through prominently posting the library's policy at several service points throughout the library or on the backs of the library cards issued to each patron as well as by ensuring a relatively private, respectful, and nonjudgmental atmosphere in providing reference assistance.

THE BIBLIOGRAPHIC BARRIER

Another barrier limiting equality of access for gay and lesbian library users emerges from the techniques employed by librarians in implementing bibliographic access to materials. Since few lesbian and gay periodicals are indexed in mainstream publications, libraries are reluctant to buy such materials, thus effectively denying users access to massive amounts of important information on gay and lesbian issues produced by gay and lesbian sources. While petitioning publishers to index gay and lesbian material has led to more inclusive indexing,[18] currently no publisher indexes more than 10 gay and lesbian publications.[19] Though the recent release of the *Gay/Lesbian Periodicals Index* attempts to rectify this situation by indexing a wide range of gay and lesbian publications, unfortunately as of this writing, the producers have yet to find a publisher and have issued a microfiche edition indexing 1990 publications only. The 1990 edition contains almost 33,000 entries culled from the following 29 publications: *The Advocate, Bay Area Reporter, BLK, Christopher Street, Common Lives, Lesbian Lives, Equal Time, Gay Community News, The James White Review, Journal of Gay and Lesbian Psychotherapy, Journal of Homosexuality, Lambda Book Report, Lesbian Contradiction, Lesbian Herstory Archives Newsletter, NAMBLA Bulletin, New York Native, Our Stories, Out/Look, Partners, PWA Coalition Newsline, RFD, San Francisco Bay Area Gay & Lesbian Historical Society Newsletter, The Second Stone, Sinister Wisdom, Treatment Issues, Trikone, Visibilities, The Washington Blade, and Womanews.* Unless librarians demonstrate their support of such a project by purchasing the index, future editions may not be forthcoming.[20]

Cataloging practices also compromise access to gay and lesbian materials. Because most libraries use the obsolete, biased, inadequate, and inappropriate terminology utilized by the Library of Congress Subject Headings (LCSH) or Sears Subject Headings (SSH), much information of interest to lesbian and gay library users is needlessly difficult to identify. For example, while popular usage has favored the word "gay" over the synonymous term "homosexual" since the early 1970s, it was not until 1987 that the Library of Congress initiated such changes to LCSH. Another example concerns LCSH's employment of sexist and inaccurate terminology in its preference of the umbrella term "gays" over the generally accepted terminology "gays and lesbians" when referring to these communities as a whole. Such subject headings obscure the lesbian content of materials pertaining to both gay men and lesbians.[21]

Librarians can help remedy this situation by urging the Library of Congress and Sears to use current, unbiased, and accurate terminology in formulating their subject headings. The Cataloging Consumers Network (CCN) led by Sanford Berman is an organization which petitions the Library of Congress to reform its subject headings.[22] Since such lobbying is often a lengthy process, libraries inclined to immediately improve access to their collection could add appropriate cross-references to their catalogs.

The near-universal library practice of not assigning subject headings to fictional works also interferes with access to lesbian and gay literary works, limiting patrons to titles and authors with which they are already familiar. While this practice has begun to change lately with projects by Library of Congress and OCLC to add subject headings to new works of fiction, the bibliographic records for older works still lack such access. Librarians can help patrons identify these older lesbian and gay literary works by producing bibliographies and booklists. In fact, this is about the only way to provide one-step access to such materials.

Another bibliographic obstacle for gay and lesbian library users is the negligence of cataloging agencies to record the contents of anthologies in their catalog records. Such contents information is easily keyword—searchable in many online catalogs and would be a definite boon in identifying specific essays, articles, poems, or short stories. Since a large percentage of books with gay and lesbian themes are published in the anthology format, this failure to reflect their contents is an especially significant access barrier. Librarians can remedy this situation at their own libraries by insuring that contents information is made available in bibliographic records.

THE ACCESS BARRIER

Many libraries, particularly school and public libraries, have traditionally limited physical access to lesbian and gay library materials, housing them in closed stacks or staff-only areas. Requiring patrons to ask a staff member for these materials compromises the privacy of lesbian and gay library users, effectively blocking them from obtaining these materials.

Librarians sensitive to gay and lesbian patron information needs will remove restrictions on as much material as possible. In a library committed to intellectual freedom, the only defensible reason for treating access to some library materials differently than access to others is to protect them from mutilation or theft. Simultaneously maximizing both access and security for any irreplaceable, particularly expensive, or high-demand item (regardless of its content) is a difficult challenge with no ideal solution. Sometimes unusual and regrettable security measures must be taken to provide *any* type of access to *anyone:* if someone steals a particular book or magazine, no one else can use it, regardless of its content, regardless of how carefully it was ordered, and regardless of how easy it was for a patron to find it listed in the library's catalog.

Librarians can, however, use the library's catalog to inform their users about a restricted item in the collection by clearly noting the item's special status, stating the reason for the item's restricted status, and describing where it is kept. A notice or "dummy" containing similar information can be placed where the restricted item would have been shelved to further alert browsers of the item's existence. Again, staff should be trained in how to properly handle requests for such items, and confidentiality policies should be prominently posted and enforced.

Librarians must bear in mind that restricting access to materials should never occur simply because some patrons—or staff members—find them irrelevant, disagree with them, or are offended by their content. No library patron, organized group of citizens, or library official should be allowed to dictate what others may and may not read, listen, or view in "their" library.

Removing access barriers to library service to lesbians and gays is largely an ethical issue, not a technical or a financial one. Librarians should value the right of every library user to make up his or her own mind about what is relevant or worthless, illuminating or disgusting, fit or unfit to read about, listen to, or look at. Personal reactions to the full record of human experience, activity, reflection, expression, and aspiration are properly none of the librarian's business, and no librarian should willingly or carelessly try to placate one group of library users *at the expense of* another group of users. Librarians should apply a non-exclusionary principle not only to library collections, but also to library programming, library book displays, library publications, and library outreach efforts.

THE CHALLENGES AHEAD

While the focus of this article has been on various barriers to quality service confronting gay and lesbian library users, the fact remains that the most important single remedy for the unmet information needs of any library's gay and lesbian patrons would be the methodical collection of library materials written or recorded with these readers, listeners, and viewers in mind. Formulating a collection development policy with this goal is the initial step in this process. The next step is to inventory the library's collection, weeding inappropriate or outdated materials and noting gaps. Important retrospective titles can be identified in bibliographies of recommended titles on gay and lesbian issues.[23] Current items can be identified through book reviews in such periodicals as the *Advocate, Journal of Homosexuality, Lesbian and Gay Studies Newsletter, GLQ: Gay and Lesbian Quarterly, GLTF [American Library Association Gay and Lesbian Task Force] Newsletter, Women Library Workers, Journal, Lesbian Review of Books,* and the *Lambda Book Report,* the foremost source of gay and lesbian book reviews. Many of these periodicals, including the *Lambda Book Report,* are indexed in *Book Review Index.*[24]

BECOMING ACQUAINTED WITH THE TERRITORY

Librarians with access to either BITNET or the Internet can subscribe to The Gay/Lesbian/Bisexual Librarians Network (GAY-LIBN),[25] an electronic forum for discussions of interest to gay, lesbian, and bisexual librarians (and friends). GAY-LIBN is an excellent networking tool, exposing subscribers to current issues and concerns in the field, practical advice, and research and information sharing.

Started in December 1992, GAY-LIBN grew to over 500 subscribers in its first 18 months.

Another Internet reference source is the Queer Resources Directory (QRD) which is accessible via electronic mail, BBS, gopher, WAIS, FTP, and WWW (lynx and Mosaic).[26] The QRD contains a wealth of information including: a directory for each state and the District of Columbia with information of local interest (/pub/QRD/usa); a directory containing the texts promulgated by the anti-gay movement including the Traditional Values Coalition and the Family Research Council (/pub/QRD/religion); directories containing information about resources for youth (/pub/QRD/youth); a filmography of movies with same-sex themes (/pub/QRD/media/film/glbo.films.list); information about lesbian and gay groups and happenings all over the world (/pub/QRD/world); and much more.

The *GLTF Newsletter*, published quarterly by the Gay and Lesbian Task Force of the American Library Association, is another good way to stay informed about gay and lesbian library issues. It is an excellent resource, covering library and publishing news, pointing to current publications in the field, and containing a large section devoted exclusively to book reviews. It is intended not only for gay and lesbian librarians but also for any library or librarian serving gay and lesbian patrons.[27] Publications targeted to women's concerns, such as *Women Library Workers' Journal, Women in Libraries,* and *Feminist Bookstore News,* are also wonderful sources of information about lesbian library and publishing issues and often contain reviews of lesbian-related materials.

COLLECTION PROMOTION AND OUTREACH

Library staff members can also increase the *use* of whatever gay- and lesbian-related materials they currently provide with the same methods employed to target other user groups: bookmarks, book lists, pathfinders, displays, browsing guides, and programs.[28] Additionally, librarians should consider compiling and adding the names of local gay and lesbian service organizations to the library's community information and referral file. The American Library Association's Gay and Lesbian Task Force has identified over three *dozen* additional methods or projects that individual librarians can undertake to make their libraries more user-friendly for gays and lesbians.[29]

The following examples illustrate ways in which particular libraries have raised awareness about lesbian and gay materials and issues in their libraries. The Pikes Peak Library District in Colorado sponsored a five-part series of panel discussions about the topic of tolerance and intolerance in the community including a panel discussion on sexual orientation issues.[30] Each of these discussions was telecast live on a local cable station, with provision made for both the attending audience and the viewing audience to question the panelists. Videotapes of these telecasts are available for check-out.

Many libraries create exhibits highlighting their collections. For example, the University of California, Los Angeles library staged an exhibit of historically significant gay and lesbian books dating from the sixteenth century until the present and produced a catalog for the event.[31] National Lesbian and Gay Book Month in June is a popular time for exhibits.[32] The University of California at Santa Cruz's exhibits committee, for example, staged an exhibit entitled: "Lesbian and Gay Book Publishers in Northern California: Celebrating National Gay and Lesbian Book Month," filling eight display cases with publications from 20 active small press publishers of lesbian and gay focus.

Libraries can publicize their gay- and lesbian-related materials in the local gay community by supplying local service organizations with copies of their library's gay/lesbian-related bookmarks, booklists, bibliographies, or pathfinders. Librarians can write a feature story or a letter to the editor—or even a regular book review column—for a local or regional gay or lesbian publication.

Libraries can become involved with local Gay Pride celebrations. For example, the Seattle Public Library participated in Seattle's Gay Pride Festival by bringing its mobile unit to the Gay Pride Parade as well as housing a concurrent exhibit of its gay and lesbian materials. Some libraries sponsor Gay/Lesbian Pride film series.

Librarians can also develop, or help a local community group develop, a library program or other event of interest to gay and lesbian patrons such as a reading by a visiting gay or lesbian author; a speaker on the history of the local gay or lesbian community; a panel on legal issues facing gay and lesbian citizens; or an exhibit of drawings, paintings, sculptures, or crafts by local gay or lesbian artists.

SENSITIZING STAFF

Beyond the collection development and collection promotion possibilities that individual librarians could pursue immediately, library managers should find ways to sensitize their staff members—non-professional and professional alike—to the unique information- and service-related needs of gay and lesbian library patrons. Each library worker should handle requests for gay- and lesbian-related information in a profcssional manner: nonjudgmentally, pleasantly, efficiently, helpfully, and thoroughly.

Administrators should ensure that sexual orientation is addressed in the library's cultural diversity workshops. And special sensitivity sessions should be available to personnel after any particular incident. For example, after the controversy surrounding its observation of Gay/Lesbian History Month in 1991, the Los Angeles Public Library initiated sensitivity training for all its employees.[33]

As with other efforts in librarianship to raise employee consciousness on a particular issue, to fill previously overlooked or neglected gaps in collections, or to improve service to a previously unserved or ill-served group of library users, there can be no "quick fix" for achieving and maintaining quality collections and quality service to gays and lesbians. As with other reforms on behalf of other library users throughout the profession's history of providing better library service, individual efforts to improve the usefulness of libraries to gays and lesbians will cost time and money. Librarians pursuing these efforts may sometimes encounter resistance or provoke conflict. But as with previous reforms in librarianship, this one is long overdue.

NOTES

1. It would amend Article 2 of the Colorado Constitution by the addition of Section 30, which states: NO PROTECTED STATUS BASED ON HOMOSEX-UAL, LESBIAN OR BISEXUAL ORIENTATION. Neither the State of Colorado, through any of its branches or departments, nor any of its agencies, political subdivisions, municipalities or school districts, shall enact, adopt or enforce any statute, regulation, ordinance or policy whereby homosexual, lesbian or bisexual orientation, conduct, practices or relationships shall constitute or otherwise be the basis of, or entitle any person or class of persons to have or claim any minority status, quota preferences, protected status or claim of discrimination. This Section of the Constitution shall be in all respects self-executing.

2. *Atlanta Constitution,* February 27, 1993

3. National Park Service figure. Estimates of attendance at marches provided by the National Park Service have been traditionally conservative. At this writing, the National Park Service was reviewing its figures for the 1993 March on Washington.

4. March organizers' estimate.

5. For more information see: Martin Duberman, *Stonewall* (New York: Dutton, 1993) and Toby Marotta, *The Politics of Homosexuality* (Boston: Houghton Mifflin, 1981), 71-76.

6. *San Francisco Examiner,* June 4, 1989.

7. See Barbara Gittings, "Gays in Library Land: The Gay and Lesbian Task Force of the American Library Association: The First Sixteen Years," *Women Library Workers Journal* 14 (Spring 1991), 7-13.

8. Resolution passed by ALA Council and ALA membership, June 1971.

9. Audre Lorde, "There is No Hierarchy of Oppressions" *Interracial Books for Children Bulletin* 14 (1983), 9.

10. Over 80 percent of the participants in one study were unable to identify accurately the sexual orientation of strangers—even when those guessing were gay men or lesbians themselves. See Gregory Berger and others, "Detection of Sexual Orientation by Heterosexuals and Homosexuals," *Journal of Homosexuality* 13 (Summer 1987), 83-100.

11. And lesbians of color have been triply oppressed historically.

12. Press release, "Re: ICA Initiative Review," State of Idaho, Office of the Attorney General, Boise, Idaho 83720-1000, 18 March 1993.

13. See *American Libraries* 24 (March 1993), 208-213.

14. See Dwight McInvaill and others, "Censorship: A World View," *Public Image* 4 (Winter 1992), 1-3, 6-7, which discusses censorship policies concerning Madonna's *Sex* in Ireland, Australia, and England. See also "Justify My Purchase: To Buy Madonna's *Sex* or Not," *American Libraries* 23 (December 1992), 902-904.

15. Lesléa Newman, *Heather Has Two Mommies* (Boston: Alyson Publications, 1989); Michael Willhoite, *Daddy's Roommate* (Boston: Alyson, 1990). See Dwight McInvaill and others, "Censorship: A World View," *Public Image* 4 (Winter 1992), 1-3, 6-7, for accounts of attempted censorship of *Daddy's Roommate* in Washington, New Mexico, and Pennsylvania. See also Mary Jo Godwin, "Conservative Groups Continue Their Fight to Ban *Daddy's Roommate,*" *American Libraries* 23 (December 1992), 917, 968.

16. DaVinci Metcalf, "Censorship Has a Place," *American Libraries* 24 (February 1993), 120-121.

17. See Gordon Flagg, "[Use of] Langston Hughes Poem [in a Lesbian/Gay History Month Display] Divides Gays, Blacks at Los Angeles Public Library" *American Libraries* 22 (July/August 1991), 610-611, 613.

18. A petition campaign spearheaded by Polly Thistlethwaite of ALA's Gay and Lesbian Task Force is underway at this writing to persuade the H.W. Wilson Company and others to index such magazines and newspapers as the *Advocate, BLK,* and *Lesbian News.* See "GLTF Petitions H.W. Wilson to Include [Indexing of] Gay/Lesbian Press [in the *Reader's Guide to Periodical Literature*]," *American Libraries* 22 (April 1991), 365; "*Reader's Guide* and the Lesbian/Gay Press," *SRRT Newsletter,* 99 (March 1991), 5; Graceanne A. DeCandido and Michael Rogers,

"Gay/Lesbian Task Force Seeks Index Access" *Library Journal* 115 (September 15, 1990), 16-17.

19. "Electronically Accessible Indexing of Gay/Lesbian Periodicals," compiled by Michael Montgomery, Princeton University, and Polly Thistlethwaite, Hunter College, for RASD/MARS/User Services open forum panel on "Electronic Access to America's Diversity," ALA Midwinter 1993. Major gay and lesbian periodical indexers include: *CARL UnCover,* 10 titles; *Alternative Press Index,* 8 titles; *Expanded Academic Index,* 6 titles; *Book Review Index,* 4 titles; *Magazine Index,* 3 titles; and *ProQuest Periodicals Index;* 3 titles.

20. The *Gay/Lesbian Periodicals Index,* compiled by Alan M. Greenberg, is available from Integrity Indexing, P.O. Box 33094, Charlotte NC 28233-3094.

21. [Ed. note: For more on this topic see: Ellen Greenblatt, "Homosexuality: The Evolution of a Concept in the Library of Congress Subject Headings," in *Gay and Lesbian Library Service,* ed. Cal Gough and Ellen Greenblatt (Jefferson, N.C.: McFarland, 1990), 75-101.]

22. For more information or to obtain petitions, contact: Sanford Berman, Convener, Cataloging Consumers Network, 4400 Morningside Road, Edina, MN 55416.

23. Bibliographies are available from the Library Information Clearinghouse of the American Library Association's Gay and Lesbian Task Force, ALA Office for Outreach Services, 50 East Huron Street, Chicago IL 60611. [Ed. note: See also Cal Gough and Ellen Greenblatt, "Gay and Lesbian Bibliographies" in *Gay and Lesbian Library Service* ed. by Cal Gough and Ellen Greenblatt (McFarland, 1990), 210-213.]

24. Further assistance regarding collection development strategies is available via publications ordered from the GLTF Clearinghouse, address above. [Ed. note: see also Cal Gough and Ellen Greenblatt, eds. *Gay and Lesbian Library Service* (Jefferson, N.C.: McFarland, 1990).]

25. GAY-LIBN@USCVM (BITNET); GAY-LIBN@VM.USC.EDU (Internet). [Note: Information current as of May, 1994.]

26. The QRD is found in /pub/QRD at vector.casti.com. For more information see Frequently Asked Questions about the QRD in /pub/QRD/OFREQUENTLY-ASKED-QUESTIONS. [Note: Information current as of May, 1994]

27. Subscription requests should be addressed to: The American Library Association, Office of Library Outreach Services, Gay and Lesbian Task Force, 50 East Huron Street, Chicago, IL 60611.

28. Examples of these tools used in other libraries are available from the Gay and Lesbian Task Force Library Information Clearinghouse, ALA Office for Library Outreach Services, 50 East Huron Street, Chicago, IL 60611.

29. [Ed. note: "What One Librarian Can Do to Improve Services for Lesbian and Gay Library Users," by Cal Gough and John M. Littlewood, is available from the Library Information Clearinghouse of the American Library Association Gay and Lesbian Task Force, address above.]

30. *Freedom Watch: The Citizens Project Newsletter* 2 (April-May 1993), 1. Panelists included: Roc Bottomly, senior pastor of Pulpit Rock Church; R.T. "Terry" Jackson, independent legal counsel; Robin Miller, past president of Pikes Peak Gay and Lesbian Community Center; Kevin Tebedo, executive director of

Colorado for Family Values; Greg Walta, trial lawyer; and Rev. Dr. James White, First Congregational Church.

31. Dan Luckenbill, *With Equal Pride: Gay & Lesbian Studies at UCLA: Catalog of an Exhibit, University Research Library, January-March 1993* (Los Angeles: Department of Special Collections, University Research Library, University of California, 1993).

32. Eric Bryant, in "Making Things Perfectly Queer," *Library Journal* 118 (April 15, 1993), 106-109, offers several wonderful ideas.

33. "Los Angeles Public Library Rebuked [by Local Human Relations Commission] on [Langston Hughes/Gay Pride Week] Controversy," *American Libraries* (February 1992), 134; *GLTF Newsletter* (Gay & Lesbian Task Force, American Library Association) 4 (Spring 1992), 4; and City of Los Angeles Human Relations Commission, *A Report on the Controversy Regarding Allegations of Homophobia within the Los Angeles City Public Library* (Los Angeles: City of Los Angeles Human Relations Commission, 1991).

LIVING DIVERSITY: MAKING IT WORK

Cheryl LaGuardia, Christine K. Oka and Adán Griego

... when I think about recruiting, I think about the colleagues I want to work with in the future on [the] critical issues of funding, technology, and access. I want to be confident that the best people—people with the background, character, education, and experience to understand these immensely difficult forces—are ready at all levels of our profession to make wise decisions based on fact rather than illusion. I want to confer with people who will see all sides of any problem, who have the creativity and energy to think new thoughts, who can motivate those around them, yet who will accept real constraints and be willing to change their opinions when necessary (from Anne K. Beaubien's "Recruiting the Best and the Brightest").[1]

INTRODUCTION

Having worked within a diverse library setting for the past few years, and having witnessed the "explosion" in the library literature about promoting diversity and multicultural environments, a group of us at the University of California, Santa Barbara Library decided it was time to review our collective and individual experiences within this setting.

The term diversity has as many shades of meaning as there are people in the room. The generally accepted premise is that working in a culturally diverse work environment offers personal and institutional rewards. Our experiences and personal knowledge strongly reaffirm this premise. However, the process of creating such a work environment can create tensions within an organization, both for minority and "majority" employees, unless the individuals involved build mutual confidence and successfully focus on their shared goals.

As we began the process of sifting through what had happened in our professional lives over the past few years, we had many discussions of just what pivotal events had shaped our experiences. Our recollections ranged all over the map—we couldn't pin down exactly what we wanted to say—so we turned to the library literature to see if we could find a wheel that someone else had come up with, so we didn't have to reinvent it.

We didn't find it. Our review of the literature found nothing that truly reflected just what our group had gone through. We found plenty of statistics that failed to express the experiences of individuals. Those accounts detailing individual experiences varied a great deal from what had happened to us at UCSB. So we had to change the focus of what we were looking for. We searched instead for a conceptual outline: something established in the literature around which we could narrate our story.

We found an outline in a handout from the Association of College and Research Libraries Bibliographic Instruction Section (ACRL BIS) "Cultural Diversity and Higher Education: Bibliographic Instruction in a Multicultural Environment" preconference at ALA 1991. The handout, entitled "Diversity: Necessary Conditions for Educational Excellence," had been distributed by one of the conference facilitators, G. Satyendra-Holland, and one of our number remembered this session as the best meeting she had ever attended at any ALA meeting.

In her document, Ms. Satyendra-Holland listed nine factors for reducing resistance to diversity. We traced all nine factors within our organization: the parallels were there—slightly variant, but present, nonetheless—and thus her list became the outline around which we detailed our experience.

FACTORS INFLUENCING DIVERSITY

The exact title of Ms. Satyendra-Holland's list is, "Suggested Factors in Reducing Resistance to Diversity," and the list reads as follows:[2]

1. Clear Goals.
2. Compatibility with Institutional Values.
3. Compatibility with Organizational Structure.
4. Open, Two-Way Communication.
5. Climate of Readiness.
6. Ownership.
7. Support at the Top.
8. Rewards.
9. Respect for Opposition.

For our purposes, we decided to rearrange consideration of these factors in an order that best followed the process we underwent. But first let us describe some of the background at UCSB.

THE MINORITY FELLOWSHIP AT UCSB

Over the past few years, the UCSB Library has been developing diversity in its professional staff mainly through a Minority Fellowship Program aimed at increasing new minority librarians' opportunities for careers in academic libraries. The Minority Fellowship Program (formerly the Minority Library Internship Program) began in 1985 when two recently graduated minority librarians came to the UCSB Library as one-year interns. Since that time, seven more Fellows have gone through the program, working in various Library departments for one or two years (the Program is described in a 1987 Library Journal article by Boisse and Dowell).[3]

"FACTORS" AS THEY INFLUENCED OUR SITUATION

Climate of Readiness

In 1990 the Library lost about one-third of its reference librarians to an early retirement program. Collectively these individuals had over 200 years of library experience. Half the remaining librarians had been at UCSB less than four years, and their collective library experience totaled fewer than fifteen years. After these reference librarians retired, the Library administration announced a downsizing plan that would leave many vacant positions unfilled.

The result of this short-staffing had considerable effect on new Library Fellows: they had to "hit the ground running." Most began serving at the Main Reference Desk within a few weeks of their arrival on campus, many undertook collection development and faculty liaison responsibilities within the first year of their fellowships, and others became regular members of an instructional team teaching both credit-bearing and subject-specialized classes.

The Fellowships have turned out to be more like entry-level professional jobs than formal educational experiences. We're lucky to have found Fellows sufficiently prepared (and sufficiently game!) to undertake regular librarian duties. Although we lost professional positions, demands on our services have risen.

We recently brought up a new online catalog that users (and librarians) must learn how to use. Collections' responsibilities increased exponentially after the retirements: there were fewer bodies available to handle the various guidelines. Our newly restructured, revitalized instructional program brought in many more requests for library classes than in past years. There was plenty for everyone to do, and the Fellows got their full share of professional assignments.

Some librarians outside the Fellowship program weren't sure just what roles they could play in working with the new Fellows. For example, the new library instruction coordinator was looking for new instructors to add to the teaching roster shortly after she undertook the assignment. She remembers:

> I'd been a librarian for some time but I was relatively new to this university, and I had just been asked to put together a new Library Instruction program. I wasn't sure just how much the Library Fellows could be expected to contribute, or where their time was supposed to be spent.
>
> When I drafted the initial syllabus for the course, I asked a former Library Fellow with considerable graduate teaching experience to read it. He was very supportive. He also offered suggestions on how to make the curriculum more widely accessible to different cultures. I wasn't very experienced in teaching and his support came at a time I really needed it.
>
> Then later, after we'd taught the new Skills course a couple of terms, I was given the green light to recruit two new Library Fellows for instruction. It took a little convincing to bring one of the Fellows into the program—she was leery at first, having had no teaching experience up to that time. But she joined the group, and later that year three of us revised the entire course. The Fellows authored several portions themselves. I was lucky to be working with talented people who were eager to contribute so much to the communal effort.

In my mind, their willingness to contribute to the whole became the backbone of an evolving team approach in reference.

Clear Goals

The major goals of the Minority Fellowship were as follows: to improve the employability of minority librarians in academic research libraries; to provide role models for UCSB minority undergraduates; to create a more heterogeneous group within the UCSB library; and to provide librarians at UCSB an opportunity to be involved in training new librarians.[4]

Implementation of these goals was not as clear cut, however. Individuals have had different experiences within the Program. Some candidates were under the impression during their interviews that the fellowship would be just a learning experience, that they would essentially be students continuing to learn about academic library work.

The Fellowship is designed to "provide the recent graduate an opportunity to work in a culturally diverse environment; to gain experience in at least two areas or departments of the library; and to learn about academic libraries."[5] Many Fellows have started the program by working in Main Reference, learning the "ropes" of the University Library there, then moving on to one or two other areas of their choice. But it has never been established ahead of time just where each Fellow would work nor exactly what they would do—much has been left up to the individual Fellow to carve out their own experience.

This can be both frightening and liberating for a new librarian. As one former Library Fellow notes,

> I expected more structure in the program than what I initially encountered. I thought I'd be learning more than "doing," that there would be more active teaching and formal mentoring than there was. As it turned out, within a term of my coming to UCSB I was teaching in the credit-bearing Library class program. A term later I was revising the course with the coordinator and writing some of the original materials being used. It set an exhilarating pace: after the success we had with the credit courses we got lots of requests for one-shot classes. I literally had to learn to teach day by day, on the run!

Compatibility with Institutional Values

In 1989, the Library established an Affirmative Action Committee, charged with increasing the representation of underrepresented employees, creating an environment that facilitates retention of same, facilitating an understanding of intercultural dynamics, and promoting librarianship among underrepresented UCSB student and staff groups.[6] The Library Minority Fellowship Program brochure summarizes institutional values expressed by the program:

> The University of California, Santa Barbara Library system has a strong commitment to affirmative action and is seeking to increase the minority representation in all areas of the library. The Minority Fellowship Program forms a major component of the library's overall affirmative action plan to increase that representation and to encourage the professional growth and development of minority librarians within the profession.[7]

In their 1987 article, Boisse and Dowell detail some of the ways in which UCSB Library has made a strong commitment to diversity: through support for interns to national conferences, involving interns in library operational committees, and developing special training programs to orient Fellows quickly in many areas of academic librarianship.[8]

Compatibility with Organizational Structure

We have mixed feelings about how these values fit into the organizational structure at the Library. This is for a number of reasons. Any large institution has bureaucratic imperatives that can blur the outlines of that institution's value system: a kind of "you can't see the forest for the trees" situation in which emerging philosophies struggle with the institutional history and past practice. The basic structure at the UCSB Library has excited different opinions about our implementation of diversity.

The reference department at UCSB has two ethnic studies units— Black Studies and the Coleccion Tloque Nahuaque (Chicano Studies)—which are housed and staffed separately from the rest of the reference collections. Several of the Library Fellows worked in these units early in their time at UCSB.

Several Fellows worked a few hours a week in the ethnic studies units to provide release time for the Black Studies and Chicano Studies librarians. Some librarians and Fellows interpreted this to be "ghettoizing" the new minority Fellows, treating them differently and separately from other librarians, channeling them into ethnic studies only. However, this is not at all how other Fellows viewed the experience themselves.

One of these former Fellows notes:

> When my internship began, I was told that both Fellows were being asked to work in the ethnic studies units that year. I was asked if I had a preference for working in the Black Studies or Chicano Studies Unit. I had erroneously assumed that, as a Chicano, I would be working in Chicano Studies. But we had a choice, and neither of us expressed a preference, so the other intern and I flipped a coin and I went to Black Studies. It was only by this accident I worked there.

Another issue emerged surrounding this situation. Although we had Fellows who were Native American and Asian American, the Library has no special units that serve these groups. One of these Fellows had Asian American students approach her at the Reference desk repeatedly, asking "Where is the Asian American studies unit?" This has raised the question in our minds of whether we are serving all underrepresented groups equally.

It is not unusual for non-black, non-Latino students to approach any of us at the Reference desk and ask, "Am I allowed to go into Black Studies and Chicano Studies and use those collections?" This raises a further question with some of us: are we creating greater cultural divisions by having these units separate from the rest of the collection?

We have no answer, not even a consensus, among ourselves on this question. There is no right answer—the jury is still out on which approach to teaching and supporting the teaching of multiculturalism is most effective and least divisive.[9] We raise the issues simply because they are important to consider in any discussion of diversity.

Support at Top

Support and leadership from the top in this area are well documented at our Library. Joseph Boisse, the University Librarian, established the Minority Fellow Program at UCSB, as well as the Library Affirmative Action Committee. In the last two years, four Target of Opportunity appointments for minority librarians have been made under Dr. Boisse's direction. During his tenure as President of ACRL, a Task Force on Recruitment of Underrepresented Minorities was established within the organization.

The Library has also held several diversity workshops and seminars on valuing diversity. But the greatest support for diversity we have encountered is probably best described in the next section: Ownership.

Ownership

The Climate of Readiness factor directly influenced the way we have lived diversity. The ultimate goal for the Library, above and beyond living diversity, is, of course, to get the work done. Two years ago in the Reference department we found ourselves in a situation in which we all—librarians and Minority Fellows—had to scramble to get the work done. There were so few of us that we had to double- and triple-up on collections' assignments. To tell the truth, we didn't have much time to ruminate over whether or not we wanted to work with anyone, nor could we be choosy about the roles we would take.

In other places we had worked, individuals had assumed certain set roles within the organization according to the requirements of their positions. But with us, an unusual pattern emerged. We'd assume a role, then "trade it off" for another, one day being a mentor, the next day a mentee. Where one of us had substantial experience or skill in an area, we would act as a mentor to several others to build up their confidence. As mentees we were all anxious to absorb whatever knowledge others were willing to share with us. Since we came from different socioeconomic, ethnic, and educational backgrounds, we had a wide variety of skills and experience upon which to draw.

The novice instructors who had never taught before in their lives teamed up with expert teachers and learned how to get comfortable in front of a class. Computer gurus gave troubleshooting and technological support to Luddites. Old hands showed new reference librarians tricks of the trade at the desk (how and where to find who and what). New reference librarians showed old hands where to find information they'd never had to look for in the past: Native American reaction to the Columbus 500-year anniversary, observances of the fiftieth anniversary of Japanese-American internments during World War II, the origins of the Mexican Dia de los Muertos (Day of the Dead) celebration, for example.

Other factors were, obviously, at play here for us to succeed in such trying circumstances. Support came not only from the top but from closer to home.

Our department head was the coach of the team. She set the collegial tone for the department. She especially encouraged each of us to try new approaches, and to carry out projects as we thought best. Her trust became the focus of our work: the fact that she trusted our professional judgment gave us greater confidence to "go and do" (although she was continually available for advice and help). This attitude set the tone for the department, and rather than concentrating on our differences, we spent time working on and achieving our common goals.

This constant encouragement, combined with professional freedom, created an atmosphere in which we naturally came to trust each other, while at the same time taking ownership for our part in the work of the department. We each had a clearly-established stake in the survival of the department, although our roles were not so overly-defined as to hinder us from experimenting creatively. Our only adversary became the work itself.

Open, Two-Way Communication

In the early days of our working together, we were concerned only with the interpersonal communication that was taking place in the department: how each of us related to the others, and how well personal dynamics worked among the Reference librarians. We realize in retrospect, however, that we were dealing with issues of communication on many levels throughout our organization, and this communication had a profound effect on the group's ability to embrace diversity as matter-of-factly as we did.

In the Reference department communication was very open. Many of us were new to the organization, which actually helped in our interpersonal dynamics: we didn't share an institutional history, nor were we in the mainstream of "organizational information sharing." This worked in our favor: no one had bad past history with others; neither did anyone have definite answers to the problems we faced daily. So we started to shift responsibilities among ourselves as needs arose and as our strengths fit each situation. At the same time we also started our own highly efficient information network.

Sharing information is sharing power and responsibility within an organization. Without informal feedback and encouragement from longer-term members within an organization, newcomers will not be effective in becoming part of the organization: they are being excluded from the bastions of power, the "information loop" within the system.[10]

The fact that we enjoyed working together meant that we often spent time outside the Library together. We came to share information with each other as a matter of course—not confidential matters, but the essential bits of institutional knowledge that don't always get passed around equally within a group. All of us were involved in different committees, task forces, and projects. We each held important pieces of the jigsaw puzzle that we were working in. By sharing these bits we all got a clearer vision of the big picture. As a side benefit, we learned a lot about different aspects of the Library that we would never have access to in any other way.

Respect for Opposition

There are very few people on the face of the earth who have no prejudices, no biases. We were not the exceptions. And prejudice is not confined to "majority" group members about minorities. As a former Library Fellow of Chicano heritage notes:

> Working in Black Studies helped me face my own racial bias. I learned to interact successfully with African-Americans. I had to teach Black Studies classes and provide reference service within the Unit; I was working with many African American research materials, and it was necessary for me to learn about the African American experience to teach library classes. I had never known what the Harlem Renaissance was, for example. I knew a little about Josephine Baker before this, but I had never placed her within the context of a larger Black Renaissance Culture in the 1920s.
>
> I got over my prejudices about African American culture by taking the time to learn more about it. And working in the Unit brought me into contact with the Black Studies Librarian, my first UCSB mentor. She was very generous professionally—working closely with me, teaching me all the 'informal' rules of academic librarianship, the kinds of things they never cover in library school.

So prejudice was, at the beginning, still an issue for all of us. But as we worked so closely and shared so many difficult and challenging times, our prejudices lost some of their importance. When you work side-by-side every day with someone who helps you achieve more and better work, ethnicity fades in importance. As noted above, we do not agree about everything: but for the sake of our individual and collective goals, we have agreed to disagree and get on with the work.

Admittedly, if our prejudices were such that they interfered with our ability to get on with the work, we would have to face them in a more "head-on" style than we have had to up to this point. But as long as we continue to work along the principles that there really is no THEM, only US, we feel we've achieved at least a pragmatic level of diversity.

Rewards

Bringing fresh viewpoints to any organization usually has its rewards. In our case, the librarians' and Fellows' views embodied the American experience. As we worked together and felt more at ease with one another, any initial reluctance we may have had about sharing these views disappeared, and differences of opinion surfaced.

How do we cope with our differences? Usually, as mentioned previously, we agree to disagree. We are not confrontational about our differences: instead we discuss them and clear up problems pretty quickly, before they become barriers to our working together. Considering the differences in our personalities and communication styles, this is a major coup. But our ability to work this out is the direct result of our shared goals, commitment, and values.

There have been very practical rewards, too. For example, in the process of working on a major rewrite of the Library credit-bearing classes, one Library Fellow with extensive teaching experience mentored the librarian who had been put in charge of the rewrite. She then mentored two new Library Fellows, who, in turn, became her assistants in coordinating the bibliographic instruction program. One of them has already moved on to become a coordinator of bibliographic instruction at another academic library; the other has been offered a similar position at a prestigious university library.

Having as diverse a group of librarians working together in one place as we do relieves the pressure for each of us to fit the librarian "image"—we have much greater latitude in how we present ourselves as professionals. Diversity actually has made it easier for us to be ourselves, rather than a single norm out of a mold. It has broken down the chain of conformity within the institution, making different kinds of ideas and people welcome rather than feared.

SUMMARY

In her "The Way I See It" column quoted at the beginning of this chapter, Anne Beaubien talked about finding colleagues she wanted to work with on critical library issues. She seeks the best people, "people with the background, character, education, and experience…people who will see all sides of any problem, who have the creativity and energy to think new thoughts, who can motivate those around them, yet who will accept real constraints and be willing to change their opinions when necessary." We believe we have found many of them here, among our diverse but united ranks.

NOTES

1.   Anne K. Beaubien, "Recruiting the Best and the Brightest," *College and Research Libraries News* 53(5)(May 1992): 321,323.

2.   G. Satyendra-Holland, "Diversity: Necessary Conditions for Educational Excellence," from the ACRL BIS "Cultural Diversity and Higher Education: Bibliographic Instruction in a Multicultural Environment" preconference of the American Library Association Annual Meeting, Atlanta, Georgia, 1991.

3.   Joseph A. Boisse and Connie V. Dowell, "Increasing Minority Librarians in Academic Research Libraries," *Library Journal* 112(7)(April 15, 1987): 52.

4.   Ibid., 53.

5.   *Library Minority Fellowship Program,* (brochure) University of California, Santa Barbara, 1992.

6.   Ibid.

7.   Affirmative Action Committee Charge, University of California at Santa Barbara Library, 19 December 1989.

8.   Boisse and Dowell, "Increasing Minority Librarians," 53.

9.   Sharon Bernstein, "Multiculturalism: Building Bridges or Burning Them?" *Los Angeles Times,* 30 November 1992.

10.   J. P. White, "Diversity's Champion," *Los Angeles Times Magazine,* 9 August 1992.

POSITIONING FOR CHANGE:
THE DIVERSITY INTERNSHIP AS A GOOD BEGINNING

Linda DeBeau-Melting and Karen M. Beavers

POSITIONING FOR CHANGE—A GOOD BEGINNING

Citizens throughout the United States are beginning to gather voluntarily in groups called "Study Circles" to discuss a number of issues needing urgent attention in our society today. Prominent among these is racism. One of the study guides written for study circle participants reads in part,

> [T]he large wave of Latino and Asian immigration that began in the 1980s is changing the makeup of our nation. In some western states, whites may be a minority within a generation or two; by the turn of the century, one in three Americans will be a person of color. This diversity has brought new energy and talent, but some Americans—concerned that ethnic groups aren't doing enough to "blend in"—have felt threatened by it.[1]

Public discussion of diversity, inclusiveness and racism continue to occupy significant space in news broadcasting and publishing media across the nation. In a recent opinion piece, published in the

Star Tribune, Cheri Register, author of *Are Those Kids Yours? American Families with Children Adopted from Other Countries,* writes,

> the demographic shift will undo majority status, but it will not likely eliminate racism. We who call ourselves white need to become not colorblind, but more aware of how we are colored by the position of privilege we have occupied as the norm for "American." My presumed racelessness has allowed me to be ignorant, a privilege I must now forgo.[2]

These discussions are a response to a changing society. In some cases, they have the potential for supporting significant change in the lives of individual participants and their communities. In others, they could initiate a new view of an old problem along with a determination to propose new solutions.

CHANGING THE HOMOGENEOUS CAMPUS

The challenge and opportunity for organizations is to move beyond discussion into action. The University of Minnesota Libraries created such an opportunity for itself by developing the Affirmative Action Internship Program in 1990. This program was a deliberate act intended to begin to change a largely homogeneous population within the Libraries to one which would become a more diverse and inclusive population.[3]

During this same period, the University of Minnesota was in the midst of several activities to build diversity within its community. This background is well described in a document issued in 1993 by the University's Commission on Women:

> Since 1988, the University of Minnesota has launched several major initiatives to increase and foster diversity within the academic community, to diversify the University's curricular and research mission, and to create and maintain work and learning environments where all members of our community can thrive.[4]

The internship proposed by the University Librarian was well supported within the University administration. Over the winter and spring the essential elements of the program were articulated and the search begun. In August 1990 the first Affirmative Action Intern began work in the University of Minnesota Libraries.

This treatise will focus on the voice of the intern herself to describe and assess the outcomes of the program. Shulamit Reinharz, in *Feminist Methods in Social Research,* cites Canadian political scientist Naomi Black's position that feminist research "insists on the value of subjectivity and personal experience."[5] Reinharz goes on to formulate a definition of research as "the production of a publicly scrutinizable analysis of a phenomenon with the intent of clarification."[6]

AN AFFIRMATIVE ACTION INTERN

I am a twenty-eight year old African American woman. The relationship between an intern and the institution depends upon the particular attributes each brings to the experience. In order to understand my intern experience you first have to understand who I am.

I grew up in a predominately white neighborhood in Los Angeles, California. I attended ethnically and racially integrated public schools, but was tracked into college preparatory courses in which I was usually one of a handful of students of color, and often the only African American female. My experience did not seem too strange to me. My brothers attended the same schools and took many of the same classes I did. My mother also grew up in a predominately white neighborhood in Los Angeles and attended predominately white public schools. Even my maternal grandparents, whom I knew only through my mother's stories, grew up and lived in predominately white communities in Minnesota. I continually react in amazement when my mother reminds me that my grandfather, who during the 1920s and 1930s owned a pharmacy in Minneapolis, spoke enough Swedish to communicate with his neighborhood customers.

My family is middle class. Class should be spoken about in discussions about diversity. My grandfather and great-uncle were pharmacists in Minneapolis until the advent of super-drugstores that had policies of not hiring Negroes. My grandfather relocated to Los Angeles where he started a catering business; my great-uncle went to law school at the University of Minnesota. My aunt is a teacher. My father worked for his family's insurance business. My mother is a psychologist. I first became aware of librarianship as a career option when my mother revealed to me that it was a career path she had been interested in but had chosen not to follow.

I frequently tell my family story to people I meet in Minnesota. I tell it both because I am proud of my family and because I know it will surprise them. It surprises people because it doesn't match the stories that are told about African Americans in newspapers and on television.

Growing up I had a hard time reconciling what I knew to be true about my family and myself with the stereotype about African Americans that existed in mainstream culture. Kids I met in school, church and other activities often made comments like "you don't act black" or, because of my light skin color, asserted "you're mixed, right?" in their efforts to match me with what they knew about the black people they were exposed to in newspapers and on television.

My experiences left me feeling as if I and my family somehow existed outside dominant definitions of what it is to be an African American. I view our outsider position as a strength and an advantage. I have been determined not to be limited or confined by expectations or definitions imposed from others.

My desire to resist limitations has affected my attitudes toward my professional life. Although I felt pressure to focus on one area of librarianship during library school, I chose to develop my interests in cataloging *and* reference work. When I decided to start looking for a job in the spring of 1990, I sought to avoid choosing one specialization over the other by applying to an internship program that would allow me to explore both areas.

I applied to two minority internship programs. One was at the University of California and the other was the University of Minnesota program. At the time, I was completing an M.A. in English at the University of Michigan and working part time as a reference librarian in the undergraduate library. I was interested in the University of California internship because of the quality of the academic campus and because it would have enabled me to move back home. I was attracted to the University of Minnesota program because of the opportunity to work in a variety of library units and because of my interest in moving to a city where I had some family history. I chose the University of Minnesota internship program because of the variety of experiences it promised and the challenge and excitement of moving to a new city. It wasn't until after I accepted the position that I began to have doubts about the choice I had made.

My friends in Ann Arbor were surprised that I would choose Minneapolis over Berkeley. I dismissed their surprise until a colleague of mine at the University of Michigan showed me the map in *We the People: An Atlas of America's Ethnic Diversity* that illustrated the distribution of blacks in the United States.[7] Minneapolis was shaded in tan—which meant that it had at the time of publication a black population of 2.5 to 5 percent; but it was surrounded by a sea of white which meant that the rest of the state had a less than 1.25 percent black population. I looked at the maps that showed the distribution of other ethnic groups and noted that other ethnic/racial groups were not well represented either. I don't think that I realized until then what I had always taken for granted growing up in California; diversity is really important to me. I have always had what my mother called a "United Nations" group of friends. My thoughts went back to the vacation I had taken in Minneapolis the previous May. I traveled with a friend of mine who is Japanese American. In the course of our week there we gradually came to feel that people were staring at us. At one point a stranger came up to us and told us he had never seen a black and Asian person together as friends; at another, an elderly woman, that we had held a door open for, told my friend that she had a hard time telling Japanese and Chinese people apart. I feared that I would be on display when I moved to Minneapolis. My apprehensions grew about moving to a place that likely would not have the arts, food and culture that results from a multicultural environment.

As I reconsidered my decision, I reflected upon my family history. While my fears about Minneapolis were somewhat diminished by the fact that it is my mother's family's home, I needed to think about the reasons that my mother's family left. My grandfather and great-uncle were part of a community of middle class blacks who lived and worked in a majority white city. While many of my grandfather's and great-uncle's customers were white, their community of friends consisted of other blacks who were active in black fraternal, church and community organizations. I believe that my grandparents and great-uncle were able to live and work in a homogenous community like Minneapolis because they belonged to a community of people who gave them a sense of identity and strength. Maintaining ties with the black community was particularly important for my grandfather and great-uncle because all of their mother's brothers married white women and passed for white.

Eventually, however, my grandparents, as well as many of their friends, had to leave Minneapolis. My grandfather and great-uncle found that they could no longer be part of the profession that they had spent years of school preparing for; their business was displaced by corporate drug stores with discriminatory hiring practices that did not allow my grandfather or uncle to work for them.

I also found that in order to invoke my mother's experiences of functioning in predominately white school environments in Los Angeles I needed to talk to her about the racism she encountered.

My mother did well academically, but endured many hurtful experiences. She has often told me how uncomfortably on display she felt in elementary school when the class would sing Stephen Foster songs like "Old Black Joe" and all of her classmates' eyes would be on her.

The high school she attended redrew the district lines so that my mother, my aunt and her twenty black classmates no longer lived within the district. My mother and her friends spent two weeks of school hours on the bleachers of the high school field while their parents fought for and eventually won the right to have their children let back into school.

The experience that strikes me most hard is the time when my mother was told by her teacher that she could not board the school bus that was taking her classmates to the Huntington Library, because blacks were not allowed in the library.

Like my grandparents, my mother found strength and identity by forming friendships with her black classmates and by becoming involved in her black church and sorority. However, she sometimes found it difficult to find a place for herself between the two cultures. In elementary school, for example, at the same time she faced racism from the whites at school, she and my aunt were beaten up by several black children in her neighborhood that felt that she and my aunt were trying to pass for white by attending predominately white schools.

My mother's experiences required that she develop the ability to operate in both white and black culture. I grew up watching her interact with white people at work and in our neighborhood and watching her talk with black people in our extended family, at church, and at the beauty parlor. My mother's language, intonation, and gestures changed depending upon with whom and where she was. That's not to say that my mother became different people depending upon the setting, but that different parts of her were manifested depending upon the setting. She continues to utilize her flexibility today as a psychologist in a downtown Los Angeles high school where she works with students and parents from diverse cultures. I have watched and learned from my mother.

My community of friends in school were other women of color. I shared with my friends the struggle to understand where we fit in, given that we all had chosen to work and socialize in predominately white communities. What scared me most about moving to Minneapolis was that I would be moving alone and that the community of blacks and other people of color was small in comparison to the California communities I grew up in.

I finally decided to go through with my initial decision to move to Minneapolis because I was interested in the library work opportunities and the challenge of making a place for myself in a homogenous work and social community.

I began the internship in August of 1990. Almost from the start, I experienced the same feelings of being on display and falling outside of expected notions of African Americans that have come up for me at various times in my life.

My first two weeks were spent becoming oriented to the University of Minnesota Libraries. The size of the libraries made this an enormous task; the University of Minnesota Libraries hold the fifteenth largest research collection in the United States with over five million volumes located in 18 separate locations, serving a student body of 45,000. For the first week almost every minute of my day was spent with one group or another of strangers—I had morning visits, group lunches and then afternoon visits. I experienced it all with a mixture of excitement and anxiety. On the one hand, there was a real sense of welcoming and celebration. People made me feel that they had been looking forward to my arrival and they were eager to work with me in the future. On the other hand, I felt that I was under a microscope. I was looked to with an expectation that I often experienced as tiring. I was asked all kinds of questions about the libraries I had worked in in the past, my expectations for the internship and my long-term career goals. I went back to my house every night completely exhausted. Some of my anxiety was alleviated by my mentor who took a lot of interest and care with me. When she did not actually accompany me on my visits she at least delivered me to my destination. She was the one constant during that initial period; and she became an important presence and influence during the course of my internship.

I sensed that the library staff I met were surprised by me because I didn't fit stereotypical notions of what an African American woman is like. The application process did not include an in-person interview, so my orientation period was the first time most of the library staff laid eyes on me. During the search process I suspected that the search committee might question what my ethnic background was because nothing on my resume indicated that I was an African American. I had not belonged to any African American organizations in college or library school. In the midst of a telephone conversation, the personnel assistant in the University Libraries paused and asked me whether or not I was aware that I was applying for an affirmative action position. I just answered "yes." Why didn't I declare that I was an African American? The answer lies in my early experiences. I wasn't comfortable making that declaration because I was afraid of the assumptions that might be made about me based on stereotypical ideas about African Americans. I also enjoyed the idea of subverting what I perceived of as an attempt to classify me based on my race.

I began my work after the initial two weeks of orientation. My program had been planned for me. I would spend the first six months in the Central Technical Services department and then spend the next six months in the reference unit in the largest library on campus. After the initial year I would choose one area in which to spend my entire second year. I was pleased with my program even though I didn't play a part in the planning. While I was in library school I had completed a brief internship in serials cataloging so that I knew I would like to learn more about cataloging. I had a feeling I would ultimately choose reference as my focus for the second year, but I had a sense of the value of technical services knowledge in providing reference service.

There was another layer to my experience during this time. I accompanied my mentor to all of the committee meetings she attended. Her committee work involved people at different levels and functions within the library and the university community whom I would not have interacted with had I been confined to cataloging. It was during this period that I realized the internship would be more than just an opportunity to explore different career options; it also gave me access to levels of the library and the

University community that I would not have if I had entered via more traditional channels.

I began the second phase of my internship in reference in February of 1990. I was made to feel welcome by many acts on the part of the reference librarians. The most memorable was made by a colleague who gave up some of her office space in order to make room for me.

Many of my colleagues at other institutions have expressed concern that they receive different responses from patrons in the reference area than their white colleagues do. For the most part, my experience has been quite positive. There were times, particularly in the first few months that I worked on the reference desk, that people did not approach me because they thought that I, like they, was waiting for reference help. But I believe that had more to do with how young I look and how unsure I was as a new member of the reference staff, than it had to do with my race. Now that I have been working on the desk for over two years I am not met with much confusion. If anything, I notice that many young students seem more willing to come up to me and ask me questions—particularly students of color. These students seem to be more comfortable about asking questions of someone who looks like them.

CREATING A DIVERSITY LIBRARIAN POSITION

The second year of my internship was to be the time I got to focus on developing my skills in one area of the library. I had anticipated becoming more entrenched in the established services and programs in the reference unit—possibly becoming more involved in the unit's bibliographic instruction or guides program. I did not anticipate that a new opportunity would be presented to me.

Toward the end of my first year in the Libraries, the University Librarian asked me if I would consider becoming the Libraries' Diversity Librarian the next year. This person was to have the responsibility of creating links between the Libraries and the diverse University community by establishing contacts with the services and programs targeted to students of color.

My response to his offer was quite mixed—at least internally. On the one hand, I felt this was an exciting opportunity I didn't want to miss out on. I felt that the University Libraries was taking another positive step toward inclusiveness by making a proactive effort to make connections within the University community. In the course of my experience on the reference desk, I witnessed firsthand all the barriers the size and complexity of the University Libraries present to students—and felt that those problems were multiplied for students of color because they did not see themselves reflected in the library staff. In terms of my career goals, the position seemed to free me from my fear of being confined to one area of the library. In addition to improving outreach to students of color, I would be responsible for responding to their collection development needs. I would still be based in reference services which would allow me to work on the reference desk and teach some bibliographic instruction sessions. The variety of my work would be matched by the variety of people I would be able to interact with in the course of my job. In addition to working with the reference librarians and bibliographers throughout the University Libraries, I would be able to work with people with diverse responsibilities throughout the University community.

On the other hand, I was afraid that the job would represent another kind of confinement. The words "marginalized" and "ghettoized" came to mind. I questioned why it was necessary to create a position that stood outside of the rest of the University Libraries structure. If the goal of the position was to make the Libraries more inclusive and welcoming, did it make sense to accomplish this through a vehicle that was separate from established services? I also questioned whether it was appropriate to have one of the few persons of color in the library be responsible for diversity. I feared that my taking the diversity position might invite other people to think that diversity was only the responsibility of people of color. I was afraid that other library staff might not take responsibility for issues related to diversity, racism, and privilege.

I decided to take the position. I wanted to work toward making the University Libraries more inclusive. I felt that I had a responsibility as a person of color to reach out to others; and I felt that because I have always had a multicultural group of friends that I was a natural for interacting with students and staff from diverse cultures. The alternative, having a white diversity librarian, did not seem appropriate to me. I try to be careful, however, not to promote the idea that I am the only person in the Libraries responsible for diversity.

I have been working in this capacity for the Libraries over the past year and a half. I have formed many relationships with students and staff of color in the University community. I have found that the people I meet are often as surprised by me as my library colleagues were. I don't fit into their stereotypes of what a librarian is like either. My exchanges with students and staff of color—African Americans, Asian and Pacific Americans, Chicanos, Latinos and American Indians—have provided me with an opportunity to learn more about other cultures and sparked a renewed interest in me to learn about my own culture. I feel that I am becoming involved in a community of people on campus that can offer me support in much the same way black organizations provided support for my mother and grandparents.

The doubts I had about taking the position are not gone, however. I struggle over them internally and with colleagues from other institutions all the time. I believe that as an African American, I have a unique perspective to offer the library and the ability to reach out to diverse communities on campus. Part of my responsibility is to voice the conflicts that arise from this action. I don't think you can go forward without some conflict; it is important for this conflict to be voiced and addressed, not silenced.

ASSESSING THE INTERNSHIP

An internship can open up an institution. It provides an alternative entrance point into an organization and enables an individual to come into contact with levels of an organization that are usually closed to those who enter through more traditional career paths. An internship can be an effective tool for opening a library to diversity. I can talk about the success of the University of Minnesota Libraries Affirmative Action internship in terms of how much the institution was opened for me and how much it was opened to diversity.

The internship did open the institution for me. I came to the Libraries with the expectation that I would have the opportunity to explore different aspects of academic librarianship and to develop a depth of concrete skills and experience in one area. I did. In the first year, especially, I had the luxury of working on two projects in cataloging and working on several different reference projects. These were opportunities that would not have been available if I had entered the Libraries through a traditional entry level library position.

The internship went way beyond my expectations in terms of the access I was given to the various levels, departments and people in the University Libraries. The visibility I had often found torturous resulted in many opened doors for me. People from various parts of the library approached me and wanted to share with me the work they performed. People at all levels were receptive to whatever questions I had for them. They seemed to view my intern position as an opportunity for them to share their particular expertise.

The unusually large size of the Libraries often makes it difficult for people in technical services to know people in reference; or people on one side of the campus to know people from another side of campus. Because of my position I got to know a lot of people in different parts and levels in the University Libraries. Although it is hard to quantify, the personal interactions and relationships I have with all of these people have a great impact on how I feel at work. It makes me more willing to take risks such as trying new approaches to reference work, bibliographic instruction and outreach service. Because I have these relationships, people are unusually supportive of what I do and say.

Was the institution opened to diversity? My internship was the first in a series of steps the University Libraries needs to take toward diversity. I want us to take more steps.

I do not want to give the impression that there are no other people of color working in the University Libraries. There are a few of us. One African American librarian, in particular, took a special interest in me and offered her expertise and encouragement to me. But, there do need to be more of us.

There need to be more interns. The internship was conceived of as an ongoing program. It was planned that another intern would begin in the second year of my program—the idea being that I would pass on some of my knowledge to this person. Budget constraints have postponed the arrival of a second intern.

I think the impact I had was felt most by library staff. A lot of my impact was the result of my just being an African American woman/Affirmative Action intern who was present and visible in all parts of the libraries. My visits to people in library units and my involvement in projects in different units created opportunities for people to reflect on their work in the Libraries and think about affirmative action and diversity. It also gave staff the opportunity to experience my particular communication style. I am very expressive; but I often communicate more through my body language than I do verbally. My style has everything to do with my culture. I found library staff to be receptive to my style.

The Libraries took a first step toward diversity but in many ways I think it was a cautious step. They opened their institution to an African American woman, yes, but an African American woman with all the credentials that have been traditionally valued by academic librarians. I don't think the Libraries will truly be opened to diversity until they take a critical look at the way valuing these credentials can be used to exclude diverse people from the Libraries.

I have a B.A. in English from the University of California, Berkeley, an M.L.I.S. from the same institution and an M.A. in English from the University of Michigan. Throughout my orientation and first months in the Libraries people often commented on my academic credentials. I was commonly introduced to new people with the preface, "She has an M.A. in English" or "She went to U.C. Berkeley and the University of Michigan." I understood that the emphasis on my credentials came out of the fact that library staff first came to know me from my resume; before I arrived it had been passed around the Libraries. For most people in the Libraries, I was defined by my resume.

I define myself in ways that tend to de-emphasize my academic credentials. Growing up in Los Angeles, having a diverse group of friends, being African American, being a woman—all of these qualities and experiences have shaped me as much if not more than my going to U.C. Berkeley and the University of Michigan. I do not want to discount my education, but I need people to understand that there is much more about me than my academic degrees.

It's my cultural experiences that students I see on the reference desk, in bibliographic instruction sessions and at the cultural centers seem to respond to. They don't know or don't care about my credentials; but they feel comfortable approaching me at the desk, seeking me out in my office or coming up to me when I am in other parts of the library.

Emphasis on my academic credentials took me back to the comments from my childhood like "you don't act black." Particularly during my first few weeks in the library, I felt that sometimes I was being treated as if I were an exception.

My academic credentials may have been overemphasized when I was first introduced to people because staff were uncomfortable with introducing me as the "Affirmative Action Intern." I even felt uncomfortable with introducing myself as that to non-library staff. I usually opted to just tell people that I was an intern. The term "affirmative action" seemed to qualify or lessen my position. I feel conflicted about that. On the one hand, I wanted to just be known as the intern. On the other hand, it's the "affirmative action" part of the internship that is necessary and important. If affirmative action wasn't so widely misunderstood I believe that we could have all felt comfortable with saying it. One of the first phrases I learned about Minnesota culture was "Minnesota nice"—the idea that Minnesotans strive to avoid conflict. Minnesota nice was most strongly manifested for me in this desire to avoid talking about affirmative action.

In looking back over the internship, there are not a lot of things I would do differently. I would have benefitted from having an in-person interview—if nothing else it would have made me feel less like I was walking into a totally unknown environment on the first day of my internship. I would have felt most comfortable having the opportunity to meet the people I would be working with and allowing them to see the whole person I am. I would like for future interns to have that opportunity.

The program that was planned for me turned out to be right for me. I was able to accomplish my goals in the program. I would not suggest the same program for every individual intern; for that reason future interns might want to take a more active role in planning their programs.

The change I want to see in the future is more diverse interns. I want the opportunity to be impacted by someone who is very different from myself.

CONCLUSION

In the introduction to this chapter, the University of Minnesota Libraries was credited with creating the Affirmative Action Internship with the expressed intention of *bringing change to a largely homogeneous population.* Did we succeed? Did change occur, as a result of the intern's presence among us? Did we shift any behaviors, attitudes or engage in serious questioning of our established values as a long-term largely homogeneous staff?

There are certainly individuals among the staff who have begun to question their assumptions regarding their understanding of how to provide reference services and build collections that reflect the needs of a diverse student population because of their contacts with our intern. These are valuable insights gained which signal the beginning of the major change which needs to occur.

To continue the change, we need to engage in a remarkably different educational process with the objective of truly opening the staff to inclusion of people of diverse backgrounds, including academic preparation. This includes at the onset a reexamination of the belief that individual ethnic groups need to "blend in" with the mainstream—with the perceived "norm for American." It would seek to support the values of inclusiveness and to highlight the strength that such a strategy ultimately affords individuals and the organizations to which they contribute their ideas and efforts. The need for this educational process was stated succinctly by a writer quoted earlier, who is herself of Scandinavian American ethnicity, who says," My presumed racelessness has allowed me to be ignorant, a privilege I must now forego."[8] Only with these changes in staff can we expect marked changes in the services that we deliver and in the values which undergird and drive those services.

The academic credentials of the intern, which she commented upon earlier, served as a sign that this was a person with whom we could expect to speak the same language and with whom we anticipated being able to share similar viewpoints. She was within a safe range of difference. It seems to be understating the case at this point to say that our intern brought more than was originally expected. We gained a person with a multi-cultural life experience. We gained an individual who was willing to assume a leadership position with the assignment of Diversity Librarian, overcoming her personal and professional conflicts to do so. We are truly just beginning to feel the impact of the greater dimension of our gain. Our future is beginning to change.

NOTES

1. *"Can't We Just All Get Along?"-A Manual For Discussion Programs On Racism And Race Relations,* Study Circle Resource Center [SCRC] (Pomfret, CT: Topsfield Foundation, 1992), 2.

2. Cheri Register, "In Her Family, She is the Person of Color," *Star Tribune* (Minneapolis/St. Paul, MN), 10 February 1993.

3. Of 332 academic and civil service (non-student) library employees, 28, or 8.5 percent, were members of a racial minority, according to January 1993 statistics released by the University of Minnesota Office of Equal Opportunity and Affirmative Action.

4. "Working Paper: Documenting the Quality of Life for Women at the University of Minnesota," Commission on Women, University of Minnesota, [1993], [1].

5. Shulamit Reinharz, *Feminist Methods in Social Research* (New York, Oxford University Press, 1992), 3.

6. Ibid, 9.

7. James Paul Allen and Eugene James Turner, *We the People: An Atlas of America's Ethnic Diversity* (New York, MacMillan, 1988), 145.

8. Register, "In Her Family, She is the Person of Color."

ABOUT THE CONTRIBUTORS

Karen Beavers is the Diversity Librarian at the University of Minnesota Twin Cities Campus Libraries. She has an M.L.I.S. from the University of California, Berkeley and an M. A. in English from the University of Michigan.

Lillian Castillo-Speed has been the Coordinator of the Chicano Studies Library at University of California at Berkeley since 1984. She is also the Database Manager of the Library's Chicano Database, as well as the Series Editor of the Chicano Studies Library Publications Unit. She is the compiler of *Chicana Studies Index: Twenty Years of Gender Research, 1971-1991* (Berkeley: Chicano Studies Library Publications Unit, 1992) and the principal editor of *The Chicano Index*. She has taught ethnic bibliography at the Graduate School of Library and Information Studies at UC Berkeley. In July 1992 she was appointed head of the three ethnic studies libraries on that campus.

Rafaela Castro is Ethnic Studies Librarian at Shields Library, University of California, Davis. She holds three degrees from the University of California, Berkeley: B.A., M.L.S., and M.A. in Folklore. Her special interests are Chicano folklore and popular culture.

Linda deBeau-Melting, Human Resources and Organizational Development Officer, University of Minnesota Libraries, has specialized in working with issues of continuous education for academic library staff and campus-wide efforts to focus attention and effort on creating a climate of diversity. Her academic library background includes positions in both technical and public services positions, as well as administrative responsibilities.

Danilo H. Figueredo is the director of the Talbott Hall Library, Bloomfield College, New Jersey, and a consultant on Latin American studies. He holds an M.L.S. from Rutgers University and an M.A. from New York University. A contributor to Booklist, he has also published over thirty articles and has presented papers at Princeton University, Institute for Ibero-American Studies in Germany, New York University, and the Americas Society. He teaches collection development as well as Latin American literature.

Edward D. Garten is Dean of Libraries and Information Technologies at the University of Dayton. He holds the Ph.D. in Higher Education Administration with a specialization in organizational development and has consulted widely among libraries in this and other areas since 1977. He is a consultant-evaluator with the North Central Association of Colleges and Schools, where he currently serves on the Accreditation Review Council. His most recent books include *Using Consultants In Libraries And Information Centers* and *The Challenge and Practice Of Academic Accreditation.*

Linda Marie Golian is the Serials Department Head for Florida Atlantic University's Libraries. Previously, she was the Serials Control Librarian for the University of Miami Law Library. She received her M.L.I.S. from Florida State University and is pursuing a doctoral degree in educational leadership, specializing in adult education, from Florida Atlantic University. Linda conducts a literary discussion program for a local retirement community, and has published articles on Florida history, women and literacy, volunteers, and serials management.

Cheryl Gomez is Head of Reference Services at the University of California, Santa Cruz. She has served as Chairperson of the Library's Cultural Diversity Committee, designing and implementing a library-wide education program for staff and librarians. Currently she is working with campus and community agencies to expand the role of the library in the recruitment and retention of students of color and low income students.

Cal Gough is a reference librarian and book selector for the Ivan Allen Jr. Department of Science, Industry, and Government of the Atlanta-Fulton Public Library. He helped to establish the American Library Association's Gay and Lesbian Task Force Library Information Clearinghouse, which he coordinated from 1987 to 1989. His chapter "Key Issues in the Collecting of Gay/Lesbian Materials" in *Gay and Lesbian Library Service* (McFarland, 1990) won the 1992 Blackwell North America Scholarship Award sponsored by the American Library Association's Association for Library Collections and Technical Services. He also serves on the executive board of Atlanta's local gay and lesbian history society and is the author of *The Booklover's Guide to Atlanta* (Point of Reference, 1992).

Ellen Greenblatt is the Catalog Editor at the State University of New York at Buffalo. She currently chairs the American Library Association Gay and Lesbian Book Award Committee. From 1986 through 1988, she served as the Co-Chair of ALA's Gay and Lesbian Task Force. With Cal Gough, she co-edited *Gay and Lesbian Library Service* (McFarland, 1990) and co-authored "Services to Gay and Lesbian Patrons: Examining the Myths," *Library Journal* 117 (January 1992). She has an M.A. in Library and Information Science and an M.A. in History/Archives from the University of Denver.

Adán Griego received his M.A. in Spanish and the M.L.S. from the University of Wisconsin-Madison. He is the Latin American and Iberian Studies Librarian at the University of California, Santa Barbara.

Katherine Hoover Hill holds the M.L.S. from Rutgers University and is a free-lance editor and a reference librarian at Erie Community College in Williamsville, New York. From 1981 to 1990, she was reference librarian at Widener University's Delaware Campus Library in Wilmington, Delaware. Particular interests include library instruction and reference service to nontraditional students.

David M. Hovde holds the M. A. in Anthropology from Wichita State University and an M.L.S. from Louisiana State University. He has been at the Purdue University Libraries since 1989, and is currently Sociology and Anthropology Bibliographer and Reference Coordinator in the Humanities, Social Science, and Education Library. Publications include "International Cooperation" in *Encyclopedia of Library History,* ed. Wayne Wiegand and Donald G. Davis, Jr. (New York: Garland, 1994); "Modified Shell," in *Woodland Cultures on the Western Prairies,* ed. David W. Benn (University of Iowa, 1990); and "Sea Colportage: The Loan Library System of the American Seamen's Friend Society, 1859-1967," in *Libraries and Culture* 29): forthcoming.

Cheryl LaGuardia is Coordinator for Computerized Information Services at the University of California, Santa Barbara Library. She writes the monthly column, "CD-ROM Review" in *Library Journal,* and her book, *A CD-ROM Primer: The ABC's of CD-ROM for Beginners* was published by Neal-Schuman, Inc. She served as Co-Chair of the 1994 national bibliographic instruction conference, "The Upside of Downsizing: Using BI to Cope." She speaks and writes on issues involving library instruction, computer applications in libraries, and CD-ROMS.

Poping Lin, Assistant Professor of Library Science at Purdue University, holds the M.L.S. from the School of Library and Information Science, Simmons College. Among her research interests are user instruction, library instruction for culturally diverse populations, and automation system/network evaluation. A recent publication is "Exploring Collection Development Guidelines for American Studies in China," in American Studies International, 30 (October 1992).

Scott B. Mandernack is Assistant Professor, Undergraduate Reference and Instruction Librarian at Purdue University. He holds the M.L.S. from University of Wisconsin—Milwaukee. His particular interests include library instruction, reference services, instructional design, and screen design. Other recent publications include "An Assessment of Education and Training Needs for Bibliographic Instruction Librarians," in *Journal of Education for Library and Information Science,* 30 (Winter 1990); "Selected Readings on Bibliographic Instruction, 1980-1992," with John Mark Tucker, in Hardesty, Larry, ed. *Bibliographic Instruction in Practice: A Tribute to the Legacy of Evan Ira Farber* (Pierian Press, 1993); and *The Savvy Student's Guide to Library Research,* with Judith M. Pask and Roberta J. Kovac (Purdue University Press, 1993).

Rush G. Miller is Dean of Libraries and Learning Resources at Bowling Green State University, Bowling Green, Ohio. He has been library administrator for nineteen years at three institutions and dean at BGSU for the past eight years. He holds an M.L.S. from Florida State University and a Ph.D. in Medieval History from Mississippi State University. Areas of research interest and publication include the role of paraprofessionals in academic libraries, total quality management in libraries, and professional development and credentials. He has also published in the field of history.

Christine K. Oka is Coordinator of Library Publications at the University of California—Santa Barbara. In addition to providing reference services and library instruction in the humanities, sciences and social sciences, she is the collection manager for the Asian American Studies and Environmental Studies Programs. She has written articles on diversity issues in library instruction and collection d8evelopment and several product reviews for *CD-ROM Professional.*

Donna Z. Pontau is a reference librarian and education-psychology selector at the San Jose State University library, San Jose, California. Since 1984 she has also been the Library Liaison to Patrons with Disabilities, and she has given numerous presentations to staff, students, faculty, and other librarians at SJSU and professional conferences on sensitivity, reference, services, and bibliographic instruction for patrons with disabilities. "Researching the

Information Needs and Seeking Behavior of Students with Disabilities in Academic Libraries" was presented at the 1993 Annual ASIS Conference in Columbus, Ohio. She also published "Elimination of Handicapping Barriers in Academic Libraries," *Urban Academic Librarian* 8 (Winter 1991/1992), and is active in the Association of Specialized and Cooperative Library Agencies (ASCLA), a division of ALA, as well as ASCLA's Academic Librarians Assisting the Disabled Discussion Group.

Kwasi Sarkodie-Mensah, currently Chief Reference Librarian at the O'Neill Library at Boston College, was the Bibliographic Instruction Coordinator at Northeastern University in Boston from 1989-1992. His areas of specialization include multicultural librarianship, with special emphasis on the diverse populations served by libraries. He has written several articles on multiculturalism and libraries, and written reviews on multicultural topics for the *Video Rating Guide for Libraries* and the *Horn Book Guide*. His doctoral dissertation at the University of Illinois, Urbana-Champaign in 1988 was a study of international students and libraries in the United States.

William Welburn is Assistant Dean for Graduate Studies at the University of Iowa. He has been a librarian at Indiana and Princeton Universities and at William Paterson College, and has taught in the programs in Library and Information Studies at Clark-Atlanta University, at Rutgers, the State University of New Jersey, and at the University of Iowa, where he has also taught in the African American World Studies Program. Most recently he was Diversity/ Special Services Librarian and Coordinator of the Social Sciences Division for the University of Iowa Libraries. His current research interests revolve around cultural and social aspects of information studies, libraries and librarianship.

Linda Lou Wiler is the library development officer at Florida Atlantic University in Boca Raton, Florida. She is also involved with the growing Judaica program there. She previously worked at the John Crerar Library and the Chicago Public library—where she learned much about the cultural diversity of the older generation—as reference librarian, and at the University of Chicago as cataloger. A graduate of the University of California at Los Angeles with a B.A. in History and an M.L.S. in library science, she has taken courses toward her Ph.D. in history at the University of Chicago. She has written articles about the Greenbackers, Cuba, the American Civil War, religion resources, children's' church libraries, volunteers, and the elderly.

Carol Yates has been a biomedical reference librarian at the University of California, San Francisco since 1981. She initiated and developed seminars on searching biomedical databases; served as the outreach librarian for the UCSF Area Health Education Center; and worked as librarian and manager of a specialized medical library. She has been active in professional organizations, including the Medical Library Association and the Black Caucus of ALA. As a member of the Cultural Diversity Committee for the Librarians' Association of the University of California, she co-authored the discussion paper on cultural considerations for bibliographic instruction. She retired in October 1993.

INDEX